Thank YOU

D0221020

# DAILY LIFE OF

# VICTORIAN WOMEN

**Recent Titles in**
**The Greenwood Press Daily Life Through History Series**

Women during the Civil Rights Era
*Danelle Moon*

Colonial Latin America
*Ann Jefferson and Paul Lokken*

The Ottoman Empire
*Mehrdad Kia*

Pirates
*David F. Marley*

Arab Americans in the 21st Century
*Anan Ameri and Holly Arida, Editors*

African American Migrations
*Kimberley L. Phillips*

The Salem Witch Trials
*K. David Goss*

Behind the Iron Curtain
*Jim Willis*

Trade: Buying and Selling in World History
*James M. Anderson*

The Colonial South
*John Schlotterbeck*

A Medieval Monastery
*Sherri Olson*

Arthurian Britain
*Deborah J. Shephard*

# DAILY LIFE OF

# VICTORIAN WOMEN

LYDIA MURDOCH

The Greenwood Press Daily Life Through History Series

AN IMPRINT OF ABC-CLIO, LLC
Santa Barbara, California • Denver, Colorado • Oxford, England

**Library of Congress Cataloging-in-Publication Data**

Murdoch, Lydia, 1970–
Daily life of Victorian women / Lydia Murdoch.
pages cm. — (The Greenwood Press daily life through history series)
Includes index.
ISBN 978-0-313-38498-1 (hardback) — ISBN 978-0-313-38499-8 (ebook)
1. Women—Great Britain—History—19th century. 2. Women—Great Britain—Social conditions. 3. Women's rights—Great Britain. 4. Great Britain—Social conditions—19th century. 5. Sex role—Great Britain—History—19th century. I. Title.
HQ1596.M87 2013
305.40941—dc23 2013020956

ISBN: 978-0-313-38498-1
EISBN: 978-0-313-38499-8

18 17 16 15 14 1 2 3 4 5

This book is also available on the World Wide Web as an eBook.
Visit www.abc-clio.com for details.

Greenwood
An Imprint of ABC-CLIO, LLC

ABC-CLIO, LLC
130 Cremona Drive, P.O. Box 1911
Santa Barbara, California 93116-1911

This book is printed on acid-free paper ∞

Manufactured in the United States of America

For M. Jeanne Peterson

# CONTENTS

# ACKNOWLEDGMENTS

I am grateful to my Vassar colleagues, especially to those in History, Urban Studies, Victorian Studies, and Women's Studies. Vassar librarians Deb Bucher and Carol Lynn Marshall answered my many questions, and Barbara Durniak and the interlibrary loan staff found obscure materials. Lee Bernstein, Lisa Brawley, Mita Choudhury, Lisa Collins, Beth Darlington, Rebecca Edwards, Andy Fiss, Laura Kasson Fiss, Kit French, Susan Hiner, Seth Koven, Ellen Ross, Mary Shanley, Anthony Wohl, and Susan Zlotnick offered support and shared their expertise with me. Along with the works of other scholars listed in the Further Reading, the books by Sally Mitchell, Ellen Ross, and Susie Steinbach provided invaluable models for how to write a history of Victorian women's daily life. The VICTORIA Listserv, run by Patrick Leary, has also been a vital resource. I am also thankful to my editors: Bridget Austiguy-Preschel, Denver Compton, Nina Gomez, Sharmila Krishnamurthy, and T. Malarvizhi. My greatest thanks go to my student research assistants Alexandra Zeman, Laura McCoy, and Andrea Selby, and to Andy Evans and Carol Engelhardt Herringer, who generously provided insightful suggestions on the entire manuscript.

This book is dedicated with gratitude to M. Jeanne Peterson, professor emeritus of History and Gender Studies at Indiana University, whose own research and teaching have done so much to advance the field of Victorian women's social history.

# CHRONOLOGY

| | |
|---|---|
| **1828** | Repeal of Test and Corporation Acts grants Nonconformists right to hold public office and serve in parliament |
| **1829** | Catholic Emancipation grants Catholics right to serve in parliament |
| **1830** | Liverpool and Manchester Railway opens |
| **1831** | Mary Prince, *The History of Mary Prince, a West Indian Slave* |
| **1831–1832** | Cholera epidemic |
| **1832** | Great Reform Act enfranchises middle-class men |
| **1833** | Factory Act limits children's work hours |
| **1833** | Emancipation Act outlaws slavery in British colonies followed by the "apprenticeship" system in West Indian colonies until 1838 |
| **1834** | New Poor Law |
| **1837** | King William IV dies and Victoria becomes queen |
| **1838** | Anti-Corn Law League |
| **1838** | 700,000 women petition Queen Victoria to end apprenticeship system in British West Indian colonies demonstrating how petitioning becomes an important political tool for women in the 1830s |

| | |
|---|---|
| **1839–1840** | Louis Daguerre refines daguerreotype photographic process in France and William Fox Talbot develops calotype process in England |
| **1839** | Sarah Stickney Ellis, *The Women of England: Their Social Duties and Domestic Habits* |
| **1839** | Custody of Infants Act |
| **1839** | First Chartist petition presented to parliament |
| **1839–1842** | First Opium War |
| **1840** | Uniform Penny Post |
| **1840** | Marriage of Queen Victoria and Prince Albert |
| **1840** | British Foreign Anti-Slavery Society holds first World Anti-Slavery Convention in London |
| **1842** | Second Chartist petition presented to parliament |
| **1842** | Mines and Collieries Act limits employment of women and children |
| **1842** | London Female Chartist Association |
| **1844** | Factory Act restricts hours of women and sets additional limits on children |
| **1845** | Friedrich Engels, *The Condition of the Working Class in England* |
| **1845–1854** | Irish Potato Famine |
| **1846** | Repeal of the Corn Laws signals support for free trade and Prime Minister Sir Robert Peel resigns, dividing Tory Party |
| **1847** | Factory Act (Ten Hour Act) reduces workday to 10 hours for women and children under 18 in textile mills |
| **1848** | Third Chartist petition presented to parliament |
| **1848** | Pre-Raphaelite Brotherhood |
| **1848–1849** | Cholera epidemic |
| **1849** | Bedford College for Women, London |
| **1851** | Sheffield Women's Political Association |
| **1851** | Religious census raises concern about declining church attendance and national census sparks debate about increasing numbers of unmarried "superfluous" women |
| **1851** | Great Exhibition at the Crystal Palace |

| | |
|---|---|
| **1851** | Harriet Taylor, "Enfranchisement of Women," *Westminster Review* |
| **1852–1871** | *Englishwoman's Domestic Magazine* |
| **1852** | 500,000 Englishwomen sign petition to end slavery in the United States |
| **1853** | Doctors give Queen Victoria chloroform for the birth of her eighth child |
| **1853–1854** | Cholera epidemic |
| **1853** | Vaccination Act makes smallpox vaccination compulsory |
| **1854** | Caroline Norton, *English Laws for Women in the Nineteenth Century* |
| **1854** | Barbara Leigh Smith Bodichon, *A Brief Summary in Plain Language of the Most Important Laws Concerning Women* |
| **1854–1856** | Crimean War, Florence Nightingale and Mary Seacole nurse soldiers |
| **1854** | Dr. John Snow links spread of cholera to infected water supply |
| **1856–1860** | Second Opium War |
| **1857–1858** | Indian Rebellion |
| **1857** | Divorce Act creates London divorce court, opened following year |
| **1858–1864** | *English Woman's Journal* |
| **1858–1865** | Workhouse Visiting Society |
| **1858** | Jewish Emancipation grants Jews right to serve in parliament |
| **1858** | Government of India Act abolishes East India Company and declares India a colony under rule of the British Crown |
| **1858** | Wesleyan Methodist Missionary Society begins recruiting single women as missionaries |
| **1859** | John Stuart Mill, *On Liberty* |
| **1859** | Society for Promoting the Employment of Women |
| **1859** | Charles Darwin, *The Origin of Species* |
| **1861** | Prince Albert dies from typhoid |
| **1861–1865** | Civil War in the United States creates Lancashire cotton famine |

| | |
|---|---|
| **1862** | Female Middle-Class Emigration Society |
| **1863** | London Underground opens |
| **1864** | Contagious Diseases Acts passed (extended in 1866 and 1869) |
| **1865** | Morant Bay Jamaican Rebellion |
| **1866–1867** | Cholera epidemic |
| **1866** | Ladies' Petition for women's suffrage signed by 1,500 women |
| **1866** | Transatlantic telegraph cable |
| **1866–1910** | *The Englishwoman's Review* |
| **1867** | Women's suffrage amendment defeated and Second Reform Act passed |
| **1867** | First permanent women's suffrage societies founded in London, Manchester, and Edinburgh and others in Birmingham and Bristol following year |
| **1868** | Last convicts transported to Australia |
| **1868** | Conservative Prime Minister Benjamin Disraeli's first ministry |
| **1868–1874** | Liberal Prime Minister William Gladstone's first ministry |
| **1869** | John Stuart Mill, *The Subjection of Women* |
| **1869** | Women ratepayers gain vote in municipal elections |
| **1869** | Girton College, Britain's first residential college for women |
| **1869** | Suez Canal opens |
| **1869** | Josephine Butler founds Ladies' National Association for the Repeal of the Contagious Diseases Acts |
| **1870–1890** | *Women's Suffrage Journal* |
| **1870** | Forster Act creates national system of elementary schools |
| **1870** | Married Women's Property Act |
| **1871** | Charles Darwin, *The Descent of Man* |
| **1872** | Secret Ballot Act |
| **1873** | Infant Custody Act |
| **1873–1896** | Great Depression |
| **1874–1880** | Disraeli's second ministry |

| | |
|---|---|
| **1875** | First woman poor law guardian elected |
| **1876** | Royal Titles Act declares Queen Victoria as Empress of India |
| **1878** | London University admits women to degrees and University College London becomes coeducational |
| **1878** | Matrimonial Causes Act allows magistrate courts to grant separation orders in cases of cruelty |
| **1878** | William and Catherine Booth found Salvation Army (previously East London Christian Mission) |
| **1880–1885** | Gladstone's second ministry |
| **1882** | Second Married Women's Property Act |
| **1883** | Women's Cooperative Guild |
| **1883** | Contagious Diseases Acts suspended |
| **1884** | Third Reform Act |
| **1884–1885** | Berlin Conference on Africa initiates European "Scramble for Africa" |
| **1885** | W. T. Stead, "The Maiden Tribute of Modern Babylon," *Pall Mall Gazette* |
| **1885** | Criminal Law Amendment Act raises age of consent for girls to 16 and outlaws male homosexuality |
| **1886** | Gladstone's third ministry and First Irish Home Rule Bill divides Liberal Party into Liberal and Liberal Unionist parties |
| **1886** | Contagious Diseases Acts repealed |
| **1886** | Colonial and Indian Exhibition |
| **1886** | Guardianship of Infants Act |
| **1887** | Queen Victoria's Golden Jubilee |
| **1888** | Match Girls' strike |
| **1888** | Oaths Act allows members of parliament to take secular oath of allegiance to the sovereign rather than to God |
| **1888** | *Daily Telegraph* debates "Is Marriage a Failure?" |
| **1888** | Jack-the-Ripper murders in London |
| **1889** | Giant illustration of Sara Baartman displayed at Universal Exhibition of Paris |
| **1889** | National Society for the Prevention of Cruelty to Children |

| | |
|---|---|
| **1889** | Women's Franchise League |
| **1889** | London dock strike |
| **1891** | Clitheroe Abduction Case (*Regina* v. *Jackson*) rules that husbands cannot imprison their wives |
| **1892–1894** | Gladstone's last ministry |
| **1892** | Isabella Bird becomes first woman admitted to Royal Geographical Society |
| **1895** | Trials of Oscar Wilde |
| **1897** | Mary Kingsley, *Travels in West Africa* |
| **1897** | Queen Victoria's Diamond Jubilee |
| **1897** | National Union of Women's Suffrage Societies, led by Millicent Garrett Fawcett |
| **1899–1902** | South African War |
| **1901** | Queen Victoria dies and Edward VII becomes king |
| **1901** | 30,000 women mill workers petition parliament for suffrage |
| **1903** | Women's Social and Political Union, led by Emmeline and Christabel Pankhurst |

# INTRODUCTION: VICTORIAN CONTEXTS AND IDEALS OF WOMANHOOD

"What is now called the nature of women is an eminently artificial thing—the result of forced repression in some directions, unnatural stimulation in others." John Stuart Mill, the philosopher known for his defense of classic liberalism and individual freedom, wrote these words in *The Subjection of Women* (1869). By his own account, Mill developed these conclusions in collaboration with his wife, Harriet Taylor Mill (1807–1858), and stepdaughter, Helen Taylor (1831–1907). Their views rallied support for the emerging women's movement in the 1850s and inspired vociferous attacks from women and men of diverse backgrounds. Mill went on to question the Victorian notion of a natural, universal ideal woman, arguing that "History . . . teaches another lesson: if only by showing the extraordinary susceptibility of human nature to external influences, and the extreme variableness of those of its manifestations which are supposed to be most universal and uniform. But in history, as in travelling, men usually see only what they already had in their own minds; and few learn much from history, who do not bring much with them to its study."[1]

This critique of the ideal woman serves as a reminder that no one uniform life experience for Victorian women existed. What all Victorian women shared—as Mill revealed so forcefully in *The Subjection of Women*—was not any natural or biological or even historical commonality, but rather the condition of their legal, social, and economic subjugation. Within this framework, women's experiences differed immensely as they constantly negotiated between society's expectations of a woman's nature and the circumstances of their own lives. Moreover, the very ideals of womanhood as well as women's daily experiences varied depending on class, religion, race, age, and locality. To begin to discuss the daily life of Victorian women, it is necessary first to introduce these key contexts, focusing on Englishwomen's class differences, their public and private spheres of influence, and their imperial settings from the period when Queen Victoria took the throne in 1837 until her death in 1901.

**Population of England and Wales (Rounded to the Nearest Thousand)**

| *Year* | *Total* | *Males* | *Females* |
|---|---|---|---|
| 1831 | 13,897,000 | 6,771,000 | 7,126,000 |
| 1841 | 15,914,000 | 7,778,000 | 8,137,000 |
| 1851 | 17,928,000 | 8,781,000 | 9,146,000 |
| 1861 | 20,066,000 | 9,776,000 | 10,290,000 |
| 1871 | 22,712,000 | 11,059,000 | 11,653,000 |
| 1881 | 25,974,000 | 12,640,000 | 13,335,000 |
| 1891 | 29,003,000 | 14,060,000 | 14,942,000 |
| 1901 | 32,528,000 | 15,729,000 | 16,799,000 |

*Source:* B. R. Mitchell, *British Historical Statistics* (Cambridge, UK: Cambridge University Press, 1988), 9.

## CLASS CONTEXTS

Class profoundly shaped the circumstances of Englishwomen's lives—their childhoods, their families, their health, their leisure, and their work experiences. From politics to economics, women of the upper and middle classes enjoyed distinct advantages. While, for example, the Great Reform Act of 1832 officially denied parliamentary suffrage to all women (and most men), many elite women continued to employ political influence through family and social connections. The economist and writer Harriet Martineau (1802–1876) gained access to the House of Commons Library for her research in the early hours of the morning—an exceptional case of women's contingent and limited admission into the spatial center of government. Such opportunities remained inconceivable for most working-class men and women. An elite woman could easily spend as much on a single dress as a skilled seamstress earned from several weeks of labor. Even by the end of the 19th century, the children of a woman living in one of London's poorest neighborhoods were significantly more likely to die early from disease or malnutrition than those of London's wealthiest residents.

The basic class structure in England evolved during the course of Victoria's reign. At the very top were the aristocrats and landed gentry, who together made up less than 5 percent of the population. The peerage included only those male heads of some 500 British households who passed on the hereditary titles of duke, marquess, earl, viscount, or baron and were members of the House of Lords. Aristocratic women, except for members of the royal family, held only courtesy titles. Descriptions of the aristocracy generally also include untitled families with annual incomes of at least £10,000. This massive sum was enough to maintain an extensive country estate in addition to a London house with a large ensemble of servants. (By comparison, a private box at London's Adelphi Theatre in the late 1870s cost between £1 1s. and £6 6s.; weekly bread cost approximately 1s. per person.) Many historians group the wealthier of the landed gentry with the aristocracy as well, since these families wielded significant local—sometimes national—political and social influence. Together, the peerage and landed gentry owned the vast majority of property and dominated British politics even after the 1832 Reform Act granted the vote to middle-class men. Aristocratic political influence began to decline only in the late Victorian period with the effects of the 1867 and 1884 Reform Acts that extended suffrage to some working-class men. The agricultural depression that lasted from the early 1870s into the 1890s also diminished the economic power and political clout of England's landed elite.

Most Victorians were members of the middle and working classes. The distinctions between these groups—each diverse within itself—depended much more on cultural values and the type of work

**Victorian Money (Replaced by a Decimal System in 1971)**

£1 (also written as 1l.) = 20 shillings.

1 shilling (abbreviated as 1s. or 1/-), also called a "bob" = 12 pence (abbreviated as 12d.); the singular of pence is penny; there were 240 pence in £1.

Sums were written using abbreviations. Thus, 3 pounds, 2 shillings, and fourpence would be written as £3 2s. 4d. or as £3/2s/4d.

Paper notes were very rare. A paper pound note was also called a "quid." In addition to gold pound coins (called "sovereigns"), silver shillings, and copper pence, there were many different types of coins in circulation. These included

Guinea = 21 shillings or £1 1s. (not minted after 1813)

Half sovereign = 10s.

Crown = 5s.

Half crown = 2s. 6d.

Florin = 2s. (first minted in 1849)

Sixpence = 6d. (also called a "tanner")

Groat = 4d.

Threepence = 3d.

Twopence = 2d.

Halfpenny = 1/2d.

Farthing = 1/4d.

Half farthing = 1/8d.

rather than simply on income. The older middle classes, or "middling ranks" as they were often called in the 18th century, tended to be associated with those who worked in the professions, such as Anglican clergymen, military and naval officers, lawyers, university professors, and, to some extent, doctors. The rising middle classes included those associated with forms of wealth developed or greatly expanded by Britain's industrial revolution of the late 18th and early 19th centuries: bankers, merchants, brokers, factory owners, and manufacturers. Although their wealth came from industry and commerce rather than from land, the wealthiest of the upper middle classes could rival—or, through marriage, supplement—the incomes of the aristocracy. Expectations for a "comfortable" middle-class family income at mid-century remained significantly more modest, somewhere between £300 and £500 a year. By the 1850s, however, an annual income of £150 was sometimes used as a more inclusive baseline to track the growing numbers of middle-class workers. At the lower end of the middle classes, people such as clerks, shop assistants, school teachers, and civil servants made under £100—less than what a skilled working-class carpenter, mechanic, or other male member of the so-called labor aristocracy might earn (typically in the range of £75–100 a year). By the early 20th century, about £1 a week or roughly £50 a year was the least amount required to support a family, yet many working-class women received far less. On the whole, members of the working classes made up approximately three quarters of the English population.

**Weekly Budget for a Working-class Family with Three Children, 1870s**

| *Expense* | *£* | *s.* | *d.* |
|---|---|---|---|
| Lodging | 0 | 3 | 6 |
| Bread | 0 | 3 | 9 |
| Meat | 0 | 3 | 7 |
| Tea, coffee, and sugar | 0 | 1 | 3 |
| Oil and matches | 0 | 0 | 4½ |
| Coal coke and wood | 0 | 1 | 2 |
| Rice, barley, and peas | 0 | 0 | 6 |
| Vegetables | 0 | 1 | 0 |
| Treacle | 0 | 0 | 1½ |
| Starch, soap, soda, blue, pepper, salt | 0 | 0 | 4 |
| Flour | 0 | 0 | 7 |
| Children's school and Bible | 0 | 0 | 6 |
| Burial club | 0 | 0 | 4 |
| Man's club for clothes | 0 | 1 | 0 |

*(Continued)*

(*Continued*)

| *Expense* | £ | s. | *d.* |
|---|---|---|---|
| Woman's club | 0 | 1 | 0 |
| Doctor* | 0 | 2 | 0 |
| Shoe club for all | 0 | 1 | 0 |
| Cotton, tape, and buttons | 0 | 0 | 2 |
| | 1 | 2 | 2 |

*They owed a doctor 2l. 10*s*., for which he summoned them, and Mrs. A agreed to pay off the debt 2*s*. a week.

*Source:* Ellen Henrietta Ranyard, "Dinner for the Bread-Winner," *The Missing Link Magazine* 14.2 (February 1, 1878), reprinted in Ellen Ross, ed., *Slum Travelers: Ladies and London Poverty, 1860–1920* (Berkeley: University of California Press, 2007), 202.

**Expenditure for an Income of £100 per Annum**

| *Expense* | £ | s. | *d.* |
|---|---|---|---|
| Rent and taxes, rates, and water rate | 17 | 0 | 0 |
| Housekeeping | 55 | 0 | 0 |
| Clothing | 12 | 10 | 0 |
| Incidentals, which will include traveling expenses, medicine, education of children, repairs of furniture, pew rents, and charitable gifts | 15 | 10 | 0 |
| | 100 | 0 | 0 |

**£400 per Annum Allows the Following Disbursement**

| *Expense* | £ | s. | *d.* |
|---|---|---|---|
| Rent, taxes, and all rates, including water rate (one-eighth of income) | 50 | 0 | 0 |
| Housekeeping—laundry, coal, gas charge, also wines, spirits, and beer, where used (one-half) | 200 | 0 | 0 |

(*Continued*)

(*Continued*)

| *Expense* | £ | s. | *d.* |
|---|---|---|---|
| Wages—two servants—general servant, £16; housemaid, £14, inclusive of tea and sugar. Beer, 1s. 2d. each, weekly; laundry, 1s. 2d. each, weekly | 36 | 1 | 4 |
| Clothing of all descriptions, including tailor's, milliner's, and dressmaking bills (one-eighth) | 50 | 18 | 8 |
| Incidentals | 63 | 0 | 0 |
| | 400 | 0 | 0 |

*Source: Cassell's Household Guide: Being a Complete Encyclopedia of Domestic and Social Economy, and Forming a Guide to Every Department of Practical Life*, Vol. 1 (London: Cassell, Petter, and Galpin, ca. 1869–1871), 3.

The different meanings that class groups gave to core values, including the ubiquitous Victorian ideal of "respectability," highlighted the cultural as well as the economic basis of class identity. For the middle classes, being respectable implied good social standing, discipline, thrift, industry, individualism, honesty, and sexual morality. Such values helped to unite individuals of diverse economic backgrounds. The cultivation of domesticity proved equally important, especially for middle-class women, who according to social codes of respectability were to put aside all wage labor. For working-class women, however, as well as for some women of the lower middle classes, their very work for wages could actually serve as a sign of respectability based upon their commitment as mothers to provide for their families. Some social reformers and journalists described neatly dressed working-class women as being respectable even in cases when they had illegitimate children or resided with men out of wedlock, if the women could show that they were doing their best to live within their means and secure resources for their children. Thus, depending on the class context and the particular setting, Victorian values could be remarkably flexible in their meanings.

## SPATIAL CONTEXTS: RETHINKING VICTORIAN IDEALS OF SEPARATE SPHERES

Similar to notions of respectability, 19th-century ideals of separate public and private spheres for men and women provided a framework that Victorians celebrated, negotiated, reinterpreted, and, at times, contested. Historians writing in the 1970s and 1980s, most notably Leonore Davidoff and Catherine Hall, explored how ideals of separate public and private spheres for men and women gained greater prominence among the English middle classes during the late 18th and early 19th centuries. They linked this process to the religious Evangelical revival and to England's commercial growth (see Chapter 3). Consigning women to the home became a sign of middle-class status. Gender therefore played a key role in the process of class formation. Although the ideal of separate spheres first gained prominence among the middle classes, it became widespread among the working classes as well in various forms, despite the obvious contradiction that many working-class women could not fully devote themselves to their homes and families because of their need to work for wages.

Certainly, by the early and mid-Victorian period, writers, artists, politicians, religious figures, scientists, and men and women from many different parts of society drew distinctions between what they understood to be the masculine realm of business, commerce, politics, empire, and warfare and the feminine realm of domesticity, family, morality, and spiritual guidance. Victorians adopted the title of Coventry Patmore's popular serial poem—"The Angel in the House" (1854–1862)—as a reference for the ideal woman. The poem celebrated marriage as woman's supreme destiny and valorized her submissive devotion to the needs of her husband and children without any regard for her own. In his best-selling *Sesame and Lilies* (1865), two essays first delivered as lectures in Manchester, the art critic and noted Victorian "sage" John Ruskin suggested that men and women had distinct powers and spheres of influence through which to reform society. Unlike Patmore, Ruskin condemned what he saw as the unsatisfactory, frivolous nature of middle-class education for girls in comparison with boys, although he still warned against the prideful arrogance that he attributed to women's study of theology. Ruskin encouraged women to employ their skills to society at large—to move from the domestic private sphere into the public realm in order to combat the evils of *laissez-faire* industrial capitalism. However, according to Ruskin, the goal of female education was to develop empathy rather than knowledge for its own sake, and woman's public contribution remained distinct from man's. "The man's duty as a member of a commonwealth," he wrote, "is to assist in the maintenance, in the advance, in the defence of the state. The woman's duty, as a member of the commonwealth, is to assist in the ordering, in the comforting, and in the beautiful adornment of the state."[2] Such descriptions of men's and women's supposedly natural qualities became commonplace. Even Charles Darwin, in *The Descent of Man* (1871), described unselfishness, affection, and imitation as essential female traits—characteristics that he deemed made women beneficial for society, yet ultimately inferior in mental development to Anglo-Saxon men.

**John Ruskin, "Lecture II—Lilies of Queens' Gardens," in *Sesame and Lilies*, ed. by Deborah Epstein Nord (New Haven, CT: Yale University Press, 2002; 1865), 77**

The man's power is active, progressive, defensive. He is eminently the doer, the creator, the discoverer, the defender. His intellect is for speculation and invention; his energy for adventure, for war, and for conquest, wherever war is just, wherever conquest necessary. But the woman's power is for rule, not for battle,—and her intellect is not for invention or creation, but for sweet ordering, arrangement, and decision. She sees the qualities of things, their claims, and their places. Her great function is Praise; she enters into no contest, but infallibly adjudges the crown of contest. By her office, and place, she is protected from all danger and temptation. The man, in his rough work in open world, must encounter all peril and trial;— to him, therefore, must be the failure, the offence, the inevitable error: often he must be wounded, or subdued; often misled; and *always* hardened. But he guards the woman from all this; within his house, as ruled by her, unless she herself has sought it, need enter no danger, no temptation, no cause of error or offence. This is the true nature of home—it is the place of Peace; the shelter, not only from all injury, but from all terror, doubt, and division. In so far as it is not this, it is not a home; so far as the anxieties of the outer life penetrate into it, and the inconsistently-minded, unknown, unloved, or hostile society of the outer world is allowed by either husband or wife to cross the threshold, it ceases to be home.

Noting the complex, often contradictory ways in which Victorians understood gendered spheres of influence, recent scholarship suggests that the 19th-century belief in distinct male and female characteristics did not necessarily imply a strict division between a male public sphere and a female private sphere. The binary division of life's actions into public and private spheres oversimplifies the many ways in which women actively engaged the worlds beyond their homes. In other words, rather than thinking of the public solely in terms of a male realm of business and politics, Victorians imbued "the public"—and also "the private"—with multiple, sometimes overlapping, sometimes inconsistent meanings. Many Victorians, like Ruskin, believed in essential differences between men and women, yet still encouraged women to apply their skills of sympathy and affection to those in need outside the home, particularly through work with the poor, the orphaned, the sick, the elderly, and the fallen. Drawing on the language of separate spheres, domesticity, and maternalism, middle-class Victorian women—including large numbers of single, unmarried women—dedicated themselves to various social causes ranging from housing reform and nursing to women's higher education and employment. Some historians have described such actions as taking place within the "social sphere" or the "parochial realm." These terms emphasize the familial, religious, neighborhood, and friendship networks underlying women's actions outside of the home—connections lacking within other forms of the "unknown" public. Such reformulations allow for the blurring of boundaries between public and private and help to explain how leading philanthropists such as the prison reformer Elizabeth Fry (1780–1845) or the housing reformer Octavia Hill (1838–1912) could describe their activism as "private" works based upon woman's domestic sphere of influence.

During the 1850s and 1860s, women in England organized the foundations of a feminist movement (though the term itself was not used until the late 19th century). They formed female debate societies, published journals, and advocated for female legal equality, education, work opportunities, and suffrage. Many of these women believed that they could contribute to the larger society and politics through their distinctly feminine attributes. Some continued to praise the domestic realm as the basis for civic action even as they challenged the domestic model that held women submissive to their husbands. By the 1890s, however, more and more women began to question the very ideals of "The Angel in the House" and female domesticity. In the intervening decades, women increasingly engaged public urban spaces that were rapidly expanding in size and population. Women ventured out unchaperoned, took advantage of new forms of public transportation, and presented public lectures. For many, the "New Woman" of the 1890s was so controversial because of her claim to the unknown spaces of the urban public sphere. These were the "Wild Women" condemned by the antisuffrage journalist Eliza Lynn Linton (1822–1898) in a series of articles from the early 1890s—the women who drank and smoked with men, pursued careers, traveled the world, sought a life beyond marriage and motherhood, advocated free love, and campaigned for women's suffrage in order to have a voice not only in local matters, but also in national and imperial politics.

## IMPERIAL CONTEXTS

The growth of the British Empire during the 19th century also shaped women's lives. The primary focus of this book is on women in England, but the empire is nonetheless an essential part of this history. Imperial expansion over the course of the 19th century directly affected the daily lives of Englishwomen, influencing their economic choices, their cultural activities, and their political identities.

Britain's imperial holdings increased significantly during Victoria's reign. Britain's empire, the largest in history by the end of the 19th century, included territories under a variety of different headings—direct colonies, self-governing dominions, and protectorates—as well as regions under Britain's informal imperial control, such as much of China and parts of the Ottoman Empire and South America. Formal 19th-century colonies included Canada, Australia, New Zealand, and South Africa (often construed as "white settler" colonies despite the indigenous communities devastated by imperialism), as well as territories in the West Indies, India, Southeast Asia, Singapore, the Pacific Islands, Hong Kong, Africa, and the Middle East. After the loss of the American colonies in 1783, the focus of British imperial expansion shifted eastward to Asia and then, later in the 19th century, to Africa.

**Charles Darwin, *The Descent of Man* (1871) in *Darwin*, selected and edited by Philip Appleman (New York: W.W. Norton & Company, 2001), 234–235**

Woman seems to differ from man in mental disposition, chiefly in her greater tenderness and less selfishness; and this holds good even with savages, as shewn by a well-known passage in Mungo Park's Travels, and by statements made by many other travellers. Woman, owing to her maternal instincts, displays these qualities towards her infants in an eminent degree; therefore it is likely that she would often extend

> them towards her fellow-creatures. Man is the rival of other men; he delights in competition, and this leads to ambition which passes too easily into selfishness. These latter qualities seem to be his natural and unfortunate birthright. It is generally admitted that with woman the powers of intuition, of rapid perception, and perhaps of imitation, are more strongly marked than in man; but some, at least, of these faculties are characteristic of the lower races, and therefore of a past and lower state of civilisation.
>
> The chief distinction in the intellectual powers of the two sexes is shewn by man's attaining to a higher eminence, in whatever field he takes up, than can woman—whether requiring deep thought, reason, or imagination, or merely the use of the senses and hands. If two lists were made of the most eminent men and women in poetry, painting, sculpture, music (inclusive both of composition and performance), history, science, and philosophy, with half-a-dozen names under each subject, the two lists would not bear comparison. . . . [T]he average of mental power in man must be above that of woman.

Britain's global empire emerged in tandem with the ideals of Victorian womanhood and the experiences of Englishwomen that are the focus of this book. To begin to understand the daily lives of women in England, it is necessary to approach them through this broader lens of England as a part of the British Empire. Only then do certain formerly overlooked experiences of women become visible. Awareness of the imperial context, for example, brings attention to the diversity and changing nature of the English population. By the late 18th century, between 15,000 and 20,000 people of color lived in England. They were mainly the descendants of Africans, West Indians, and South and East Asians, including former slaves, servants, sailors, and dockworkers. Imperial immigration increased during the 19th century, when it became more common for elite men and women from the colonies to travel to England. Imperial emigration also directly influenced the lives of Englishwomen, albeit in very different ways. The working-class woman transported to Australia for pickpocketing had a very different experience from the unmarried "superfluous" middle-class spinster hoping to discover new career opportunities in the colonies. Race was a key factor—historically situated and changing over time—shaping the Victorians' concepts of feminine "purity" as well as their class relationships.

The topical chapters that follow explore the social history of Victorian women with particular attention to the ways in which understandings of class, gender, and imperialism affected their lives. While the primary focus is on the years of Victoria's reign from 1837 to 1901, chapters examine earlier events that are key to understanding the actions and attitudes of Victorian women, such as the abolition movement and the Great Reform Act of 1832. The narrative also extends slightly beyond Victoria's death to provide an account of the campaign for women's suffrage into the early 1900s. As an introduction to the period, this history demonstrates the "extreme variableness" of human experience that—for Mill and others—threw into doubt any notion of woman's universal nature.

## NOTES

1. John Stuart Mill, *On Liberty with The Subjection of Women and Chapters on Socialism*, ed. by Stefan Collini (Cambridge, U.K.: Cambridge University Press, 1989), 138–139.
2. John Ruskin, *Sesame and Lilies*, ed. by Deborah Epstein Nord (New Haven, CT: Yale University Press, 2002), 88.

# 1

# WOMEN AND THE STATE

Two months after the passage of the Great Reform Act of 1832 that extended suffrage to middle-class men, the radical member of parliament Henry Hunt presented a petition to the House of Commons requesting that unmarried women taxpayers should also receive the vote. Hunt admitted that the topic might "be a subject of mirth" to members of parliament, but "was one deserving of consideration." The petitioner, Mary Smith from Yorkshire, asserted that "she paid taxes, and therefore did not see why she should not have a share in the election of a Representative." She stressed that "women were liable to all the punishments of the law, not excepting death, and ought to have a voice in the making of them; but so far from this, even upon their trials, both judges and jurors were all of the opposite sex." As Hunt predicted, the discussion devolved into a joke instead of serious debate. The Irish Conservative Sir Frederick Trench said, "it would be rather awkward if a jury half males and half females were locked up together for a night, as now often happened with juries. This might lead to rather queer predicaments." Hunt replied that he "well knew that the hon. and gallant Member was frequently in the company of ladies for whole nights, but he did not know that any mischief resulted from that circumstance." Trench answered, "Yes, but not locked up all night," thus ending for the time being the conversation and leaving the "petition laid on the table."[1]

The 1832 Reform Act transformed British politics not by bringing about a democracy—changes that would come later in the 19th and early 20th centuries. Rather, the Reform Act is significant for setting up the uniform £10 borough franchise that entitled men who owned or rented homes of at least £10 annual value to vote in England and Wales. (Separate acts reformed suffrage in Scotland and Ireland.) The previous system included much local variation, but largely restricted the vote as a privilege for landed men of the aristocracy following the tradition going back for centuries that only they had a permanent fixed interest in the country. With the Reform Act's passage, the Whigs ushered in a modern political system that prioritized national politics over local variation and valued industrial wealth alongside aristocratic landed power. The Tories opposed the Reform Act. They bemoaned that the restructuring of suffrage had, in the words of Sir Robert Peel, opened the floodgates of change, as it certainly did by establishing a precedent for subsequent suffrage extensions under the Second Reform Act of 1867, the Third Reform Act of 1884, the Representation of the People Act of 1918, and the 1928 Equal Franchise Act that finally brought full suffrage on equal terms to all adults 21 or older. The 1832 Act increased the electorate from approximately 366,000 to 653,000 voters, or from 11 to 18 percent of the adult male population. It also abolished many "rotten boroughs"—sparsely populated districts, including the infamous uninhabited cow pasture at Old Sarum, that powerful families used to send their favored representatives to parliament—and created new ones, giving northern industrial cities such as Manchester representation.

The Great Reform Act for England and Wales also stipulated for the first time that all voters should be "male persons." Prior to 1832, it had been exceedingly rare but not unknown for single or widowed women who met local property qualifications to vote. The Reform Act also put an end to the more common custom in Bristol and some other areas allowing freewomen to bestow voting privileges inherited from their fathers onto their husbands. Until recently, most historians argued that the 1832 act thus marked a closing off of formal political life to women, as it certainly did in important ways, and the establishment of an explicitly masculine understanding of political citizenship. Yet, as Hunt's petition from Mary Smith hints amidst the ridicule, the lines between political exclusion and inclusion might not be so clearly drawn, particularly in a political system that was evolving and one that, for that matter, limited the participation of the majority of men along with women.

When during the debates leading up to the Great Reform Act the House of Lords opened the galleries to elite women, Charles Greville noted that "the House of Lords was so full of ladies that the Peers could not find places."[2]

Victorian women from all classes remained active in political debates and campaigns, albeit often in auxiliary roles and as objects of mockery or worse. They attacked the legal restrictions placed by the state on women's rights sometimes by referring to women's need for male protection or sometimes by claiming equality. They joined in popular protest movements and expressed their views through other means besides the vote, chiefly with petitions and demonstrations. By the 1860s and 1870s, many—though certainly not all—female reformers understood women's suffrage as necessary to their broader political campaigns, if not a goal in its own right.

## WOMEN'S LEGAL STATUS

At the beginning of the Victorian period, the state denied women the fundamental civil as well as political rights held by men of the same class. Single women and widows enjoyed greater rights than married women, but still suffered many injustices. They could legally own property and were required by law to pay the same taxes as men, but could not vote for members of parliament. They could inherit personal property such as household goods from deceased parents, but male siblings and their descendents received prior claim to all "real property"—land and estates. Women were also excluded from most church and government offices with notable exceptions. A woman could be queen or assist in governing Britain's expanding empire by purchasing stock in the East India Company, but could not until later in the century gain accreditation to practice medicine or law.

For married women, the legal restrictions cut much deeper. According to the common law doctrine of coverture, they became nonpersons with no legal rights apart from their husbands. In her widely read pamphlet, *A Brief Summary in Plain Language of the Most Important Laws Concerning Women* (1854), the feminist reformer Barbara Leigh Smith Bodichon (1827–1891) surmised that a married woman has "no legal existence. A man and wife are one person in law; the wife loses all her rights as a single woman, and her existence is entirely absorbed in that of her husband. He is civilly responsible for her acts; she lives under his protection or cover, and her condition is called coverture."[3] A married woman could not sign her own contracts or be accountable for her debts. She could not sue or be sued unless under the name of her husband as the primary party. She could not draw up her own will without her husband's consent, which he could later withdraw at any moment before probate. All of a married woman's property—both personal items such as jewelry, clothing, and furniture as well as any real property—became her husband's. Any money that she had prior to marriage or income that she earned while married also became the sole property of her husband. (While aristocratic families had access to the legal expertise to set up complicated settlement trusts providing married women with some financial resources of their own, this was not an option for most middle-class women and far beyond the resources of working-class women.) Moreover, a married woman's very body belonged to her husband, a claim that he could legally enforce by a writ of *habeas corpus*. Married mothers had no legal custody of their children until 1839, and then only very limited claims. Even after the husband's death, the mother would not be granted custody unless he had named her as guardian. Given expectations of women's role within the home, it is unsurprising that the issue of child custody sparked many of the first challenges to married women's legal nonexistence.

### The Custody of Children

One of the earliest and certainly most spectacular challenges to married women's status came from the writer Caroline Norton (1808–1877), the granddaughter of the playwright Richard Brinsley Sheridan. Witty, striking, strong-willed, and well-connected among certain aristocratic circles if not always well-off financially or viewed as fully respectable, Norton initiated reforms of child custody, domestic violence, divorce, and married women's property rights. At the age of 19 she married George Norton, who took little time in revealing himself as a dim and violent man dissatisfied with the £1,000 a year police court judge position that Caroline secured for him through her connections with the Whig Home Secretary, Lord Melbourne. That Caroline joined her family in supporting the Whigs while George favored the Tories was only one of their sources of conflict. Beginning in the first months after their marriage, George responded to Caroline's irrepressible need to express her views with controlling violence: he kicked her when she dismissed his opinion as ridiculous, choked her when she threw his hookah from the carriage, burned her letter writing book when she conveyed complaints to her mother, and scalded her hand with the tea kettle when she refused to give up her seat so that he might better observe people strolling in the park outside. In March 1836, Caroline planned to take her three young sons to her sister's home for Easter without George. Before she left, he sent the children away, denying Caroline access to them. Later that summer, George initiated divorce proceedings and created a public scandal by charging Lord Melbourne, by then prime minister, with having "criminal conversations"—that is, an adulterous relationship—with Caroline. The court quickly dismissed the unsubstantiated charge, a ruling that vindicated Caroline yet later made it impossible for her to attain a divorce. The couple separated, but George continued to deny Caroline all contact with their sons.

Caroline Norton responded by turning to her literary talents. Already a recognized author by this point, she published several influential political pamphlets decrying women's lack of custody rights, including *Observations on the Natural Claim of a Mother to the Custody of Her Children as Affected by the Common Law Right of the Father* (1837). Gaining support from key political friends, Norton proved instrumental to the passage of the 1839 Custody of Infants Act. The legislation, although certainly an improvement, granted only very restricted custody rights to women. Married mothers could petition the Lord Chancellor for a special court hearing to determine custody of children under seven, but only if the women were wealthy enough to file a suit in the Court of Chancery and had never been found guilty of adultery in a court of law. (Adultery on the part of the father rarely mattered in custody disputes.) George begrudgingly gave Caroline limited access to the boys—though never in public. It was only after their youngest son, William, then eight years old, died following a riding accident in 1842 that the two surviving boys came to live with their mother regularly for six months out of the year.

Later reformers expanded women's custody rights, looking back to Norton as having initiated the first major challenge to English patriarchal law. The Infant Custody Act of 1873 did away with the clause excluding adulterous mothers' petitions and increased the child's age from 7 to 16 for which mothers could seek custody or visitation. However, to the great frustration of feminist reformers such as Elizabeth Wolstenholme Elmy (1833–1918), the 1873 Custody Act failed fundamentally to recognize the mother's equal right to custody and also limited appeals to Chancery, thus making them available only to the very wealthy. The 1886 Guardianship of Infants Act recognized a widow as having custody of her children upon her husband's death, although the husband could designate future co-guardians along with the children's mother. This marked an important step, but was still nowhere near Wolstenholme Elmy's vision of equal parental custody and "the establishment of the family on the basis of justice, equality, and mutual duty and love."[4]

### Divorce Reform and Married Women's Property

Caroline Norton instigated reforms of married women's property rights and divorce law in addition to custody rights. The years following her custody arrangement brought Norton a short-lived reprieve from conflict with her husband that developed anew over financial disputes. In 1848, George, having squandered his money, appealed to Caroline to let him mortgage her settlement trust property arranged by her parents upon her marriage. George agreed in exchange to provide her with a greater annual allowance of £500 a year. They drew up what Caroline understood to be a legal deed to this effect. However, when Caroline's mother died in 1851, leaving her an annual inheritance secured as her property alone of £480 a year, George stopped his annual payments, making Caroline aware of the harsh reality that their previous agreement proved legally invalid since they remained husband and wife, technically "one" under the law and not two separate parties capable of forming a contract. Caroline retaliated by refusing to pay her creditors, who turned to George for payment. The conflict went to court in 1853, when Caroline's carriage repairman sued George for compensation.

**Caroline Norton, *Caroline Norton's Defense: English Laws for Women in the Nineteenth Century*, introduced by Joan Huddleston (Chicago: Academy, 1982; 1854), 160**

The law-forms respecting property, followed the same rules as the law-forms respecting prosecution for libel. Anxious to make arrangements for a future home, less expensively than in furnished houses, I propose to take a lease; and am told, that being "non-existent" in law, *my* signature is worthless. Anxious to recover property left at home, gifts from my mother and my family, I am informed, that being "non-existent" in law, I can claim nothing, and that my husband

> intends to *sell* them. Anxious to leave what little I have through the generosity of my family, or the gifts of friends—my furniture, trinkets, books, etc., to my two sons, I am informed, that, being "non-existent" in law, it would be a mere farce my attempting to make a will; that a married woman can bequeath nothing, as she can possess nothing; and that my property is the property of the husband with whom I am still legally *"one,"* after seventeen years of separation! Anxious to end the apparently ceaseless disputes respecting a provision for me in this state of separation, I accept Mr. Norton's own terms, after demanding others; I sign a contract, dictated, corrected, and prepared under *his* instructions; which I never even saw except for the purpose of affixing my signature to it; and I am informed, that being "non-existent" in law, I have signed that which binds him to nothing.

George won the case on a technicality, but Caroline took her appeal to the public. She began with a series of letters to the *Times*, expounding on her marital clashes in shocking detail, and followed these with the privately published *English Laws for Women in the Nineteenth Century* (1854), a full account of her custody, marital, and financial conflicts with George in which she promised to publish solely on the topic of women's legal rights as long as George held possession of her copyrights. Caroline Norton differed from the later, primarily middle-class women who campaigned for women's civil rights in that she neither claimed women's equality with men nor supported women's suffrage. She repeatedly asserted that what she sought was women's "protection"—and that if this could not be provided by husbands like George who proved dishonorable and violent, then protection must be guaranteed by the law. Although her arguments differed from later reformers, however, many of Norton's solutions remained the same. She demanded changes in the law that would undo married women's legal nonexistence by empowering them to have greater custody over children, to own property, to sign contracts, to draft wills, and to be liable for their debts. In *English Laws for Women* and her later pamphlet *A Letter to the Queen on Lord Chancellor Cranworth's Marriage and Divorce Bill* (1855), she argued for reform of divorce laws that would make the procedure both more accessible and more equal for women.

As the law then stipulated, a civil divorce could only be attained through a separate act of parliament—an expensive legal process inaccessible to all but the most wealthy. Before petitioning parliament, the plaintiff first had to gain a declaration of divorce *a mensa et thoro* (granting a separation) from the ecclesiastical courts and then prove in the civil courts that there had been an adulterous relationship, which is what George Norton unsuccessfully attempted to do in his charge of criminal conversations against Lord Melbourne. While a husband could appeal for divorce on the basis of his wife's infidelity, the grounds for a woman filing for divorce remained much more prohibitive. According to Norton, only 3 women in English history had successfully petitioned the House of Lords for divorces compared with over 300 men, and the women's cases involved serious charges against the husband, such as bigamy or incest, in addition to adultery.

Norton's public appeals inspired a much broader campaign. The same year as Norton wrote *English Laws for Women,* Barbara Bodichon published her full-scale critique of coverture in *A Brief Summary in Plain Language of the Most Important Laws Concerning Women*. Dedicated to securing married women's equal rights (not simply the protection of those wronged by ruinous husbands), Bodichon joined with her close friends Elizabeth (Bessie) Rayner Parkes (1829–1925) and Anna Mary Howitt (1824–1884) in 1855 to form a committee to petition parliament. By March 1856, their petitions calling for recognition of married women's property rights had some 26,000 signatures, including those of prominent literary women such as Elizabeth Barrett Browning (1806–1861), Elizabeth Gaskell (1810–1865), Anna Jameson (1794–1860), Harriet Martineau (1802–1876), Jane Carlyle (1801–1866), and Marian Evans (1819–1880), who published under the name George Eliot. By 1857, Bodichon and Bessie Parkes emerged as leaders of the liberal feminists who together became known as the Langham Place Circle. The group took its name from Langham Place, London, the ultimate publication site of the *English Woman's Journal* (1858–1864), which served as a leading voice of British feminism. Langham Place operated as a center for middle-class feminist activism on issues of married women's rights, women's work, women's education, and, by the mid-1860s, women's suffrage, before the group disbanded in 1866. Important associated professional organizations included the Society for Promoting the Employment of Women (1859) and the Female Middle-Class Emigration Society (1862). The London Kensington Society (1865–1868), an all-female debating group, provided another useful network for reformers. Women also presented arguments for married women's property and related rights at the annual meetings of the National Association for the Promotion of Social Science—a prominent forum for professional debate on social, economic, and political issues that was exceptional for admitting women from its establishment in 1857.

The 1856 petitions for married women's property rights reached parliament in the midst of debate over the creation of a new divorce court—one that would rework the complicated judicial system and the archaic process requiring a private act of parliament. The women's petitions and the notoriety of Norton's case pushed a number of members of parliament to debate married women's property rights along with what had begun as a much more bureaucratic and administrative discussion of divorce. The 1857 Matrimonial Causes Act (also known as the Divorce Act) established a separate divorce court in London. Thus, divorce became more accessible for the middle classes, but still, because of the expense involved for travel and fees, out of reach for most of the working class. The 1857 act also reaffirmed the patriarchal structure of marriage and the existing double standard for divorce: the husband could attain a divorce on the basis of his wife's adultery alone, but the wife seeking a divorce needed to prove the husband's adultery in addition to either incest, bigamy, or physical cruelty. Feminist arguments did influence the crafting of a clause allowing the abused wife to seek a legal separation from her husband on the basis of cruelty alone. Once separated, she attained many of the legal rights of a *feme sole* (single woman)—able to own property, claim her own earnings, sign contracts, and sue and be sued. Although a far cry from upholding the property rights of all married women, this aspect of the 1857 Divorce Act proved much more important than parliament anticipated. When the Divorce Court opened in 1858, a surprisingly large number of women, primarily from the middle classes, presented requests for separation on the basis of their husbands' gross physical cruelty.

It would take over 10 years for parliament to approve legal reforms recognizing married women's property rights. The movement gained renewed prominence after the failed attempt to include women's suffrage in the 1867 Second Reform Act, a moment that led many feminists to link issues of suffrage and property rights together if they did not already. In 1868, feminists—many from the north of England, especially Manchester—joined to form the Married Women's Property Committee with Lydia Becker (1827–1890) as treasurer and Wolstenholme Elmy as secretary, along with other suffragists including Ursula Bright (1835–1915) and Josephine Butler (1828–1906). The barrister Richard Pankhurst, later married to the great suffrage leader Emmeline Pankhurst (1858–1928), joined the committee and drafted bills to be introduced to parliament. Another member of the Married Women's Property Committee, the writer and Langham Place associate Frances Power Cobbe (1822–1904), presented a powerful argument for married women's claim to property as a fundamental civil right unjustly denied in her essay "Criminals, Idiots, Women, and Minors" (1868). Her friend John Stuart Mill, who as a member of parliament had sponsored the 1867 amendment for women's suffrage, made similar arguments in *The Subjection of Women* (1869).

Thus, backed by some 15 years of feminist activism, the Married Women's Property Act became law in 1870. It, too, proved a compromise and a disappointment. The Married Women's Property Act

Frances Power Cobbe, ca. 1870s, journalist, leader of the women's movement, and the force behind the British Union to Abolish Vivisection (BUAV), formed in 1898 and still active today. (Hulton-Deutsch Collection/Corbis)

of 1870 made it legal for wives to own only certain types of "separate property." These included some inheritances, savings in registered accounts, and any wages earned after marriage, but not saved income earned prior to marriage or before the bill became law. The law did not support, as feminists had hoped, the recognition of wives' legal existence as individuals separate from their husbands. Married women still, for example, could not sign contracts, sue or be sued in court, or draft wills without their husbands' approval.

The Married Women's Property Committee renewed its campaign, ultimately gaining a significant victory with the Married Women's Property Act of 1882. This law fell short of overturning coverture. It did, however, grant married women full claim to their inheritances and property, including all earnings and savings, along with the right to make their own wills and form contracts. Such major reforms led the *Women's Suffrage Journal* to celebrate the 1882 act as "the Magna Carta" for women.[5]

## Domestic Violence and Rape

Domestic violence and rape emerged as principal issues for feminist reformers amidst the campaigns for married women's rights. Changes in the court system and the rise of the popular press gave Victorians greater awareness of domestic violence. Early Victorian discussions concentrated primarily on the working classes. The passage of the 1828 Offenses Against the Person Act permitted local police court magistrates to try spousal abuse complaints, resulting in a dramatic increase in cases featured in newspapers' regular police court reports. The press provided ample subject material for novelists such as Charles Dickens, who stunned the public with his description and dramatic readings of Sikes's vicious murder of Nancy in *Oliver Twist* (1837–1839). The Society for the Protection of Women and Children from Aggravated Assaults was founded in 1857 to observe magistrates' proceedings and campaign for national reform. When the Divorce Court opened in January 1858, the daily press similarly chronicled accusations of marital violence among the middle and upper classes, demonstrating in brutal detail that Caroline Norton's experience was by no means exceptional.

By the 1870s, liberal feminists engaged in an organized campaign against domestic violence by publishing articles, presenting papers, and petitioning parliament on the topic. In "Wife-Torture in England," published in the widely read *Contemporary Review* (1878), Frances Power Cobbe compiled a horrific account of domestic violence. Drawing from recent police court cases, she reproduced with glaring insensitivity stereotypes about drunken and brutal working-class men, while appealing to gentlemen of the middle and upper classes to act as female protectors. Cobbe's essay nonetheless also suggested that domestic violence stemmed from the subordination of women of all classes, and her essay rallied the necessary support to pass the Matrimonial Causes Act of 1878. The new law enabled wives who had been physically abused by their husbands to appeal to their local police court for a formal separation entitling them to the legal rights of a *feme sole*. Until this point, only those women who could gain access to the Divorce Court in London could be granted a separation on the basis of cruelty, so the new law opened up this avenue for working-class women. Still, if a wife left her husband because of physical abuse before receiving an official court separation, she could be charged with desertion and denied all rights to custody of her children or maintenance payments from her husband. The Summary Jurisdiction (Married Women) Act of 1895 changed this, allowing women to apply to magistrates for a separation after they left abusive husbands in cases of cruelty, neglect, or desertion. In practical terms, however, the new laws left much to be desired. Police court magistrates often showed an unwillingness to approve separations, the punishments for convicted wife beaters—even murderers—were often appallingly lenient, and divorce still remained largely inaccessible to working-class couples until after World War I.

**Frances Power Cobbe, "Wife-Torture in England," *The Contemporary Review* 32 (April 1878): 74**

*In this article calling for government legislation to create stronger punishments for domestic violence and make it easier for working-class women to leave abusive husbands, Cobbe provided summary accounts of cases reported in newspapers from September 1877 to January 1878.*

James Mills cut his wife's throat as she lay in bed. He was quite sober at the time. On a previous occasion he had nearly torn away her left breast.

J. Coleman returned home early in the morning, and, finding his wife asleep, took up a heavy piece of wood and struck her on the head and arm, bruising her arm. On a previous occasion he had fractured her ribs.

John Mills poured out vitriol [sulfuric acid] deliberately, and threw it in his wife's face, because she asked him to give her some of his wages. He had said previously that he would blind her.

James Lawrence, who had been frequently bound over to keep the peace, and who had been supported by his wife's industry for years, struck her on the face with a poker, leaving traces of the most dreadful kind when she appeared in court.

Frederick Knight jumped on the face of his wife (who had only been confined [for childbirth] a month) with a pair of boots studded with hobnails.

Richard Mountain beat his wife on the back and mouth, and turned her out of her bed and out of their room one hour after she had been confined.

Alfred Roberts felled his wife to the floor, with a child in her arms; knelt on her, and grasped her throat. She had previously taken out three summonses against him, but had never attended.

John Harris, a shoemaker, at Sheffield, found his wife and children in bed; dragged her out, and, after vainly attempting to force her into the oven, tore off her night-dress and turned her round before the fire "like a piece of beef," while the children stood on the stairs listening to their mother's agonized screams.

While the feminist critique of marriage brought widespread attention to domestic violence, few proved willing to speak out against marital rape and sexual assault. A handful of reformers did, and their comments sparked widespread discourse on the very institution of marriage, mostly in favor of its defense and women's subordination. John Stuart Mill was one of the first to raise the issue in *The Subjection of Women*. Nearly a decade later in *Marriage As It Was, As It Is, and As It Should Be* (1878), Annie Besant (1847–1933) identified the granting of husbands conjugal rights regardless of their wives' consent as "legalised rape," one of the most fundamental ways in which the state continued to deny the basic human rights of married women. She stressed, "A married woman loses control over her own body; it belongs to her owner, not to herself; no force, no violence, on the husband's part in conjugal relations, is regarded as possible by the law; she may be suffering, ill, it matters not; force or constraint is recognised by the law as rape, in all cases save that of marriage."[6]

Married women's sexual subordination became a central issue for other reformers, including Wolstenholme Elmy, who worked unsuccessfully through the 1880s and 1890s to have parliament remove the marital exemption explicitly stated in existing rape laws. Writing an essay for the radical *Westminster Review* on "Marriage" in 1888, the journalist and New Woman novelist Mona

Caird (1854–1932) suggested that the institution itself was the root cause of inequality and violence. In an argument similar to those of prominent socialists such as Friedrich Engels, she described marriage as a form of prostitution. Caird envisioned ideal marriage as a free partnership in which the wife maintained not only economic independence, but also the right of sexual consent—"the obvious right of the woman to *possess herself* body and soul, to give or withhold herself body and soul exactly as she wills."[7] Caird's essay sparked an unprecedented response in the popular press when the *Daily Telegraph* elicited and published letters from readers under the heading "Is Marriage a Failure?" The newspaper received some 27,000 letters, although none of the examples selected for publication addressed marital rape. The editor continued to print selections representing both sides of the argument from August to September 1888, when the series abruptly ceased, overshadowed by press reports of the Jack-the-Ripper (or Whitechapel) murders of female prostitutes in London. Meanwhile, Caird wrote one of the most in-depth examinations of marital rape to date in her Gothic novel *The Wing of Azrael*, which she published the following year in 1889.

The clearest affirmation of married women's right to control their own bodies came not from parliament, but the courts. In 1891, the Court of Appeals defended a married woman's right to bodily autonomy in the case *Regina* v. *Jackson*. The disagreement, better-known as the Clitheroe Case, arose from a conflict between Emily Jackson of Clitheroe in Lancashire and her husband Edmund. At the age of 42, Emily suddenly married Edmund Jackson in November 1887. Five days after the wedding, he left for New Zealand, promising to bring Emily shortly. The couple disputed during their correspondence, and when Edmund returned to England in July 1888, Emily refused to live with him. Edmund filed with the Divorce Court for restitution of conjugal rights to force his wife to cohabit with him. But before any decision could be made, he abducted her as she left church in the spring of 1891, taking her away in his carriage and holding her under lock and key in his house with scheduled visits from a physician to attest there was no physical cruelty under the law. Emily's relatives applied for a writ of *habeas corpus* to force Edmund to bring his wife before the court. The judges refused, arguing that it was not illegal for a husband to detain his wife. When Emily's relatives appealed, however, the justices overturned the previous ruling and granted a writ of *habeas corpus* requiring Edmund to release his wife. Lord Chancellor Halsbury defended his decision in the *Times*, declaring that "no English subject has a right to imprison another English subject . . . without any lawful authority."[8]

The antisuffragist Eliza Lynn Linton (1822–1898) condemned the appeal decision in the *Nineteenth Century* as signifying the end of marriage, while Wolstenholme Elmy celebrated the moment as a culminating victory on par with the 1772 Somerset Case that made slavery in England illegal. "'Coverture' is dead and buried," she wrote to a friend, "It [*Regina* v. *Jackson*] is the grandest victory the women's cause has ever yet gained, greater even than the passing of the Married Women's Property Acts."[9] Wolstenholme Elmy knew well that marital rape remained unacknowledged by the law, yet the Clitheroe Abduction Case provided a ruling from which to work that recognized women's legal right as English subjects to control their very persons.

## POPULAR POLITICAL MOVEMENTS

In addition to the campaigns for women's legal rights, women took part in nearly every Victorian political movement. For example, elite women cultivated political connections by hosting dinners and organizing fund-raisers. But beyond the home, women also petitioned parliament, published political essays, corresponded with government officials, canvassed voters, demonstrated in the streets, and in exceptional instances delivered public speeches. Women's activism was unsurprisingly most visible in the century's popular political movements that took shape outside of parliament; in these, women worked alongside working-class men who were also for much of the century denied suffrage to demand political change using tactics other than the vote. While labor historians of the 1960s and 1970s tended to overlook women's activism, more recent research demonstrates women's strong commitment to many working-class political causes. In some cases, women's roles continued to be mainly secondary and supportive, as in the Chartist and Anti-Corn Law movements of the 1830s and 1840s. In other instances, however, women took center stage. The political issues that drew all classes of women stressed common themes of individual rights, child custody, and bodily autonomy—essential principles of the abolition movement (see Chapter 8), the opposition to the New Poor Law of 1834, the anti-vaccination movement, and the campaign to repeal the Contagious Diseases (CD) Acts that introduced state regulation of prostitution.

### The New Poor Law of 1834

The New Poor Law of 1834 was one of the first major pieces of legislation passed by the newly structured parliament following the Great Reform Act of 1832. Reforming the old Elizabethan poor laws had been a decades-long process, but the 1834 act clearly represented the influence of the newly enfranchised middle classes. Attacking what they perceived as an overly generous system of poor relief, supporters of the New Poor Law stressed ideas of self-help and individualism gleaned from the Evangelical revival as well as from the liberal ideas of political economists such as Adam Smith, Jeremy Bentham, and Thomas Malthus. The result was to turn what had once generally been considered a right to basic assistance from the local parish of birth (in the form of shelter, food, medical aid, or even wage supplements) into a punishment. The changes in law had profound effects for the working classes, who frequently applied to their local parishes for help during times of family crisis, illness, and old age. Women most of all felt the effects of the punitive New Poor Law; from 1834 until the end of the century, approximately two-thirds of all adults receiving relief were women.

The New Poor Law eventually imposed sweeping changes to the system of poor relief, although some local parishes initially resisted the reforms. To make services more uniform, more centralized, and, above all else, more cost effective, the New Poor Law organized local parishes into unions managed by elected local boards of guardians. A central body, the Poor Law Commission (replaced in 1847 by the Poor Law Board and then in 1871 by the Local Government Board), supervised national poor law policy. The most fraught goal of the New Poor Law was to limit outrelief—that is, the aid traditionally distributed by parish guardians in the form of food, medical care, or wage supplements—by imposing the "workhouse test" requiring all individuals seeking state assistance to enter the workhouse. All unions were to build their own workhouses if they did not already exist. Loosely modeled on Jeremy Bentham's Panopticon plans for prisons and other institutions, the workhouse served as a punishment—a humiliating reminder that poverty supposedly resulted from a failure to work. Designers of the New Poor Law envisioned workhouses as places of confinement, discipline, and supervision where paupers might learn the value of work through demeaning tasks, such as breaking stones, grinding grain for flour, or picking oakum (pulling apart old ropes, which would then be mixed with tar and used by ship builders). In practice, many poor law recipients, especially women, continued to receive some form of outrelief until the 1870s, when the Local Government Board pressured guardians to enforce the strictures of the workhouse test much more uniformly.

The division of families within workhouses underscored more than anything else paupers' lowly status. Husbands and wives were separated into different wards. Guardians also took children from their parents and sent them to separate quarters for boys aged 7–15, girls 7–15, and younger children under 7. In most cases, only infants under two could stay with their mothers. The New Poor Law's separation of children from their mothers inspired widespread criticism and sympathy for the poor. Yet most middle-class reformers continued to view poor parents as corrupting influences and made even greater efforts to curtail their parental rights. By 1870, all London poor law unions sent long-term child inmates away from workhouses to separate schools (called district schools when they contained children from more than one poor law union), which could be miles away from their parents' workhouse or other place of residence in the city. Some poor law reformers—including those who otherwise favored women's increased political rights and suffrage—advocated cutting the legal bond between pauper parent and child entirely. Florence Davenport Hill (1828/1829–1919) proposed in 1870 that pauper parents should lose all legal rights over their children. In 1874, Jane Nassau Senior (1828–1877) suggested that parents who brought children to the workhouse for short-term stays should be detained and sent to agricultural work colonies on the Yorkshire moors—a plan that she put forth with "some hesitation . . ., knowing the tenderness of the English law with regard to the liberty of the subject."[10] Such proposals proved too extreme, but in 1889, the Act for the Prevention of Cruelty to Children (also known as the Children's Charter) empowered poor law guardians to claim custody from parents found guilty of neglect, child abuse, or desertion.

The New Poor Law's restrictions on parental rights represented for many working-class men and women a fundamental assault on the rights of English subjects. Widespread protests arose after the act's introduction in 1834 and continued with force through the 1840s. People marched in opposition to the new law, disrupted local board of guardians' meetings, and burned down workhouses in the name of individual rights, local self-government, and the sanctity of the family. Thousands of women signed anti–Poor Law petitions sent to parliament and Queen Victoria. Working-class women also boycotted shop owners who favored the law. Through the 1850s, children, too, regularly protested by destroying property and rioting within the New Poor Law schools; they even set fire to a newly opened school in Manchester.

Widespread opposition against the New Poor Law declined during the second half of the century, but mothers and fathers still asserted their custodial claim to children as a fundamental English right and protested when they felt officials treated children improperly. In 1894, for example, the nurse at the poor law Brentwood infants' school in Hackney, London, killed a young girl by pushing her down the steps. The school initially overlooked the child's death, but the girl's mother demanded an official investigation that revealed the nurse's history of sadistic, cruel abuse of children in the school. The mother's call for justice—or at least legal recourse—resulted in the nurse's trial and a five-year prison sentence. The school superintendent and matron resigned, but when the Hackney Board of Guardians agreed to give them their pensions anyway, local members of the community came out in large numbers to demonstrate vehemently until the board denied the pensions.

In less dramatic but nevertheless important examples, mothers struggling with poverty oversaw the daily care of children maintained within poor law institutions. Without the influence of wealth or the vote, they did so by using the political means available to them: they petitioned local officials, wrote letters to poor law guardians, appealed to the local police courts, and, when necessary, sought support from the local press. Mothers complained when teachers beat children unduly or treated them unkindly. They supervised their children's medical care and religious education, requesting, for example, that Roman Catholic and Jewish children receive proper instruction. They wrote to school officials asking for children to be transferred or that visiting days be extended. These actions, too, represented expressions of social citizenship demonstrating a deeply held belief not only in poor law relief as a basic entitlement rather than a punishment, but also in the rights of parents to oversee the care of their children.

### Chartism

In many cases, women who opposed the 1834 Poor Law turned to the popular movement known as Chartism in order to attain a direct political voice for the working class in government. The movement took its name from the 1837 People's Charter in which working-class radicals demanded political rights that continued to be denied to them following the enfranchisement of middle-class men under the 1832 Reform Act: universal manhood suffrage, annual elections, the secret ballot, equal electoral districts, the abolition of property qualifications for membership in the House of Commons, and the payment of members of parliament. Chartism at its height was a mass radical movement widely supported by women. Over one and a quarter million people—including tens of thousands of women—signed the 1839 National Petition to parliament, making it the largest petition ever received by parliament at that time. The second National Petition of 1842 gained even more support with 3,315,752 signatures. Despite overwhelming popular backing, the House of Commons voted resoundingly against the Chartists' demands.

In addition to circulating and signing petitions, women turned to more assertive and militant tactics. Female mill workers concentrated in the north of England numbered among the strongest supporters along with women from artisan families. As the government arrested, imprisoned, and transported hundreds of men during the violent Chartist demonstrations of 1839–1840, 1842, and 1848, women marched in protest and sometimes joined men in attacking police, government officials, and strikebreakers. Denied membership in the leading national committees such as the London Workingmen's Association, women formed over 150 all-female

A *Punch* cartoon from 1848 depicts "How to Treat the Female Chartists: Cockroaches, Rats and Mice Should See Off the Most Ferocious Crowd of Females." (Mary Evans Picture Library/The Image Works)

English Chartist associations and also joined mixed-sex organizations when allowed. They published Chartist tracts, raised funds, boycotted unsupportive merchants, and attended and delivered lectures when most people still regarded women's public speaking as a curiosity at best, a scandal at worst. Chartist women also organized cultural activities in support of the movement. To create community and raise money, they held tea parties and balls, theatrical and musical events, newspaper readings, and temperance society meetings. Connecting the domestic with the political, women headed Chartist schools and Sunday schools for children. While most women joined the movement to support the extension of political rights to working-class men, some demanded the vote as a natural right for women too.

By the mid-1840s, however, women became much less prominent within Chartism. Women's declining role stemmed in part from changes in working-class forms of political protest in the 1840s as committee groups and delegations gained importance. Unlike the mass demonstrations, processions, and petitions that depended on women's participation to demonstrate widespread support, the official national committees limited women's involvement, as well as that of migrant and unskilled workers. Chartists also typically held meetings in public alehouses and inns—locales where women may have felt unwelcome, especially as the temperance movement gained momentum in the 1840s.

An even more important factor in women's declining role rests in Chartists' acceptance of a gendered masculine definition of working-class political rights. Although several male Chartist leaders supported women's suffrage, only a handful did so prominently, and many openly rejected the idea. By the early 1840s, Chartist men stressed more and more the domestic role of working-class women in an attempt to refute the middle-class objection that workingmen's lack of respectable family life made them undeserving of political rights. Sacrificing egalitarianism in the hope of gaining acceptance, male Chartists increasingly argued that women should not work for wages and celebrated the supportive position of women within the home and family.

At the October 1842 inaugural meeting of the Female Chartist Association in London, for example, one of the male speakers argued that women should not have the basic political rights to vote or hold office—that their proper station "was the pride and ornament of 'the domestic hearth,'" rather than "the political arena." His comments caused a "sensation among the ladies," eliciting brilliant replies from Susanna Inge and Mary Ann Walker, who had previously written on the evils of the New Poor Law.[11] The crowd of women and men heartily supported Walker as she defended women's political rights and the principles of the People's Charter. In the following year, both Walker and Inge traveled the Chartist lecture circuit, Walker speaking on occasion alongside the great Chartist leader Feargus O'Connor (no supporter of women's suffrage). However, the middle-class and, at times, even the working-class press ridiculed the women. After 1843, there is no trace of their activism. That same year, the National Chartist Association revised its rules to replace the term "persons" with "males," leaving no doubt as to the movement's official position.[12]

The exclusion of women as political agents in their own right undermined Chartism's strength and potential as a working-class mass movement. In 1848, the Chartists' last major attempt to petition parliament ended with far fewer signatures than anticipated, and parliament again rejected their demands. Chartists continued to campaign for reform though without the popular support of earlier years. In 1851, the Quaker abolitionist Anne Knight (1786–1862) encouraged Chartist women of Sheffield to draft the first-ever parliamentary petition for universal women's suffrage and create a new organization devoted to women's enfranchisement, the Sheffield Women's Political Association. An anonymous political pamphlet, likely written by Knight, stated the problem most clearly in 1847: "Never will the nations of the earth be well governed, until both sexes, as well as all parties, are fully represented and have an influence, a voice, and a hand in the enactment and administration of the laws."[13]

**"Meeting of Female Chartists," *Times* (October 20, 1842): 3**

A meeting of female Chartists was held on Monday evening, in the National Charter Association-hall, Old Bailey, for the purpose of forming a "Female Chartist Association," to co-operate with the male association, and for other objects connected with the interest of the People's Charter. . . .

Mr. COHEN . . . could not help saying that woman, in his (Mr. Cohen's) opinion, would be more in her proper character and station at home, where she was the pride and ornament of "the domestic hearth," than in the political arena. (Sensation among the ladies.) He acknowledged the high and useful talents of Miss Martineau; but he did not consider that nature intended woman to partake of political rights. She was not, physically considered, intended for it. He had the highest respect for the character of woman, and sense of what was due to her in every point of consideration; but he would put it to the mothers present, whether they did not find themselves more happy in the peacefulness and usefulness of the domestic hearth than in coming forth in public, and aspiring after political rights. ("Hear, hear," murmurs, interruptions, and cries of "Order.") . . .

Miss SUSANNA INGE, secretary to the association, should like to ask Mr. Cohen why he considered women not qualified to vote, if they were not qualified to fill public offices? ("Hear, hear.") It did not require much "physical force" to vote. ("Hear," and applause.)

Mr. COHEN would, with all humility and respect, ask the young lady what sort of office she would aspire to fill? (Order, order.) If she would fill one, she would fill all. He was not going to treat the question with ridicule (hear, hear), but he would ask her to suppose herself in the House of Commons, as member for a Parliamentary borough (laughter), and that a young gentleman "a lover," in that House, were to try to influence her vote through his sway over her affection, how would she act? whether, in other words, she could resist, and might not lose sight of the public interests? (Order, order). He (Mr. Cohen) wished to be in order. He was for maintaining the "social rights" of woman. "Political rights," such as he understood that meeting to aspire to, she could never, in his opinion, attain.

Miss M.A. WALKER was astonished at the question put by Mr. Cohen, and at the remarks made by that gentleman. (Hear, hear.) She repudiated, with indignation, the insinuation that if women were in Parliament, any man, be he husband, or be he lover, would dare be so base as to attempt to sway her from the strict line of duty. ("Hear, hear," cries of "Bravo" from the men, and much applause.) She would treat with womanly scorn, as a contemptible scoundrel, the man who would dare to influence her vote by any undue and unworthy means (cheers from the men); for if he were base enough to mislead her in one way, he would in another. ("Hear, hear," and renewed cheers.) The events which were at that moment taking place in the north, where their sisters and brothers were being cruelly and unjustly transported, or else plunged into dismal and pestiferous dungeons, for no other cause than standing up for their rights and demanding bread to appease their hunger and save themselves from dying of starvation in their native land, were unfortunately of a nature to drag woman from her retirement, and call upon her to lift up her voice against such deeds. (Great cheering from the men, and cries of "Bravo, Miss Walker," and "Hear, hear," from the ladies.) . . . The spirited young lady . . . declared herself a Chartist in name and feeling; and having appealed to her fellow-countrywomen to "come out" in favour of the Charter, and, however ungrammatical their language, not to be dismayed by any shafts of ridicule that might be pointed against them, concluded by giving them the encouraging hope, that if it were only from the curiosity to hear "a woman" speak, the young men would come out and speak to them. (Laughter, and long-continued applause, amidst which Miss Mary Ann Walker resumed her seat.)

### The Anti-Corn Law League

Along with the anti–Poor Law agitation and Chartism, the Anti-Corn Law League represented one of the most important popular political movements of the early Victorian period. Created in Manchester in the late 1830s, the league called for the repeal of the Corn Laws—tariffs on all imported grain ("corn" in England refers to grain generally, not maize) that had been in place for centuries and were most recently revised at the end of the Napoleonic Wars in 1815. A foundation of Tory economic policy, the Corn Laws served the interest of the English landed aristocracy by keeping the domestic price of wheat high at the expense of the working and middle classes, who were forced to pay higher prices for food and higher wages to workers. While the league's supporters included working-class men and women, it was dominated by the interests of middle-class employers who favored liberal free trade. When, in the midst of the Irish famine, the Tory Prime Minister Sir Robert Peel eventually repealed the Corn Laws in 1846, his actions represented the rise of economic liberalism in England—and resulted in his resignation from office and the division of the Tory party.

Similar to their ultimately subordinate role within Chartism, women's participation in the Anti-Corn Law League tended to be defined by ideals of female domesticity and dependency. From the beginnings of the league in 1838, women attended political meetings and lectures, in some cases listening from a separate ladies' gallery. Women became most active in the movement from 1840 to 1842—a period when male organizers encouraged the formation of local female committees that drew on preexisting antislavery, missionary, and religious networks. During these years, tens of thousands of liberal and radical women expressed their opposition to the Corn Laws by signing petitions to the Queen, demonstrating how petitioning emerged as an important political outlet for women in the 1830s and 1840s. Women also canvassed for contributions and, most importantly for the league's success, organized charity bazaars that brought in impressive sums of money. The Covent Garden bazaar of 1845—the national culmination of women's effort—raised £25,000. Like the Chartists, women supporters of the Anti-Corn Law League organized cultural events, such as tea parties and dances. Most of all, by focusing on how the high cost of bread devastated the family economy, women used the domestic realm as a source of authority for public political action. The Anti-Corn Law movement thus not only reinforced women's association with the domestic, but also helped make political activism respectable for middle-class women by presenting national issues of trade and taxation as central to women's interests. Many middle-class women who later became involved in other campaigns regarded their early involvement with the league as having provided them with their first training in political organizing.

### The Anti-Vaccination Movement

During the second half of the 19th century, the anti-vaccination movement coalesced around many of the same themes as earlier popular political battles: the liberty of the subject, the rights of parental custody, and the freedom of bodily autonomy. Dr. Edward Jenner invented a smallpox vaccination in the 1790s using cow lymph, after witnessing in rural Gloucestershire that milkmaids exposed to cows with cowpox rarely became infected with smallpox. Medical professionals soon regarded Jenner's method as a safer, more effective improvement over the existing practice of variolation or inoculation—a procedure that Lady Mary Wortley Montagu (1689–1762) brought to England from Turkey in the 1720s in which doctors and laypersons used a razor or needle to insert smallpox matter from those with the disease into the arms of the healthy in order to create resistance.

The 1853 Vaccination Act made infant vaccination compulsory within three months of birth in England and Wales. Many opposed the state mandate of a practice still questioned on scientific grounds and simply disobeyed the act or continued the outlawed practice of inoculation. Popular resistance grew after another act passed in 1867 enforced compulsory vaccination much more stringently by appointing public vaccinators and increasing the penalties for noncompliance. Parents who refused to vaccinate infants could be fined up to 20s. Wealthier families could easily pay the 20s. fine, but working-class families who could not afford the fine (in addition to court costs) risked having the state claim their household possessions. If the public sale of such goods did not provide enough funds, one of the parents would be imprisoned for as long as 2 weeks—punishments that could, after the 1867 law, be imposed repeatedly until the child turned 14.

As a prime example of class-based legislation, the Vaccination Acts sparked protest primarily among the working classes, but the movement also gained support from the lower-middle classes in northern England and from the middle and upper-middle classes in London and the south. Leading politicians such as the radical John Bright and Conservative Prime Minister Lord Salisbury critiqued compulsory vaccination, showing it was by no means merely a fringe issue. By the 1890s, less than 10 percent of infants in Leicester (the center of the movement) were vaccinated. Popular protest eventually led the government to create a clause for conscientious objection to vaccination in 1898, which in 1907 could be proved by a simple oath before a local magistrate, thereby effectively eroding compulsory vaccination in England.

Much of the anti-vaccinationists' literature and rhetoric stressed that compulsion represented an attack on workingmen's paternal authority within the home, presenting working-class fathers as both loving and ready to defend their children. However, women asserted their political rights as parents too, along with their claim to personal liberty as English subjects. Women wrote for the anti-vaccinationist press, disrupted public auctions selling the seized possessions of convicted anti-vaccinators, marched in public demonstrations that could turn violent, and defended their actions in court. Fathers were more likely to be imprisoned for disobeying the acts, but mothers defied vaccination officers as well and took their terms in prison.

Women especially stressed the dangers that vaccination posed to children, citing cases of infants and youth believed to have died from smallpox or other blood-transmitted diseases soon after the procedure. The dead child and grieving mother emerged as dominant reference points and symbols for the movement. At the enormous Leicester demonstration in March 1885 attended by some 20,000 people from all over England, the procession began with a group of men who had been imprisoned under the acts followed by a hanged effigy of Jenner and a child's coffin. Earlier that year, after a child in Hackney died following vaccination, women in London organized a march across the city. The march took the form of a funeral procession with the women dressed in mourning clothes, several mourning coaches, a brass band, and the child's coffin. The banner draping the hearse read, "In memory of 1,000 children who have died this year through vaccination."[14]

While the Chartists' emphasis on women's domesticity ultimately overshadowed the female claim to political enfranchisement, this was not the case among the anti-vaccinationists. Women specifically drew on their maternal role and potential grief for dead children to justify their prominent public participation in political protests. The context had changed by the 1870s and 1880s, and many anti-vaccinationists supported women's suffrage as key to their cause. These included women such as Jessie Craigen (1834/1835–1899), Frances Power Cobbe, Elizabeth Wolstenholme Elmy, Ursula Bright, and Millicent Garret Fawcett (1847–1929), as well as many men. Female anti-vaccinationists also devoted their energies to similar issues framed around threats to women's bodily freedom, including the legal reform of married women's rights along with the antivivisection movement, the social purity movement, and especially the campaign to repeal the Contagious Diseases (CD) Acts. The anti-vaccinationist leader Mary Hume-Rothery (1824–1885), daughter of the Liberal member of parliament Joseph Hume, highlighted such connections in her pamphlet *Women and Doctors: Or, Medical Despotism in England* (1871). The work presented a broad call for Englishwomen's rights in areas ranging from women's suffrage to higher education and control over childbirth and reproduction. Hume-Rothery condemned both the Vaccination Acts and the CD Acts for overturning traditional English liberties and creating a political structure "under which free-born Englishwomen can no longer call their bodies or their babes their own."[15]

### Repeal of the Contagious Diseases Acts

More than any other issue besides slavery, the state regulation of prostitution (legal in the United Kingdom) instituted under the CD Acts of 1864, 1866, and 1869 galvanized the feminist movement, by bringing together women and men from the working and middle classes and in many cases reinforcing their commitment to women's suffrage as the ultimate means to guarantee women's constitutional rights. Both the antislavery movement and the campaign to repeal the CD Acts (a crusade also referred to as "abolition" by the repeal leader Josephine Butler) provided women with the experience of public speaking and political organizing for a just and righteous cause. Opponents of the CD Acts combined religious and moral rhetoric with the language of political rights to demand women's full liberties as citizens. Like many other feminist reformers active in the 1870s and 1880s, the repealers directly challenged the double sexual and legal standards for men and women.

Initially passed as military provisions, the CD Acts at first received little debate and discussion even though they marked an extreme restriction of women's rights in Britain as well as in the numerous British colonies that adopted similar laws generally with much more extensive regulatory powers. (The first such legislation was implemented in Hong Kong in 1857.) After a government study of the British military found soldiers suffering from remarkably high rates of venereal disease, parliament passed the first CD Act of 1864 to regulate prostitution in select ports and garrison towns in southern England and Ireland. The subsequent acts extended regulation to 18 ports and military districts in the United Kingdom. The CD Acts empowered plainclothes policemen in these areas to detain any women suspected of prostitution and force them to undergo regular fortnightly medical examinations to check for venereal disease. A woman who refused voluntarily to submit to the examination had to present her case before the local magistrate to prove she was not a prostitute. If, as often happened, the court rejected her statement and she still refused the exam, she could be sent to prison. Officials initially instituted regular medical exams for soldiers and sailors as well, but eventually jettisoned this plan as too degrading for the men. When doctors diagnosed the detained woman as having syphilis or gonorrhea, she was sent to a hospital for venereal disease patients (known as a "lock hospital") for as long as nine months. Furthermore, the CD Acts required women identified as prostitutes to register as such. Although many working women turned to prostitution periodically in times of economic crisis rather than as a full-time profession, by publicly identifying these women as prostitutes, the CD Acts contributed to their isolation as an outcast group.

Florence Nightingale (1820–1910) condemned the acts early on, but widespread public opposition began only in 1869 and lasted through the suspension of the CD Acts in 1883 and their eventual repeal in 1886. By 1867, doctors and sanitary reformers proposed an extension of the legislation to the north of England (where opposition to the Vaccination Acts was strongest), suggesting that they envisioned the CD Acts as a model of new state powers for all of the United Kingdom rather than simply reforms limited to ports and garrisons. Some prominent women supported regulation, including the physician Elizabeth Garrett Anderson (1836–1917), a member of the Langham Place Circle and the only female member of the British Medical Association for 19 years after her admission in 1873. In 1869, however, opponents of the CD Acts formed the National Association for the Repeal of the Contagious Diseases Acts—a group that excluded women from its first meeting and thus prompted Josephine Butler and Elizabeth Wolstenholme Elmy to create the Ladies' National Association for the Repeal of the Contagious Diseases Acts (LNA). Both organizations worked to gain support through petitioning, holding large public meetings, forming local branch associations, and lobbying members of parliament and the electorate. They wrote pamphlets and circulated information through their official journal, *The Shield*. Josephine Butler in particular emerged as a dynamic and persuasive public speaker. Yet even Butler's sharp intelligence, renown beauty, elite social position, and devout religious faith did not exempt her from newspaper attacks of being a woman "unsexed" by speaking in public.

The repealers drew support from working- and middle-class radicals and liberals to challenge the CD Acts on religious and political grounds. On January 1, 1870, the LNA published a "Women's Protest" in the *Daily News* with the signatures of 124 well-known female reformers, including Florence Nightingale, Mary Carpenter (1807–1877), and Harriet Martineau. The LNA's protest put forth the main arguments against the CD Acts in clear language. The laws gave plainclothes police—called "spy police" by the repealers—unprecedented powers over women, establishing a system that challenged women's basic civil rights while the men who solicited their services remained unscathed. Repealers also argued that the CD Acts gave state sanction to the moral vice of prostitution, all the while ensuring that only women, not men, experienced the social shame and repercussions.

**"The Women's Protest [against the Contagious Diseases Acts]," *Daily News*, January 1, 1870, reprinted in Josephine Butler, *Personal Reminiscences of a Great Crusade* (London: Horace Marshall & Son, 1896), 17–19**

We, the undersigned, enter our solemn protest against these Acts.

1st.—Because, involving as they do such a momentous change in the legal safeguards hitherto enjoyed by women in common with men, they have been passed, not only without the knowledge of the country, but unknown, in a great measure, to Parliament itself; and we hold that neither the Representatives of the People, nor the Press, fulfil [sic] the duties which are expected of them, when they allow such legislation to take place without the fullest discussion.

2nd.—Because, so far as women are concerned, they remove every guarantee of personal security which the law has established and held sacred, and put their reputation, their freedom, and their persons absolutely in the power of the police.

3rd.—Because the law is bound, in any country professing to give civil liberty to its subjects, to define clearly an offence which it punishes.

4th.—Because it is unjust to punish the sex who are the victims of a vice, and leave unpunished the sex who are the main cause, both of the vice and its dreaded consequences; and we consider that liability to arrest, forced medical treatment, and (where this is resisted) imprisonment with hard labour, to which these Acts subject women, are punishments of the most degrading kind.

5th.—Because, by such a system, the path of evil is made more easy to our sons, and to the whole of the youth of England; inasmuch as a moral restraint is withdrawn the moment the State recognises, and provides convenience for, the practice of a vice which it thereby declares to be necessary and venial.

6th.—Because these measures are cruel to the women who come under their action—violating the feelings of those whose sense of shame is not wholly lost, and further brutalising even the most abandoned.

7th.—Because the disease which these Acts seek to remove has never been removed by any such legislation. The advocates of the system have utterly failed to show, by statistics or otherwise, that these regulations have in any case, after several years' trial, and when applied to one sex only, diminished disease, reclaimed the fallen, or improved the general morality of the country. We have, on the contrary, the strongest evidence to show that in Paris and other Continental cities where women have long been outraged by this system, the public health and morals are worse than at home.

8th.—Because the conditions of this disease, in the first instance, are moral, not physical. The moral evil through which the disease makes its way separates the case entirely from that of the plague, or other scourges, which have been placed under police control or sanitary care. We hold that we are bound, before rushing into experiments of legalising a revolting vice, to try to deal with the *causes* of the evil, and we dare to believe that with wiser teaching and more capable legislation, those causes would not be beyond control.

Like the anti-vaccinationists, opponents of the CD Acts highlighted issues of bodily assault authorized by the laws. *The Shield* and repealers' propaganda pamphlets published vivid accounts of the medical examinations forced on registered prostitutes, describing the exams as "instrumental rape" or "rape by speculum." While the movement revealed undeniable fractures among working- and middle-class women, on this issue, the working-class women directly affected by the CD Acts tended to agree with the elite members of the LNA. When asked the difference between prostitution and the medical exams, one woman replied, "Ain't it a different thing what a woman's obliged to do for a living because she has to keep body and soul together, and going up there to be pulled about by a man as if you was cattle and hadn't no feeling, and to have an instrument pushed up you, not to make you well (because you ain't ill) but just that men may come to you and use you thersils [sic]." Choosing prison over the medical examination, another woman told Josephine Butler, "We ought all to show the officers that we have some respect for our own persons."[16]

The successful repeal of the CD Acts in 1886 marked a profound victory for British feminists, but the length of their campaign underscores the entrenched resistance they faced. The repeal crusade provided later feminists with a model of women's public extra-parliamentary political action, as well as the female networks necessary to sustain it. The crusade to repeal the CD Acts was also significant for bringing together women from the middle and working classes, while revealing rifts echoed within the movement for women's suffrage.

## WOMEN'S SUFFRAGE

Although histories of women's political activism tend to focus on the question of suffrage, early and mid-Victorian women were much more likely to engage in issues of legal reform and popular politics. Some of these women would come to regard suffrage as key to their goals, while others would not. Certainly, there are examples of women demanding suffrage throughout the late 18th and 19th centuries, including, most notably, radicals such as Mary Wollstonecraft; socialist followers of Robert Owen who believed in sexual equality; women such as Mary Smith who protested their exclusion from the Great Reform Act of 1832; and Chartists such as Mary Ann Walker. Months after Chartist women created the Sheffield Women's Political Association in 1851, Harriet Taylor Mill (1807–1858) published an essay in the *Westminster Review* calling for the "Enfranchisement of Women." But large-scale, sustained support for a British women's suffrage movement did not develop until the debates leading up to the Second Reform Act of 1867.

Supporters of women's suffrage introduced the issue amidst intense national debate of reforms that would ultimately enfranchise many men of the labor aristocracy, or the better off among the working classes. The 1867 Second Reform Act gave the vote to nearly all urban male householders as well as to urban ratepayers—lodgers who paid £10 a year in rent and occupiers of dwellings taxed for the poor rates—and also lowered property qualifications in rural districts. These changes doubled the electorate to nearly two million men in England and Wales. Seeking to introduce once again the issue of female suffrage, Barbara Bodichon and John Stuart Mill's stepdaughter, Helen Taylor (1831–1907), with help from Emily Davies (1830–1921), Jessie Boucherett (1825–1905), Rosamond Hill (1825–1902), Elizabeth Garrett Anderson, and Elizabeth Wolstenholme Elmy, organized local women's suffrage committees in London and Manchester to circulate a Ladies' Petition arguing that women property owners should gain the vote on the same terms as men. Their position rested on the constitutionalist grounds that current practice denied the rights of "freeborn Englishwomen"—rights formerly granted under the ancient unwritten British constitution.

In the summer of 1866, John Stuart Mill presented to the House of Commons the Ladies' Petition signed by nearly 1,500 feminist leaders. Then in May 1867, he proposed an amendment to the suffrage bill that "person" replace "male person," which parliament resoundingly rejected. The 1867 Reform Act did substitute "male person" with "man"—a change that inspired thousands of women to test the law by arriving at the polls to vote in the general election of 1868, since "man" legally included women in nearly all other cases. A handful of Manchester women actually cast their votes, but the courts soon rejected women's claim to vote in parliamentary elections under the new law. However, the campaign initiated the development of local women's suffrage organizations in London, Manchester, and Edinburgh in 1867, as well as in Birmingham and Bristol the following year. Founded in 1870, *The Woman's Suffrage Journal* published in Manchester became a main voice of the movement under Lydia Becker's editorship.

Rather than supporting universal adult suffrage, the women's suffrage societies formed in the 1860s and late Victorian period tended to favor gradualist approaches advocating that women receive the same property-based voting rights as men. Suffragists developed rifts over the question of property qualifications and whether to support suffrage for married as well as for single women. Many of their public arguments for suffrage drew on ideas of separate spheres by suggesting that women—particularly elite women—could apply their domestic knowledge to the political realm. Even John Stuart Mill and Helen Taylor stressed such approaches. In her 1867 *Westminster Review* essay on "The Ladies' Petition," republished as *The Claim of Englishwomen to the Suffrage Constitutionally Considered*, Taylor focused on the constitutional arguments for suffrage highlighted in the essay's title. She suggested that the restrictions on female property-owners' voting rights proved "un-English" and "Oriental"—an example of how suffragists drew upon imperial rhetoric to make their case. However, Taylor concluded her essay with an appeal that would prove even more popular: a celebration of the domestic virtues women might bring to venues generally regarded by the 1860s as appropriate for women—settings such as schools and workhouses, parks and picture galleries.

**Helen Taylor, "The Ladies' Petition," *Westminster Review* (January 1867): 78–79**

Ladies accustomed to the government of households and the management of their families, will scarcely find political affairs petty, or calculated to exercise a narrowing influence on their sympathies. Whether we consider that women ought to be especially devoted to what is beautiful or to what is good, there is much work in the interests of either to be done in politics; and if the ladies were only to take schools, workhouses, public buildings, parks, gardens, and picture galleries under their special protection, and try to send to Parliament a few members who would work efficiently at such subjects, the rest of the community would have cause to be glad of their help, without their being themselves in the smallest degree vulgarized by such a task.

But, in fact . . . it is too late to be afraid of letting Englishwomen share in the life of Englishmen. We cannot shut up our women in harems, and devote them to the cultivation of their beauty and of their children. . . .

It is, indeed, remarkable how large a part of the subjects which occupy most attention in modern politics are of this quasi-domestic

> character; and how growing a tendency there is for them to become ever more so. The homes of the working-classes, education, factory acts (regulating the labour of women and children), sanitary laws, water supplies, drainage (all municipal legislation in fact), the whole administration of the poor-laws, with its various subdivisions—care of the pauper sick, pauper schools, &c.,—all these are subjects which already, by common consent, are included in the peculiarly feminine province of home and charity. If the possession of a vote should induce more women to extend their interest to the comfort and happiness of other homes besides their own, it will certainly not have exercised a deteriorating influence on their character.

Such arguments based on assumptions of women's unique domestic skills did help women gain the vote in local settings. By the 1890s, some 1,500 Englishwomen held locally elected positions primarily related to schools, poor law boards, and municipal and rural councils. In 1869, women ratepayers gained the right to vote in municipal elections (legislation later restricted to include only unmarried women). Women could also vote for the new school boards created under the 1870 Education Act, which established a national system of elementary education. In 1870, the suffragists Emily Davies, Elizabeth Garrett Anderson, and Lydia Becker were the first women to serve on the new school boards for London and Manchester. Beginning in 1875, many elected women worked as poor law guardians and, in 1889, served on county councils. Most suffragists viewed women's local vote and office holding as necessary steps toward national suffrage. However, even the *Anti-Suffrage Review* and the 104 prominent women who signed and published their 1889 "Appeal Against Female Suffrage" in the *Nineteenth Century* agreed that women's work on elected school boards, poor law boards, and other local councils generally proved beneficial for the nation and in keeping with women's proper sphere of influence.

Despite reforms on the local level, parliament refused to include women in the continued expansion of national suffrage. The Third Reform Act of 1884 further increased the male electorate by extending the lower 1867 property qualifications in boroughs to rural counties, although still only some 60 percent of adult males could vote after the act. By this point, however, women's suffrage had become a national issue. Radical suffragists, including Wolstenholme Elmy, Emmeline Pankhurst and her husband Richard Pankhurst, and Ursula Bright and her husband Jacob Bright, joined the Women's

Franchise League founded in 1889 in Manchester. Unlike most other organizations of the time, they supported suffrage for married as well as for single and widowed women, underscoring the fundamental connections between the challenge to coverture and the vote.

Meanwhile, radical working-class women concentrated in the north of England organized their own campaign calling for universal adult suffrage. They drew upon connections with socialist, trade union, and nascent Labour Party organizations, such as the Women's Cooperative Guild (founded in 1883). The anti-vaccinationist Jessie Craigen, who began working as a fairy in pantomime theater when only four years old, traveled the country in the 1870s and 1880s speaking to women workers outside their factory gates, in their homes, and, by 1879, in large public halls on the repeal of the CD Acts and women's suffrage. She became a favorite speaker among audiences (if not always among middle-class suffragists) and did much to bring working-class women into the movement. Similarly, in the 1890s, Esther Roper (1868–1938), whose factory worker father had abandoned her at an early age, joined with her life partner Eva Gore-Booth (1870–1926) to campaign for suffrage among working-class female textile workers in Lancashire. In 1901, Roper and Gore-Booth presented parliament with a petition for women's suffrage signed by 30,000 women, followed by another petition in 1902. Other radical working-class women, such as the socialist dressmaker Hannah Mitchell (1872–1956), held out the hope for universal adult suffrage that would include all women, not only those with property.

The more moderate National Union of Women's Suffrage Societies (NUWSS), established in 1897, demanded the vote for women on the same terms as men, meaning that the group accepted property qualifications at least for the short term. The NUWSS soon gained recognition as the principle national suffrage organization. Its leader Millicent Garrett Fawcett, younger sister of the doctor Elizabeth Garrett Anderson, first attended a speech by John Stuart Mill in 1865. In May 1867, when only 19, she witnessed from the ladies' gallery the House of Commons debate his amendment to include women's suffrage in the reform bill. Fawcett became a lifelong supporter of Mill's ideas, and under her direction, the NUWSS pursued primarily constitutionalist reform methods using petitions, writing campaigns, public speeches, and parliamentary appeals.

In the years directly following Queen Victoria's death, some supporters of women's suffrage adopted more aggressive tactics

Suffragettes walk Fleet Street, the newspaper district of London, selling *Votes for Women*, the WSPU's weekly newspaper. The paper was founded in 1907 and continued until 1918 when women (aged 30 and above) finally got the vote. (Mary Evans/Women's Library/The Image Works)

that gained widespread publicity even as the NUWSS remained by far the largest suffrage organization in terms of membership. Emmeline Pankhurst and her daughter Christabel (1880–1958) founded the Women's Social and Political Union (WSPU) in 1903 after becoming disillusioned with the lack of success gained by the more moderate tactics of the NUWSS, although the two major suffrage organizations continued to share many similarities. Like the NUWSS, the WSPU pursued the vote for women on the same terms as men. But Emmeline Pankhurst's vision of the suffrage campaign as "guerilla warfare" marked a significant departure from the NUWSS's "law-abiding" stance and drew support from early radicals, including Wolstenholme Elmy and Ursula Bright, as well as from many working-class women. The "suffragettes"—as members of the WSPU and other more militant groups, such as the democratic Women's Freedom League founded in 1907, were called—employed increasingly aggressive tactics. Adopting as its motto "Deeds, Not Words," the WSPU publicly protested candidates who did not support women's suffrage regardless of their party affiliation. Between 1905 and the outbreak of the Great War in 1914, some 1,000 women suffrage campaigners (most of them from the WSPU) and 40 men suffered prison sentences for acts of civil disobedience, including heckling, marches on parliament, and destruction of property.

Partial victory came at the end of World War I. The 1918 Representation of the People Act enfranchised all men 21 and over (except for conscientious objectors to the war) and all women over 30 provided that they were householders, married to householders, renters of dwellings with a yearly rent of at least £5, British university graduates, or military nurses or members of the Women's Auxiliary Army Corps who had served abroad during the war. Finally, in July 1928, parliament passed legislation granting full voting equality for all adults 21 and over. The experience of total war no doubt pushed parliament to question older ideas of political citizenship based on property and sex. While historians continue to debate the effects of the suffragettes' more militant tactics, it is clear that their attacks on property, their public processions, and their conscious use of prison sentences for a moral cause drew upon earlier women's working-class and radical political traditions from the 19th century.

## NOTES

1. "Rights of Women Petition," *Hansard's Parliamentary Debates*, 3rd series, Vol. 14 (London, August 3, 1832), 1086.

2. Charles Greville, as quoted in Kathryn Gleadle, *Borderline Citizens: Women, Gender, and Political Culture in Britain, 1815–1867* (Oxford: Oxford University Press, 2009), 162.

3. Barbara Leigh Smith Bodichon, *A Brief Summary in Plain Language of the Most Important Laws Concerning Women; Together with a Few Observations Thereon* (London: John Chapman, 1854), 6. I refer to women by their better-known married names, even when (as in this case) discussing moments in their lives prior to marriage.

4. Elizabeth Wolstenholme Elmy, *The Infants Bill* (Manchester, U.K.: A. Ireland and Col, 1884), 12, as quoted in Mary Lyndon Shanley, *Feminism, Marriage, and the Law in Victorian England* (Princeton, NJ: Princeton University Press, 1989), 145.

5. *Women's Suffrage Journal* 13 (September 1882), 131, as quoted in Shanley, 124.

6. Annie Besant, *Marriage As It Was, As It Is, and As It Should Be: With a Sketch of the Life of Mrs. Besant* (New York: A.K. Butts, 1879), 42, 12, as

quoted in Lisa Surridge, *Bleak Houses: Marital Violence in Victorian Fiction* (Athens: Ohio University Press, 2005), 192, 188.

7. Mona Caird, "Marriage," *Westminster Review* 130 (1888): 198, emphasis in original.

8. Lord Halsbury, as quoted in Elizabeth Wolstenholme Elmy, *The Decision in the Clitheroe Case, and Its Consequences: A Series of Five Letters* (Manchester, U.K.: Guardian Printing Works, 1891), 4.

9. Elizabeth Wolstenholme Elmy to Harriet M'Ilquham, March 21, 1891, Elmy Collection, British Library, as quoted in Shanley, *Feminism, Marriage, and the Law in Victorian England*, 182.

10. Jane Nassau Senior, as quoted in William Chance, *Children under the Poor Law* (London: S. Sonnenschein and Co., 1897), 319.

11. "Meeting of Female Chartists," *Times*, October 20, 1842, 3.

12. Anna Clark, *The Struggle for the Breeches: Gender and the Making of the British Working Class* (Berkeley: University of California Press, 1995), 245.

13. Anonymous [Anne Knight], as quoted in Edward H. Milligan, "Knight, Anne (1786–1862)," in *Oxford Dictionary of National Biography* (Oxford: Oxford University Press, 2004).

14. *Vaccination Inquirer* (January 1885): 193, as quoted in Nadja Durbach, *Bodily Matters: The Anti-Vaccination Movement in England, 1853–1907* (Durham, NC: Duke University Press, 2005), 63.

15. Mary Hume-Rothery, *Women and Doctors: Or, Medical Despotism in England* (Manchester, U.K.: Abel Heywood & Son, 1871), 16.

16. Quoted in "Report from the Royal Commission on the Administration and Operation of the Contagious Diseases Acts, 1866–9 (1871)," *P.P.* XIX, Q. 20297 and Josephine Butler, "The Garrison Towns of Kent," *Shield* (April 25, 1870), as quoted in Judith Walkowitz, *Prostitution and Victorian Society: Women, Class, and the State* (Cambridge, U.K.: Cambridge University Press, 1980), 202.

# 2

# RELIGION, SPIRITUALISM, AND DEATH

"We poor gals ain't very religious, but we are better than the men."[1] This is what an 18-year-old apple seller told Henry Mayhew, according to his early sociological study of the London working classes, *London Labour and the London Poor* (1861–1862). Her comments came in the midst of widespread fear of religious decline in the face of industrialization, urbanization, and scientific discoveries—most notably Charles Darwin's theories of evolution eventually published in *On the Origin of the Species* (1859). On March 30, 1851, the national census included a separate survey of religious practices in England, Wales, and Scotland. The findings, presented in 1854, shocked the public by reporting that almost half of the population had not attended any Christian church or Sunday school service on the census Sunday. Of those who observed religious services, nearly half (44%) were Nonconformist Protestants, who (particularly in industrial cities) appeared to be gaining over Anglicans, or members of the Established State Church of England, who made up just over half (51%) of attendees. Roman Catholics represented 4 percent of worshippers. The official report provided some measured hope in suggesting that among the aristocracy, regular church attendance had become one of the essential proprieties of life, if not always an act of deeply felt devotion. Yet, overwhelmingly, religious leaders interpreted the report as proof of declining faith among the working classes. Church observance was lowest in London and, with few exceptions, in England's great industrial textile and coal towns.

The findings of the 1851 religious census sparked substantial programs to build more churches and chapels in the second half of the century and, more importantly, energized religious leaders to find new ways to reach out to the working classes. The focus on religious attendance in the 1851 census, however, created a misleading sense of an increasingly secular society. The statistics—based on one Sunday out of many—failed to capture the importance of religion to the lives of Victorians, especially Victorian women. The young, London apple seller's claim that "we are better than the men" reflected not simply the fact that more women than men attended nearly all religious services. Her statement emphasized women's religiosity as a fundamental basis for female identity. Religious faith influenced nearly all areas of women's lives—their education, family, childrearing, leisure, charity, work, and mourning practices—albeit not always in ways that corresponded with official doctrine. Even women who did not regularly attend religious services likely said prayers with their children or marked the deaths of family members with the hope that they rested safely in God's presence. Religion served in many circles to justify female subordination, but women also transformed the religion of their day to become religious teachers, philanthropists, missionaries, and even female preachers.

**Major Denominations in England and Wales from the 1851 Census of Religious Worship**

**Table 2.1**

| *DENOMINATION* | *NUMBER OF PLACES OF WORSHIP* | *TOTAL ATTENDANCES ON CENSUS SUNDAY, MARCH 30* |
|---|---|---|
| **BRITISH PROTESTANT CHURCHES:** | | |
| **Church of England** | 14,077 | 5,292,551 |
| **Scottish Presbyterians:** | | |
| *Church of Scotland* | 18 | 11,758 |
| *United Presb. Church* | 66 | 31,628 |
| *Presb. Church in England* | 76 | 37,124 |

(*Continued*)

**Table 2.1:**
*(Continued)*

| *DENOMINATION* | *NUMBER OF PLACES OF WORSHIP* | *TOTAL ATTENDANCES ON CENSUS SUNDAY, MARCH 30* |
|---|---|---|
| **Independents (Congregationalists)** | 3,244 | 1,214,059 |
| **Baptists:** | | |
| *General* | 93 | 22,096 |
| *Particular* | 1,947 | 740,752 |
| *Seventh Day* | 2 | 83 |
| *Scotch* | 15 | 1,947 |
| *New Connexion, General* | 182 | 64,321 |
| *Undefined* | 550 | 100,991 |
| **Society of Friends (Quakers)** | 371 | 22,478 |
| **Unitarians** | 229 | 50,061 |
| **Moravians** | 32 | 10,874 |
| **Wesleyan Methodists:** | | |
| *Original Connexion* | 6,579 | 1,544,528 |
| *New Connexion* | 297 | 99,045 |
| *Primitive Methodists* | 2,871 | 511,195 |
| *Bible Christians* | 482 | 73,859 |
| *Wesleyan Methodist Association* | 419 | 94,103 |
| *Independent Methodists* | 20 | 3,120 |
| *Wesleyan Reformers* | 339 | 91,503 |
| **Calvinist Methodists:** | | |
| *Welsh Calvinistic Methodists* | 828 | 264,112 |
| *Lady Huntingdon's Connexion* | 109 | 44,642 |
| **Sandemanians** | 6 | 756 |
| **New Church** | 50 | 10,352 |
| **(Plymouth) Brethren** | 132 | 17,592 |
| **Isolated Congregations** | 539 | 104,675 |
| **OTHER CHRISTIAN CHURCHES:** | | |
| **Roman Catholics** | 570 | 383,630 |

*(Continued)*

**Table 2.1:**
*(Continued)*

| *DENOMINATION* | *NUMBER OF PLACES OF WORSHIP* | *TOTAL ATTENDANCES ON CENSUS SUNDAY, MARCH 30* |
|---|---|---|
| **German Catholics** | 1 | 700 |
| **Catholic and Apostolic Church** | 32 | 7,542 |
| **Latter Day Saints (Mormons)** | 222 | 35,626 |
| **JEWS** | 53 | 6,030 |

*Source:* Horace Mann, *Census of Great Britain, 1851: Religious Worship in England and Wales* (London: Eyre and Spottiswoode, 1854), 110.

## WOMEN AND THE MAJOR RELIGIOUS GROUPS

Victorian women's primary religious affiliation was usually developed through one of the many existing religious institutions. The Anglican church, corresponding to the Episcopalian church in the United States, is the established state Church of England. As monarch, Queen Victoria served as head of "the Church," as it was frequently called, and local church parish divisions provided the basic geographical organization for government. While most Victorians were identified as Anglicans, many associated with one of the proliferating Protestant sects, collectively known as dissenters or Nonconformists, who attended "chapel" as opposed to "church." These included older groups from the 16th and 17th centuries: the Unitarians, Baptists, Congregationalists, Presbyterians, and Society of Friends (originally called Quakers as a pejorative reference to their trembling with religious fervor). Other Nonconformist groups, most notably the Methodists, developed during the 18th-century Evangelical revival. Still other dissenting sects, such as the fast-growing Salvation Army, arose in the 19th century. Catholics accounted for roughly 5 percent of the English population. There was also a small, but established Jewish community (under 1% of the population) that grew with immigration from Eastern Europe in the last decades of the century and remained concentrated in major cities, especially Liverpool, Manchester, Leeds, Birmingham, and, most of all, London.

During the 19th century, liberal reforms gradually chipped away at Anglicans' exclusive hold on political power, overturning the

17th-century Test and Corporation Acts that restricted all military and government positions to Anglicans. In 1828, Nonconformists were officially allowed to hold public office and serve in parliament. (Some had previously held office under "acts of indemnity" passed by parliament.) Similar legislation granted political rights to Catholics in 1829, Jews in 1858, and atheists after 1886 with Charles Bradlaugh's admission to parliament and then the passage of the Oaths Act in 1888.

### The Church of England

The religious practices of women within the Church of England varied depending in part on their particular form of Anglicanism. "High Church" Anglicans placed greater importance on the sacraments, ecclesiastical authority, and ceremonies similar to Catholic practice, whereas "Low Church" Anglicans focused more on individual interpretation of scripture and Evangelical social reform. Those associated with "Broad Church" moderate principles stressed the Church's inclusiveness and acceptance of a multiplicity of theological positions and practices. On the whole, Anglicanism signified social respectability and status. The vast majority of aristocrats and gentry were Anglicans, as were many of the upper-middle classes. Until the 1836 Marriage Act, the Anglican church was the sole institution that could perform legal marriages, the only previous exceptions having been made for Jews and Quakers. The Church of England maintained a dominant presence in English villages, where the parish church typically towered over all other buildings, but its greatest stronghold continued to be in rural areas, particularly in the south of England.

Anglican women played a key role in directing their family's religious observation. Within the domestic setting, women represented moral and spiritual models. On Sundays, women usually attended the morning church service or, less frequently, the Evening Prayer service. (Evening and afternoon services tended to be more popular with Nonconformists, especially Methodists and Baptists.) Only the most pious Anglican women would attend both. During the week, many Anglican women also joined with their families for family prayers and devotionals at least once each day.

Among the leisured classes, Sunday observance required putting aside all work, amusements, and, for children, boisterous play. Women would read the Bible or religious texts such as *Pilgrim's Progress* to their children, but generally not indulge in novels.

After the midday Sunday dinner, they might take a family walk to observe God's work through nature, followed by silent prayer or the singing of hymns. Less observant families engaged in more festive activities, such as a country outing or picnic. Not all Anglicans favored strict Evangelical Sabbath restrictions on businesses and amusements. Privately opposing Sabbatarian legislation, Queen Victoria declared, "I am not at all an admirer or approver of our very dull Sunday."[2] Even after 1880, when scrupulous observance of the Sabbath waned and church attendance among Anglicans declined at a faster rate than among other groups, nearly all Anglicans still marked their connection to the Church of England and elite society through major rituals such as christenings, confirmations, weddings, and funerals.

### Nonconformists

While women dissenters represented a wide array of different religious beliefs and practices, the 1851 census revealed certain general social similarities. Nonconformists tended to be most popular in England's industrial regions and cities—notable exceptions being Liverpool, where Catholics were the majority, and London, Birmingham, and Portsmouth, where Anglicans roughly equaled Nonconformists. Dissenting women tended to come from less-elite social backgrounds, although this, too, depended on the particular denomination. Quakers, Unitarians, Congregationalists, and (to a lesser extent) Baptists drew members from the rising middle classes, including families associated with industry, business, the professions, and politics. Members of the pottery-making Wedgwood family, for example, were prominent Unitarians; John Cadbury, the founder of Cadbury Brothers chocolate, came from a long line of Quakers; and the Colman mustard manufacturers were devout Baptists.

The several branches of Methodism—together comprising the largest group of dissenters, roughly one quarter of all English churchgoers—drew an even more socially mixed following. From the early beginnings of Wesleyan Methodism in 1739 when the Anglican clergyman John Wesley began preaching to followers in open-air fields, Methodism became perceived—and often feared—as a religion of the masses. The Methodists formally separated from the Church of England after Wesley's death in 1791. Rejecting the teaching of predestination, Methodists stressed that individual salvation comes from feeling God's presence and that this personal relationship with God is free to all, regardless of social status or education. By the Victorian period, Methodism had strong support among the middle classes and artisans. However, some of the fastest growing Methodist sects, such as the Primitive Methodists and offshoots such as the Salvation Army, appealed primarily to the working classes. Methodist services and revivals embraced music and singing as central expressions of faith in the chapel and in the home, as well as, on occasion, in the streets and in the factory. Believers expressed their personal communion with God through emotional channels—weeping, public preaching, and even vocal outbursts.

For women, the emphasis that dissenters placed on the individual relationship with God and, to varying extents, social equality often translated into a greater degree of gender equality. Quakerism had a long tradition of women religious leaders going back to its 17th-century origins when the gentlewoman Margaret Fell (1614–1702) spread the faith along with George Fox, whom she eventually married. Fell campaigned against religious persecution and, in *Women's Speaking Justified* (1666), claimed the spiritual right for women to act

Sketch of a Quaker women's meeting in 1881 from *The Quiver*. (Mary Evans Picture Library/The Image Works)

as preachers. There were no ordained preachers in Quaker meetings. Friends believed that any member, male or female, could be guided by God's inner light to speak. Nineteenth-century Quakers, although relatively small in number, emerged as leaders of reform movements. Quakers Elizabeth Heyrick (1769–1831), Anne Knight (1786–1862), and Elizabeth Pease (1807–1897) sustained the abolition movement, and Elizabeth Fry (1780–1845) practically singlehandedly inspired the reform of England's prison system. Like the Quakers, Unitarians enthusiastically supported female education. Out of this tradition arose such activists as the industrial novelist Elizabeth Gaskell (1810–1865), the education and juvenile prison reformer Mary Carpenter (1807–1877), and the feminist journalist Harriet Martineau (1802–1876). For nonelite as well as elite Nonconformist women, education provided a main outlet and site for religious community. Women attended weekly prayer gatherings, Bible study groups, and mothers' meetings. By the late Victorian period, practically all families—especially among the working classes—sent their children to Sunday schools, which organized youth groups and outings to the countryside, prize competitions, and lending libraries, in addition to providing the foundations of Christian instruction.

### Roman Catholics

Roman Catholics in Victorian England generally fell into one of three groups: Old Catholics, Irish Catholics, and Anglican converts. Many of the Old Catholic families, also referred to as "English Catholics," had lived in England for centuries. These families included prominent aristocrats as well as those from the middle classes. Greater Irish immigration starting in the 1830s and increasingly rapidly during the famine years of the 1840s and early 1850s significantly increased England's Roman Catholic population. By the time of the 1851 census, the ratio of Irish Catholics to Old Catholics in England was roughly three to one. Although Catholics made up only 5 percent of the total English population, Irish immigration gave them an even greater presence in certain urban areas—not only in Liverpool, but also in much of Lancashire, particularly Preston and Wigan, as well as in Manchester and south London. The vast majority of Irish Catholics in England were not only urban, but also working class.

Irish immigration fueled new forms of anti-Catholicism that overlapped with anti-Irish prejudices, but the last category of Roman Catholics—those who converted from Anglicanism—perhaps sparked the most debate and fear about weaknesses within the established Church of England. From the beginning of what became known as the Oxford Movement in 1833, a small but influential group of elite Anglicans, many of them associated with Oxford University, stressed the Church of England's underlying historic Catholic identity. These Anglicans, also called Tractarians in reference to the 90 tracts published in support of their arguments between 1833 and 1841, called for reforms of the established church: a dedication to the Catholic doctrine of apostolic succession, a greater emphasis on church ceremony, and the creation of Anglican sisterhoods, among others. In the 1840s and 1850s, a number of prominent High Church Anglicans converted to Roman Catholicism, including John Henry Newman in 1845 and Henry Manning in 1851, who both later became cardinals. The public responses to such prominent conversions revealed how all Roman Catholics faced severe, deep-seated prejudices in Victorian England long after Catholic emancipation in 1829 allowed them to hold public office. Evangelical Protestants in particular decried the Roman Catholic emphasis on church ceremony over scripture and suggested that Roman Catholics' allegiance to the Pope threatened their national loyalty. Evangelicals regularly referred to Roman Catholics as "pagans."

Many Protestants also critiqued Catholic beliefs involving the Virgin Mary, suggesting that these, like Catholic attention to saints in general, veered into idolatry. Marian devotion reached new heights in the Victorian period following Pope Pius IX's proclamation of the Immaculate Conception, which declared that Mary had been conceived free from original sin by the miraculous intervention of the divine. Marian shrines and street banners carrying such messages as "Hail, Queen of Heaven" appeared in Irish, working-class neighborhoods.[3] Divergent Protestant and Catholic views on the Virgin Mary underscored the contested nature of Victorian ideals of womanhood. While Protestant accounts of Mary emphasized her self-effacing position as an ordinary woman, her role as (the sometimes flawed) mother of Christ, and her subordination to men, the Catholic Mary provided a model of a powerful, virtuous woman. Far from simply embodying a passive, domestic ideal, the Catholic Virgin Mary suggested women might attain a greater public role and authority through their religious devotion.

### Jews

Like Roman Catholics, Jews in Victorian England represented a minority group in which recent immigrants added to an already established, generally more elite population. The Anglo-Jewish community numbered approximately 20,000 at the beginning of the century. By the century's end, some 180,000–250,000 Jews lived in Britain, most of whom immigrated from Russia and Eastern Europe to escape the pogroms during the 1880s and 1890s. The older Anglo-Jewish communities, including prominent professional families such as the Rothschilds, and the newer immigrants differed not only in terms of class, but also in their religious affiliations and politics. Elite and middle-class Jews tended to follow the moderate Orthodoxy of the United Synagogue (founded in 1871). Politically, they generally supported the Liberals who campaigned for Jewish emancipation under which Lionel de Rothschild became the first Jew to take his seat in parliament in 1858. (The great Conservative Prime Minister Benjamin Disraeli converted from Judaism to Anglicanism at the age of 12 and was thus able to join parliament when first elected in 1837, although he later described himself as the blank page between the Old and New Testaments.) Working and lower-middle-class immigrants from Eastern Europe were on the whole more Orthodox and politically radical, advocating trade unionism and socialism.

As with other religious groups, the relationship between women's domestic and public spiritual roles remained contested and open to interpretation. Eastern European Orthodox Jewish law and custom forbid women from leading public prayers. Women's primary religious duties took place in the home—through such acts as the lighting of Shabbat candles to mark the Sabbath and the preparation of food according to Jewish dietary practices—rather than in the synagogue. Many Anglo-Jews called for a greater role for Jewish women in public religious services and practices, as well as for a more in-depth education of Jewish women in religious texts. However, by the end of the century, reformers regretted that a woman still did not count in a *minyan* (the quorum of 10 adult males required for certain religious ceremonies) and that the daily prayer for men thanked God for not making them women.

Earlier in the century, the writer Grace Aguilar (1816–1847) rejected a simplistic separation of public and private spheres by asserting that Jewish women's domestic identities provided the foundation for a more expansive public role as spiritual leaders. Aguilar grounded her arguments firmly in the English middle-class ideal of domesticity developing in the 1830s and 1840s and in the Bible, using the Old Testament to appeal especially to Evangelical English Protestants. Born in Hackney, London, to Jewish parents, Aguilar achieved great success as a writer of domestic fiction, poetry, history, and theology, before her premature death from a spinal disease at the age of 31. Among her best-selling books were works of domestic fiction that emphasized the underlying connections between Jewish and Protestant middle-class domestic ideals: *Home Influence: A Tale for Mothers and Daughters* (1847), *Woman's Friendship* (1850), and *The Mother's Recompense* (1851). Her works on Jewish history stressed that Anglo-Jews shared English cultural values—most notably feminine domesticity—and thus were deserving of equal political rights. In *Women of Israel* (1845), Aguilar rejected Orthodox Jewish practices that limited women's religious authority as without basis, turning instead to the Hebrew Bible for guidance. Reflecting on the accomplishments of the prophetess, judge, and warrior Deborah, Aguilar concluded that to "a really great mind, domestic and public duties are so perfectly compatible, that the first need never be sacrificed for the last." Addressing contemporary Anglo-Jewish women, Aguilar claimed: "many and many a Jewish woman is intrusted [sic] with one or more talents direct from God; and if she can stretch forth a helping hand to the less enlightened of her people, let her not hold back, from the false and unscriptural belief that woman cannot aid the cause of God, or in any way attain to religious knowledge. His word is open to her, as to man."[4]

**Grace Aguilar, "History of the Jews in England," *Chamber's Miscellany of Useful and Entertaining Tracts*, Vol. 18 (Edinburgh, U.K.: William and Robert Chambers, 1847), 17–18, as quoted in Nadia Valman, "Women Writers and the Campaign for Jewish Civil Rights in Early Victorian England," in *Women in British Politics, 1760–1860*, ed. by Kathryn Gleadle and Sarah Richardson (New York: St. Martin's Press, 2000), 103**

The domestic manners of both the German and the Spanish Jews in Great Britain, are so exactly similar to those of their British brethren, that were it not for the observance of the seventh day instead of the first [as the Sabbath], the prohibition of certain meats, and the celebration of certain solemn festivals and rites, it would be difficult to distinguish a Jewish from a native household. . . . The virtues of the Jews are essentially of the domestic and social kind. The English are noted for the comfort and happiness of their firesides, and in this loveliest school of virtue, the Hebrews not only equal, but in some instances surpass, their neighbours.

## RELIGION AND PHILANTHROPY

For women like Grace Aguilar and those of all faiths, philanthropic service represented a vital area of religious devotion. Charity work had long been important to the lives of middle-class and aristocratic women as expressions of female piety, selflessness, and maternal caring for the poor. But the extent of women's philanthropy among all classes grew to new heights in the Victorian period. As philanthropic work became professionalized, women took on more roles as volunteers and, eventually, as organizers and directors. Initially barred from the meetings of many national charities, women formed their own auxiliary groups. By mid-century, there were hundreds of national organizations run entirely by women, and many others where women joined men as central committee members.

Women's financial contributions also increased considerably during the period. Women contributed significantly to missionary and Bible societies and subscribed in great numbers to charities focused on children, servants, and other women. The Society for the Relief of Distressed Widows (founded in 1823), the Governesses' Benevolent Institution (1841), the Workhouse Visiting Society (1858), and the Institution for the Employment of Needlewomen (1860) all had histories showing a preponderance of female subscribers. Working-class women also donated to voluntary societies, in addition to providing aid to friends in need by offering childcare, burial fees, and emergency funds through trade unions and friendly societies. Charity subscription lists document their anonymous contributions with such annotations as "a poor woman's mite," "a servant girl," or "a laboring woman."[5] By the 1890s, contemporaries estimated that over half a million women worked regularly as volunteers or semiprofessionals for British charities.

The flourishing of Victorian philanthropy stemmed from the interdenominational Evangelical revival that spread throughout England in the late 18th and early 19th centuries. Most Victorian charities held an affiliation with a specific denomination; some philanthropic groups restricted aid to members of their denomination, but others sought to help all in need of assistance. Evangelical Anglicans shared a dedication to social activism and individual salvation with Evangelical Dissenters—of which the Methodists, Baptists, and Congregationalists were the most numerous. But philanthropy also developed as an important religious activity among non-Evangelical Dissenters—that is, among those who did not actively seek converts, groups such as the Quakers and the Unitarians—and among Roman Catholics and Jews.

The ubiquitous influence of the Evangelicals even inspired many humanists who came to reject traditional ideas of God and the afterlife. For example, although the writer George Eliot (Marian Evans, 1819–1880) eventually renounced the beliefs of her Evangelical Anglican upbringing, she continued to elevate human service and communication as forms of the divine. Becoming critical of religious teachings that separated the "sinners" from the "saved," Eliot maintained the Evangelical emphasis on worldly deeds, arguing "the great end of the Gospel is not merely the saving but the educating of men's souls, the creating within them of holy dispositions, the subduing of egoistical pretensions, and the perpetual enhancing of the desire that the will of God—a will synonymous with goodness and truth—may be done on earth."[6]

**District Visitors and Biblewomen**

Women of the upper ranks had for centuries practiced philanthropy by visiting the homes of the poor. They brought food and fuel, provided medical assistance and household advice, and offered religious instruction. In the 19th century, such voluntary opportunities developed from more informal acts of charity into services provided by professionalized organizations run according to published guidelines with central committees and fleets of volunteers.

By the early 19th century, all major English cities and towns had organized visiting societies that divided localities into districts. Within districts, each volunteer would be in charge of regularly visiting approximately 20–40 households. Male committees ran most of the early visiting societies, though increasingly women formed their own organizations in addition to serving as visitors. Most of the earliest female-run organizations focused on helping women through childbirth and illness, but these broadened to address the strains of poverty more generally. While the Methodists likely established the first societies in the late 18th century, most other major religions followed suit. London in the late 1870s could claim the (Church of England) Metropolitan Visiting and Relief Association with over 2,000 visitors, as well as hundreds of smaller groups such as the South London Visiting and Relief Association, the Sisters of Charity in Spitalfields, and the Jewish Ladies' Benevolent Loan Society in the East End. Starting around 1850, middle-class women also organized what were called mothers' meetings, where they met with working-class women to study the Bible and pass on advice about housekeeping, budgeting, and childrearing, or, in some cases, simply to sing hymns, pray, or talk together over tea. These widespread meetings created new types of female religious communities for women. Whether working in association with an established society or on their own, visiting the homes of the sick and poor remained a principle activity for religiously minded women.

Along with district visitors, Biblewomen emerged as early leaders of Victorian philanthropy. Their specific goal, in addition to visiting working-class homes, was to ensure that even the poorest of families possessed their own Bible. Ellen Henrietta Ranyard (1810–1879), the eventual founder of the London Bible and Domestic Female Mission in 1857, first came to the work through personal tragedy. A Congregationalist whose grandmother was active in the nondenominational British and Foreign Bible Society (1804), the 16-year-old Ranyard, joined by her friend Elizabeth Saunders, set off after attending a Bible meeting to distribute Bibles to the poor. Both girls became infected with the typhoid fever that killed Elizabeth. Recalling her friend's death, Ranyard associated this moment with her life's mission. "I remember thinking," she wrote, "that the Bible work was the one work to which I had been called by God, and to which I must keep faithful as one who had been baptised for the dead."[7]

**Ellen Henrietta Ranyard, *The Missing Link; or Bible-women in the Homes of the London Poor* (London: James Nisbet and Co., 1859), 291**

**LONDON FEMALE BIBLE AND DOMESTIC MISSIONS**

**GENERAL RULES**

1.—The work having now considerably extended itself, it is thought desirable to give it the general designation of "LONDON FEMALE BIBLE AND DOMESTIC MISSIONS."

2.—The *objects* of these Missions are twofold, viz., to supply the very poorest of the population with copies of the Holy Scriptures, and also to improve their temporal condition by teaching them to help themselves rather than look to others; the former to be attained by taking payment for the Bible in small weekly instalments [sic], and the latter by assisting them to procure better food, clothing, and beds in the same way.

> 3.—None shall be employed in this Mission but women of thoroughly respectable and Christian character, of active habits, kindly manners, and but little encumbered with family cares.
>
> 4.—The Districts shall be of regulated extent; and the Bible-women shall reside in or quite near their respective Districts, having a room in a central position for the general purposes of the Mission, for which the rent will be paid by their Superintendent.
>
> 5.—Each Bible-woman shall be placed under the careful superintendence of a Lady who may be found willing to undertake the work, and who is a resident on [sic] the District, or within a reasonable distance from it.
>
> 6.—The Bible-woman shall present a Weekly Report of her labours to the Superintending Lady, who will receive such Report, pay the salary, and give such direction as the local circumstances may require.

Ranyard more than fulfilled this promise, continuing to volunteer for the Bible Society during her youth and early-married life. After settling in Bloomsbury, London, she developed the innovative scheme for the London Bible and Domestic Female Mission based on principles of self-help and cross-class collaboration. For Ranyard, the Bible supplied the path not only to religious salvation, but also to domestic and moral reform. Proudly displaying a Bible in the home served as a sign of respectability. Ranyard's prejudices toward the poor and nonwhite colonial subjects were unmistakable; her writings frequently compared London's working classes to colonial "savages" in India, China, and New Zealand. She also realized that the elite status of many district visitors could make them seem patronizing at best, meddling and intrusive at worst, and thus arranged for working-class women to visit poor neighborhoods and sell Bibles through small weekly installments. By 1867, the London Bible and Domestic Female Mission employed over 200 Biblewomen (supervised by "lady" volunteers). As the first to pay female home visitors, Ranyard led the way to paid professional female philanthropy. By selling, rather than donating the Bibles (and later other items such as clothing, furniture, and cooking materials), she also viewed her efforts as reinforcing a spirit of independence and self-sufficiency among the poor. By the 1860s, there were similarly structured Bible missions throughout England, which spread to North America, Australia, and Southeast Asia. In 1868, overwhelmed by the dire need for better medical care among the poor, Ranyard organized trained nurses to visit working-class homes (carrying their Bibles with them) and created one of London's first organizations of district nurses (see Chapter 4).

### Women and the Growth of Victorian Charity

In addition to their work as district visitors and Biblewomen, Victorian women entered countless new fields of voluntary service. Religious faith nearly always shaped women's philanthropic motives and tactics. Women volunteered for Sunday schools, prison reform organizations, abolitionist societies, and missionary groups. Workhouse visiting emerged as a main area of interest for elite women in the 1850s. Homes for "fallen women"—prostitutes or those otherwise thought endangered by vice—proliferated. By 1879, London alone supported numerous "rescue" societies, such as the Female Aid Society (for "penitent fallen women"), the Female Mission to the Fallen Women of London, the Home for Deserted Mothers and Infants, the Homes of Hope, the London Auxiliary of Penitentiary, and the Midnight Meeting Movement.

Social purity and anti-vice societies grew in the 1880s. These included groups such as Ellice Hopkins's White Cross Army (1883), which called on men to commit to the same sexual standards as women, as well as the National Vigilance Association and the Jewish Association for the Protection of Girls and Women, both established in 1885 in the wake of William T. Stead's sensational exposé of child prostitution, "The Maiden Tribute of Modern Babylon." Many women's charities concentrated on mentoring girls in the broadest sense—not only protecting them from sexual exploitation, imagined and real, but also creating opportunities for instruction, leisure activities, and employment services along with spiritual guidance. The Young Women's Christian Association (created by the 1877 merger of two separate organizations, both formed in 1855) and the Girls' Friendly Society (1875), an Anglican group primarily focused on helping servants, were two of the largest, most influential female charities. (See Chapters 6 and 7 for additional discussion of female philanthropists, and Chapter 8 for discussion of female abolitionists and foreign missionaries.)

The charity bazaar emerged as one of the most significant sources of philanthropic revenue. Also called "fancy fairs" or "ladies' sales," they first became popular in the 1820s. By the end of the century, women throughout England organized bazaars for all sorts of charitable initiatives. The sales could be fashionable events held in large venues such as London's Albert Hall, or smaller affairs in churches, schools, or even a lady volunteer's drawing room. The more elaborate bazaars drew crowds with promises of lively songs and speeches, theatrical productions, and pantomimes. Middle-class women typically sold fine ornaments and crafts at stalls, encouraging patrons to pay a higher price for a good cause. They made some of the products themselves, including lace and embroidery, and purchased others for resale. Some groups sold goods crafted by the working-class and foreign recipients of aid. The bazaar represented an important field of women's public and commercial activity. Some critics resented women's dominant role, but rarely to the extent that they were willing to forgo the substantial revenues women raised.

**Select List of London Charities from Charles Dickens, *A London Dictionary and Guide Book for 1879* (London: Howard Baker, 1972; 1879), 34–46**

BLIND, HOME FOR CHILDREN, Train blind children

BRITISH AND FOREIGN ANTI-SLAVERY SOC.

BRITISH AND FOREIGN BIBLE

BRITISH LADIES, FOR REFORMING FEM. PRIS.

BRITISH NURSING ASSOCIATION, Provides Protestant nurses

BRITISH ORPHAN ASYLUM, For orphans of those once in prosperity

CATHOLIC (ROMAN) CHARITIES:

- CATHOLIC POOR SCHOOL COMMITTEE, Training and primary schools
- CONVENT OF FAITHFUL VIRGIN, Orphanage for girls
- CRECHE, THE B. BENEDICT JOSEPH'S, Infants from 3 weeks to 3 years
- NIGHT HOME, For girls of good character
- REFUGE OF THE GOOD SHEPHERD, For penitent women
- REFUGE OF THE GOOD SHEPHERD, Female prisoners
- ST. ANN'S INDUST. SCHOOL & ORPH., For poor girls
- ST. ANSELM, To disseminate books
- ST. JOHN & ST. ELIZ., HOSP. OF, Incurable women
- ST. MARGARET'S INDUST. SCH., Girls from London workhouses

CHILDREN'S DINNERS.—"GOOD SHEP." Teach, clothe, & feed little chil.

CHILDREN'S HOME, For orphan & destitute children

CHURCH OF ENGLAND SUNDAY SCH. INST., Improvement of Sunday Schools

CLAPHAM SERVANTS' TRAIN. INST., To train girls of good character

CRIPPLES' HOME AND INDUSTRIAL SCHOOL, For girls

DRESSMAKERS & MILLINERS' ASSO., Home for those engd. in business

EAST-END JUVENILE MISS., Adults & chil. of poorest classes

EMIGRATION.—HOME FOR DES. LIT. GIRLS, Preventive mission to girls

EVANG. PROTEST. DEACONESSES' INST. AND TRAINING HOSPITAL, The training of Christian women for nursing the sick

FEMALE AID SOCIETY, Penitent fallen women

FEM. EDUCATION IN EAST, SOC. FOR PROM., Schools for native female teachers

FEM. EMIGRANT SOC., BRIT. LADIES', Provide matrons, books, &c.

FEM. MISS. TO THE FALLEN WOM. OF LONDON, Provides female missionaries to rescue fallen women

FEMALE ORPHAN ASYLUM, For fatherless girls

FEMALE SERVANTS' PROV. PROT. SOC., Clothing on entering service

FRIENDLY FEMALE SOC., Wom. who have seen better days

FRY, ELIZABETH, REFUGE, For criminal women on release

HOME FOR DESER. MOTHERS AND INF., Servants fallen for first time

JEWISH ASSO. FOR DIFFUSION OF RELIG. KNOWL.

JEWISH INSTITUTION FOR RELIEVING THE INDIGENT BLIND OF THE JEWISH PERSUASION

JEWISH POOR, BOARD OF GUARDIANS FOR

JEWISH WIDOWS' HOME ASY.

LADIES' ASSO. PROM. FEM. EDU. AMONG HEATHEN

METROPOLITAN ASSOCIATION FOR BEFRIENDING YOUNG SERVANTS, For workhouse and other friendless girls

NIGHT REFUGE, Shelters homeless females

NURSES, NIGHTINGALE FUND FOR TRAINING, Hospital and infirmary nurses

OVERMAN'S ALMSHOUSES, Homes for widows and single women above the age of 50, and belonging to the Church of England

PRINCESS LOUISE HOME, &c., FOR YOUNG GIRLS, Young girls (not thieves)

ST. MARYLEBONE FEMALE PROTECTION SOCIETY, Young women not dissipated

SOCIETY FOR RELIEF OF DISTRESSED WIDOWS, Applying within the first month of widowhood

VILLAGE HOME FOR NEGLECTED GIRLS, Girls in danger of vice

### The Temperance Movement

The temperance movement provides one of the best examples of the evolution of women's philanthropic service, highlighting the centrality of religion and the complex way in which an appeal to female domesticity eventually enabled women to claim greater authority and physical presence in the public realm. When the movement first began in the 1820s, most reformers supported abstention from hard liquor, particularly the gin that was so prevalent, and beer and wine only in moderation. Teetotalers who advocated complete abstinence gained prominence in the 1830s and 1840s. Women, initially primarily from the working classes, joined local organizations and volunteered for youth groups such as the immensely popular Band of Hope, created in 1847 to provide entertainment and outings for boys as young as six who signed the pledge of abstinence. However, during the early stages of the movement, women were for the most part relegated to auxiliary ladies' committees and prevented from taking public or leadership roles.

Yet, increasingly, women writers and activists positioned themselves as authorities within the movement. They argued that intemperance undermined the domestic home by leading men to spend their earnings in pubs rather than on their families. Most temperance workers focused on the impoverishment and domestic violence associated with alcoholism in working-class homes, but in the early 1840s, the Quaker Sarah Stickney Ellis (1799–1872) published a series of stories graphically portraying the disastrous effects of alcoholism on middle-class families. In her three-volume collection, *Family Secrets, or, Hints to Those Who Would Make Home Happy* (1842), a lady set within the walls of the notorious insane asylum Bedlam recounted her descent brought on by drinking brandy initially prescribed for medicinal purposes. Most of Ellis's stories, like those that followed by Anne Brontë (*The Tenant of Wildfell Hall*, 1848) and George Eliot ("Janet's Repentance," 1857), linked the violence of abusive men with drink. The devoted Anglican Julia Wightman (1817–1898) published *Haste to the Rescue!* in 1859 detailing her temperance work and home visiting among the working classes of Shrewsbury. Distributed to thousands of Anglican clergymen, the book helped inspire the creation of the Church of England Temperance Society along with the entry of many elite women into temperance reform. Drawing momentum as well from the American Gospel Temperance movement that stressed above all the goal of saving souls, reformers created the British Women's Temperance Association in 1876.

During the last decades of the century, the major temperance societies remained male-dominated, but women became a vital authoritative, spiritual voice of temperance reform. The movement brought together women from different class and religious backgrounds and created a common—though by no means always harmonious—forum for those who might not otherwise agree on political questions such as suffrage. Women pursued this work in conspicuously public spaces. They lectured in public halls throughout the country. They sold cups of cocoa, tea, and coffee from temperance carts in the streets. They even stood in pairs outside of pubs waiting to convince the men seeking admission that they would be better served by saving their money and attending a mission temperance hall instead, where their souls as well as their bodies could be saved from the wickedness of alcohol.

**Catherine Mumford Booth, *Papers on Practical Religion* (London: S.W. Partridge and Co., 1879), 26–27**

I want to observe further that *THE USE OF INTOXICATING DRINKS AS A BEVERAGE IS THE CAUSE AND STRENGTH OF A VERY LARGE PROPORTION OF THE WICKEDNESS, CRIME, VICE, AND MISERY WHICH EXIST AROUND US. . . .* Unquestionable statistics have been produced which show that its stimulus is essential to the plotting and commission of almost every kind of villainy. The gambler seeks it to aid him in the craft and cunning by which he lures his victim on to financial ruin. The seducer has recourse to its deceptive power to pave the way for his cruel licentiousness. The burglar braces his courage and hardens his conscience by its exhilarating fumes. The harlot drowns in the intoxicating cup her sense of shame, and from it gathers strength to trample out the deepest, tenderest instincts of womanhood. The murderer is powerless to strike the fatal blow till maddened by its infernal stimulus. In short, all classes and sizes of criminals unite to testify, "By the influence of drink we are what we are," and missionaries, Bible-women, chaplains, jailors, magistrates, and judges, say, "Amen" to their testimony.

## ROMAN CATHOLIC AND ANGLICAN SISTERHOODS

During the English Reformation, Henry VIII dissolved England's Roman Catholic monasteries and convents. Some English religious communities continued practicing abroad, and of these, a number returned to England during the French Revolution to flee religious persecution. Twenty-four convents existed in England in 1800, but by the end of the 19th century, there were nearly 600 English and Welsh convents. Although the terms "nuns" and "sisters" are often used interchangeably in reference to all "women religious," nuns took solemn vows to follow a life of contemplative prayer within enclosed religious orders, while sisters took simple vows, lived in congregations, and devoted themselves to philanthropic service along with prayer. During the 19th century, there were over 10,000 Roman Catholic women religious in England and Wales.

Influenced by the Oxford Movement, High Church and Evangelical Anglicans also established religious communities for women. Among all of the reforms supported by the Oxford Movement, this sparked the greatest controversy. In 1841, Marian Hughes (1817–1912) took her vows and became the first Anglican nun. Several Anglican sisterhoods arose in the mid-Victorian period. First, the Sisterhood of the Holy Cross, known as the Park Village Sisterhood, was established in London in 1845 under the supervision of Edward Pusey. Inundated by internal disputes and limited by its all-male directing committee, the Park Village Sisterhood did not survive independently. Other sisterhoods, however, emerged during this period, including the Community of St. Mary the Virgin at Wantage (1848) and the Church of England Sisterhood of Mercy at Devonport (1848) founded by Priscilla Lydia Sellon (1821–1876). (The Park Village Sisterhood eventually merged with the Devonport Society in 1858.) By the end of the century, over 100 Anglican sisterhoods had been formed in England, concentrated in the south. Some of these proved fleeting, but in 1900, there remained approximately

60 active Anglican sisterhoods. Several thousand Anglican women had completed their training and taken vows of poverty, chastity, and obedience, and many more had spent at least some time living in a community.

Beginning in the 1860s, partly in response to the growing popularity of Roman Catholic and Anglican sisterhoods, Anglicans revived the position of deaconess for women. Deaconesses did not take vows. Drawing on Protestant models from Germany, they concentrated on philanthropic mission work. Most resided in the parishes they served, although some lived in communal homes. While the Low Church clergymen of the Anglican church (and later other Protestant denominations, including Methodists, Baptists, and Scottish Presbyterians) generally favored the position of deaconess over sister, the number of ordained deaconesses remained small. There were approximately 180 deaconesses working at the turn of the century. The greater female support and relative autonomy that came from living within the established sisterhoods likely provided a strong pull for women seeking to devote themselves to a religious life.

Catholic and Anglican sisterhoods and, to a lesser extent, deaconesses suffered widespread criticism arising both from religious groups who resented what they viewed as the expanding influence of Catholicism in England and from those who claimed that women's religious communities undermined the traditional family ideal. The Anglican author Penelope Holland (d. 1873), for example, condemned contemplative nunneries as threats to morality and the domestic family, asserting that "good and able" women "should know their vocation is the world, and not the convent."[8] However, by the 1870s, women's religious communities gained greater acceptance largely because of the immense contributions of their worldly philanthropic work. Active service sisterhoods established orphanages, schools, soup kitchens, and hospitals. They nursed victims of cholera epidemics, tended soldiers in Crimea, created rescue homes for prostitutes, and provided food and shelter for the poor. By stressing what they understood to be a feminine strength of benevolent care, sisters and deaconesses explored a more expansive public role for women beyond the traditional family unit. These women—particularly the deaconesses who worked more closely under the regular supervision of local vicars—remained subordinate to the male church hierarchy. And yet, within this patriarchal structure, they managed to craft a female-oriented space in which single women could pursue their religious calling and apply themselves fully to a life of prayer and service.

## FEMALE PREACHING

While nuns, sisters, and deaconesses created a space for women within male-dominated religious institutions, female preachers claimed spiritual authority for women as public speakers in ways that potentially challenged church hierarchies and thus rarely received full official sanction from male clergy and ecclesiastical bodies. Women's preaching emerged as a contested issue primarily among Protestant denominations for whom the sermon served the essential function of interpreting scripture, not among Roman Catholics or Jews. Those who opposed female preaching appealed to two main biblical passages:

> Let your women keep silence in the churches: for it is not permitted unto them to speak; but they are commanded to be under obedience, as also saith the law. And if they will learn any thing, let them ask their husbands at home: for it is a shame for women to speak in the church. (1 Cor. 14:34–35)
>
> But I suffer not a woman to teach, nor to usurp authority over the man, but to be in silence. For Adam was first formed, then Eve. (1 Tim. 2:12–13)

However, from the very beginning of the Reformation, Protestants representing various denominational perspectives questioned these limits on women, offering nuanced interpretations of the apostles' meaning in these passages, while citing support for women's preaching from different biblical passages and examples.

Women claimed the role of preacher most often in those Protestant denominations that did not require a formally ordained and educated professional clergy. Such groups also placed greater emphasis on individual interpretation of scripture and on direct communion with God. The lack of any formally ordained clergy allowed for the continued growth of a female ministry among Quakers during the 19th century. Female preachers also came from the various predominantly working-class Methodist sects that supported lay preachers alongside anointed clergy. Wesley recognized women with "an exceptional call" as preachers during his lifetime, but they, unlike the male clergy, remained unpaid and typically preached less regularly.[9]

Disagreement over female preaching in part precipitated the split between Wesleyan Methodists and other Methodist groups in the early 1800s following the Wesleyan Methodists' 1803 ban on women preachers. In the period leading up to the Great Reform Act of 1832, paid traveling female preachers earning roughly half a single male preacher's salary gained popularity among the new Methodist sects, especially the Bible Christians and Primitive Methodists. After this point, as Methodism achieved greater respectability (in part by stressing female domesticity) and developed a more professionalized clergy, the support for women preachers declined, but by no means disappeared. The last remaining Bible Christian female itinerant preacher retired in 1869—a moment that the all-male religious leadership welcomed with cheers. However, in the last decades of the century, Methodist and other interdenominational female evangelists continued to preach locally and in some instances developed long careers addressing crowds of thousands. Unlike the earlier working-class itinerant preachers, most of the female evangelists who gained prominence during the religious revival of the 1860s came from the lower-middle and middle classes.

Rather than rejecting the frameworks of domesticity and gender difference, Victorian female preachers tended to emphasize the particular feminine qualities women brought to the pulpit. Some of the most venerated models of female ministering proved less threatening because of their connection to women's philanthropic work. Although female preaching sparked much more resistance among Anglicans than among Nonconformists, the Anglican dressmaker Sarah Martin (1791–1843) became celebrated for her sermons delivered to male and female inmates in the Great Yarmouth prison. While she initially read from printed sermons, Martin wrote her own from 1832 to 1837. The greater context of her philanthropic work helping prisoners find employment, the prison setting, and the focus of her sermons on moral rather than theological topics encouraged others to hold her religious instruction in high esteem, a model of womanly service.

Likewise, Catherine Booth (1829–1890), the most famous of the Victorian female evangelists, argued that women's natural attributes supported rather than prevented their right to preach when they received God's calling. In her widely read 1859 pamphlet *Female Teaching* (revised and republished as *Female Ministry; or, Women's Right to Preach the Gospel*), Booth noted the "devotedness, purity, and sweetness" of esteemed female preachers such as Elizabeth Fry, who were far from "unwomanly or ambitious." Booth stressed

Catherine Booth, cofounder of the Salvation Army, was an advocate of women's religious leadership. (Begbie, Harold. *The Life of General William Booth*, New York: Macmillan Company, 1920)

that "these were all more or less public women, every one of them expounding and exhorting from the Scriptures to mixed companies of men and women."[10] She worked closely with her husband, William Booth, who broke from the Methodist New Connexion and, in 1865, created the East London Christian Mission, renamed the Salvation Army in 1878. More than any other Christian denomination, the Salvation Army formed a governance and theology that encouraged great numbers of women to develop careers as preachers. Thousands of working-class women joined the army as Hallelujah Lasses proselytizing in the streets, singing hymns, joining bands, and, most controversially, even administering the sacrament of communion until the Salvation Army ceased to offer it in 1883. Women Salvationists were typically paid less than men and they were not represented in the governing ranks in equal numbers, but through the work of the Booths, they created a highly visible public role for women as voices of religious authority.

**Catherine Mumford Booth, *Female Ministry; or, Women's Right to Preach the Gospel* (London: Morgan & Chase, 1859), 3–4**

The first and most common objection urged against the public exercises of women, is that they are unnatural and unfeminine. Many labour under a very great but common mistake, viz. that of confounding nature with custom. Use, or custom, makes things appear to us natural, which, in reality, are very unnatural; while, on the other hand, novelty and rarity make very natural things appear strange and contrary to nature. So universally has this power of custom been felt and admitted, that it has given birth to the proverb, "Use is second nature." Making allowance for the novelty of the thing, we cannot discover anything either unnatural or immodest in a Christian woman, becomingly attired, appearing on a platform or in a pulpit. By *nature* she seems fitted to grace either. God has given to woman a graceful form and attitude, winning manners, persuasive speech, and, above all, a finely-toned emotional nature, all of which appear to us eminent *natural* qualifications for public speaking. We admit that want of mental culture, the trammels of custom, the force of prejudice, and one-sided interpretations of Scripture, have hitherto almost excluded her from this sphere; but, before such a sphere is pronounced to be unnatural, it must be proved either that woman has not the *ability* to teach or to preach, or that the possession and exercise of this ability unnaturalizes her in other respects; that so soon as she presumes to step on the platform or into the pulpit, she loses the delicacy and grace of the female character. Whereas, we have numerous instances of her retaining all that is most esteemed in her sex, and faithfully discharging the duties peculiar to her own sphere, and at the same time taking her place with many of our most useful speakers and writers. Why should woman be confined exclusively to the kitchen and the distaff, any more than man to the field and workshop? . . .

There seems to be a great deal of unnecessary fear of women occupying any position which involves publicity, lest she should be rendered unfeminine by the indulgence of ambition or vanity; but why should woman any more than man be charged with ambition when impelled to use her talents for the good of her race. Moreover, as a labourer in the *GOSPEL* her position is much higher than in any other public capacity; she is at once shielded from all coarse and unrefined influences and associations; her very vocation tending to exalt and refine all the tenderest and most womanly instincts of her nature. As a matter of fact it is well known to those who have had opportunities of observing the private character and deportment of women engaged in preaching the gospel, that they have been amongst the most amiable, self-sacrificing, and unobtrusive of their sex.

## SPIRITUALISM AND THEOSOPHY

The rise of spiritualism and theosophy in the second half of the 19th century suggests that the mid-to-late Victorian "crisis of faith" involved the development of new beliefs and practices along with the questioning of older ones. Spiritualism gained popularity in the 1850s, first mainly among the working and lower-middle classes, particularly those with connections to radical politics who sought a middle ground between secularism and traditional Christianity. Their goal was to bridge the material and spiritual divide by making contact with the dead. Though frequently ridiculed in the press, by the 1870s, spiritualism gained popularity among the middle and upper classes as well. Believers included radicals such as the socialist Robert Owen, scientists such as the former agnostic Alfred Russel Wallace, and popular journalists such as the founder of the spiritualist journal *Borderland* (1893–1897) William T. Stead. Even Queen Victoria engaged a medium in hopes of making contact with Prince Albert after his death. The Russian-born Helena Petrovna Blavatsky (1831–1891), herself a practicing spiritualist medium, cofounded the Theosophical Society in New York in 1875. She later moved to London where she opened the Blavatsky Lodge in 1887 as a meeting place for her followers. With a center in India and others throughout the world, theosophy drew heavily from Hinduism and Buddhism along with many mystical traditions in an attempt to develop a comparative "scientific" religion. Blavatsky became largely discredited by accusations of fraud, but after her death, the former birth control advocate and Indian nationalist Annie Besant (1847–1933) led the society.

Women took center stage in the spiritualist and theosophist movements. They led séances that became fashionable in respectable, middle-class drawing rooms by claiming powers to commune with the dead through knockings, automatic writing, and vocalizations, or by making spirits visible before sitters joined around the table with clasped hands. The medium Florence Cook (1856–1904) began materializing suspended parts of spirits' bodies—hands, legs, and faces—when she was only 15. At 17, Cook became famous for repeatedly bringing forth the full-form materialization of Katie King, a young woman physically very similar in build to Cook whose 17th-century father served as governor of Jamaica. While Cook allegedly remained bound in a closeted space, King reveled sitters with details of her "earth life." King acted in ways that would never have been publicly acceptable for a middle-class respectable woman. She flirted with male sitters—even kissed them to prove her physical presence. Female mediums claimed freedoms that in most cases were otherwise denied to women: sexual liberties, as well as an authoritative voice to offer counsel on matters ranging from marriage to politics, and the material benefits associated with money, fame, travel, and access to the elite. The spiritualist and theosophist movements thus marked a rethinking not only of the material–spiritual divide, but also of male and female roles at the very time that women in the political realm were campaigning for greater professional opportunities and legal rights.

## DEATH AND MOURNING RITUALS

In ways far more prevalent than spiritualist meetings and encompassing far more diverse religious backgrounds, the Victorians' understandings of death reflected their religious faith. In a society with dreadfully high death rates where most people died at home, death remained a main fixture of daily life. Much more so than today, childhood, along with old age, was a period when the risks of death were greatest. In some late-Victorian working-class London neighborhoods, as many as half of all recorded deaths involved children under five. Death rates for children had improved tremendously since the early 18th century, when as many as 75 percent of all children died between birth and the age of 5. By the beginning of the 19th century, the child death rate for those aged 5 and under had declined to roughly 30 percent. However, while the general death rate continued to improve during the Victorian period largely as a result of sanitary reforms (see Chapter 4), the infant death rate for children under one year remained appallingly high and even increased during the last years of century. Roughly one out of every seven Victorian infants died in the first year alone. In some urban areas, late Victorians still suffered the deaths of over a third of all children aged five and under. Child mortality was most marked in impoverished districts, but all families—rich and poor, urban and rural—risked losing a child, in many cases more than one. Victorian families overwhelmingly dealt with such high death rates not—as was previous thought—by failing to love and develop affectionate ties with their children, but by finding solace when possible through faith and community.

The Evangelical revival of the late 18th and early 19th centuries spread a belief in the Christian ideal of the "good" or "beautiful" death. The dying no doubt experienced pain, but for Victorians supporting this new belief, death also held the promise of reunion with departed loved ones and peaceful rest without suffering. For children and adults, the model Christian death was marked by spiritual consciousness and resignation. Women's letters and diaries describing the death of a husband or a child often recount the last words along with some sign that the deceased had expressed an awareness of salvation through God's presence. For children too young to speak, descriptions of this key moment noted a change in the child's eyes, a turning toward God witnessed by adults, as well as a final look of peace or contented sleep.

As mothers and wives, family members, and friends, women drew on a rich culture of mourning practices to mark their sorrow as well as their loved one's salvation. Women—either paid professionals, household servants, or bereaved family members—typically prepared the corpse for burial. Viewing the dead within homes could involve a wake with guests, food, and drink—a practice that remained popular among Irish Catholics in England despite attempts of urban reformers to curtail it. Alternatively, many grieving mothers simply washed and dressed their child, whose body they sometimes held close through the night. Families who could afford to do so might arrange for a photographer to compose a postmortem photograph, especially when there were no other images of a child. When her firstborn son Henry died days after his birth in 1856, Emily Polehampton (1833–1905), the wife of an East India Company chaplain stationed in Lucknow, India, commissioned such a photograph. She also put two daguerreotypes—one of herself and one of her husband—in Henry's hands, which she crossed and placed over her family Bible, given to her by her mother, on the baby's breast before his burial. Women decorated coffins with flowers and personal items, while keeping locks of hair from their beloved to be worn within amulets or woven into jewelry.

Funeral services and the teas that often followed reinforced communal and family ties as well as religious belief. Elite women typically did not attend funerals during the early and mid-Victorian period out of concern that open expressions of sorrow might disrupt the services. Some women, however, ignored these social restrictions. By the end of the century, it became less remarkable for upper- and middle-class women to attend the church or chapel service along with the procession and burial. Yet, even in 1870, *Cassell's Household Guide* objected to the working-class women who attended funerals, claiming, "This custom is by no means to be recommended, since in these cases it but too frequently happens

Victorian mourning dress from 1861: Silk dress with square bodice, pagoda sleeves, waist, and skirt ornamented with "crape poche à la châtelaine." Circular mantle with tassels. Tulle dress featuring a skirt with diamond *bouillonne*. (Illustrated London News Ltd/Mary Evans/The Image Works)

that, being unable to restrain their emotions they interrupt and destroy the solemnity of the ceremony with their sobs, and even by fainting."[11] Even the poorest of families did their best to gather funds for elaborate funerals out of respect for the dead. A carriage and at least two horses would be hired to convey the coffin to the burial ground, which, following the cemetery reforms of the early 19th century, was almost always far from the village or city center. Working-class women usually drew a penny or two from their weekly household funds to pay for each family member's burial insurance. When these funds proved insufficient, neighbors and friends took collections to do all they could to help poor men, women, and children avoid a pauper burial in an anonymous unmarked communal grave.

Women's mourning dress served as the most visible sign of their loss—a nonverbal means of communicating their connection to the deceased, the shared experiences of grief, and the passage of time. Following Prince Albert's death from typhoid fever in December 1861, Queen Victoria withdrew from public life for a decade and wore black for the rest of her life. However, she was exceptional in her grief—compounded by the death of her mother earlier that year—and not in this case a role model for other women. Most widows from the upper and middle classes wore all black mourning dress, referred to as "widow's weeds," for two years. The first year of mourning called for dresses made from materials that did not reflect light: black paramatta (a mixture of rough silk with wool or cotton) and expensive crepe. Then came nine months of black silk dresses trimmed with crepe, and finally three months with black silk alone. During the final six months, widows might transition into half-mourning colors, such as grey and lavender. Generally, women put aside other jewelry for items made from jet, a type of black stone that could be highly polished. Women usually wore mourning clothes for the death of a child or parent for 12 months, and 6 months for a sibling. The expectations surrounding mourning dress swelled in the 1840s along with entire shops and industries catering to mourners and became less stringent by the 1870s. Working-class women unable to afford new mourning clothes would likely borrow black attire for the funeral, resort to the pawnshop, or dye one of their other dresses black. Women not only lent one another clothing, but also sewed dresses and widows' caps for friends as a sign of sympathy. When unable to attain mourning attire, women felt the loss dearly. One of the first priorities for British women escaping after the siege of Lucknow during the Indian Rebellion was to distribute a black dress to each new widow along with food and other necessities. Although at times mocked as an example of women's supposedly mindless adherence to fashion, mourning dress served a real purpose for women by allowing them to express their respect for the dead, their grief, and their piety.

**Katherine Bartrum, *A Widow's Reminiscence of the Siege of Lucknow* (London: James Nisbet, 1858), 69–71**

*In her diary entry for February 11, 1858, Bartrum described the death of her son, Bobby, after having survived the siege of Lucknow and the death of her husband during the Indian Rebellion.*

My dear child seemed so weak this morning, and I could not get him to take any food. . . . At one a.m. he began to get restless, but when I spoke to him he looked up and smiled; then I walked about with him till he began to struggle, and I was frightened and called Mrs. Polehampton. She told me to lay him in my lap: he was gasping for breath, when I turned away my head, for I *could* not see my child die. She said, "Look, how bright his eyes are growing!" and "now his eyes grew bright and brighter still, too bright for ours to look upon.—suffused with many tears and closed without a cloud," and *so* "the Lord called the child." Mrs. Polehampton took him in her arms, and when he was dressed in his little night dress and laid upon the bed, he looked so perfectly happy, that for him I could not mourn, and of myself I dared not think. "So He giveth His beloved sleep." When the morning came, we gathered some orange blossoms and placed them round him, who was "no longer babe but angel;" and when his little coffin came we laid him in it, there to sleep until the morning of the resurrection. During the day, I had his likeness taken, as he lay in the peaceful slumber of death, his little hand enclosing a sweet white rosebud and a lock of his mother's hair; and as I sat beside him and gazed upon his happy countenance, I could not weep for my little lamb, safely in—gathered into that fold where he "shall hunger no more, neither thirst any more." For two short years had he been mine, the object of unceasing care, and then he closed his eyes for ever on this weary world of sin and sorrow.

At 5 P.M., Dr. Fayrer came and fastened down the lid, when I had given him his last kiss, and bidden him "Good night" for evermore, though not *good night* to baby; for "there shall be no night *there*." We carried him in the mourning coach to the cemetery, where many met us, who showed by their silent sympathy that they had learned to weep with those who wept. Captain Boileau and Dr. Fayrer carried the little coffin to the grave. And now, farewell, my own loved little darling, until we meet in heaven: you have soon passed the waves of this troublesome world, and are safe "In thy Father's sheltered home, Where I know that sorrow cannot come."

## NOTES

1. Henry Mayhew, *London Labour and the London Poor*, Vol. 1 (New York: Dover Publications, Inc., 1968; 1861–1862), 46. Mayhew initially published sections of *London Labour* in the *Morning Chronicle*, 1849–1850.

2. Queen Victoria, as quoted in Julie Melnyk, *Victorian Religion: Faith and Life in Britain* (Westport, CT: Praeger, 2008), 16.

3. Hugh McLeod, *Religion and Society in England, 1850–1914* (New York: St. Martin's Press, 1996), 44.

4. Grace Aguilar, *Women of Israel*, Vol. 1 (New York: D. Appleton & Co., 1851), 225–226.

5. Quoted in F.K. Prochaska, *Women and Philanthropy in Nineteenth-Century England* (Oxford: Clarendon Press, 1980), 43.

6. George Eliot, "Evangelical Teaching: Dr. Cummings," in *Essays of George Eliot*, ed. by Thomas Pinney (New York: Columbia University Press, 1963), 181.

7. Ellen Ranyard, as quoted in Lori Williamson, "Ranyard, Ellen Henrietta (1810–1879)," in *Oxford Dictionary of National Biography* (Oxford: Oxford University Press, 2004).

8. Penelope Holland, "Two Views of the Convent Question," *Macmillan's Magazine* 19 (1869): 537, as quoted in Carmen Mangion, "Women, Religious Ministry and Female Institution-Building," in *Women, Gender and Religious Cultures in Britain, 1800–1940*, ed. by Sue Morgan and Jacqueline deVries (London: Routledge, 2010), 77.

9. Jennifer Lloyd, *Women and the Shaping of British Methodism: Persistent Preachers, 1807–1907* (Manchester: Manchester University Press, 2009), 32.

10. Catherine Mumford Booth, *Female Ministry; or, Women's Right to Preach the Gospel* (London: Morgan and Chase, 1859), 4.

11. *Cassell's Household Guide* (1870), as quoted in Pat Jalland, *Death in the Victorian Family* (Oxford: Oxford University Press, 1996), 221.

# 3

# FAMILY, HOME, AND LEISURE

In 1848, a year remembered throughout Europe for revolutionary conflict, the Christmas supplement of *The Illustrated London News* featured a drawing of Queen Victoria, Prince Albert, and the royal children gathered around a tabletop Christmas tree at Windsor Castle in what became a celebrated image of domestic harmony. Soon families throughout England emulated the royal practice of trimming a Christmas tree with candles, glass ornaments, toys, and strings of raisins, making what had been a Germanic tradition a familiar part of English Christmastime festivities. In this and many other drawings, portraits, and photographs, Victoria styled herself as the middle-class domestic queen encircled by children and her beloved Albert. Unlike most portraits of earlier monarchs, these images conveyed the illusion of domestic privacy; Victoria's gaze, like Albert's, is on her children, not the viewing public. Such scenes placed religion, family, and the home as foundations of the English social order and national prosperity.

By the time Victoria ascended to the throne in 1837 and married Albert three years later, home and family had become central values of the expanding middle classes. Victoria's embodiment of these values contributed to her popularity and attested to the growing influence of the bourgeoisie. Greater importance was placed on the legal sanctions and duties of marriage and the private sanctum of the domestic hearth. The Victorian ideal of domesticity served

*Christmas Tree at Windsor Castle*, by J. L. Williams, *Illustrated London News*, Christmas Supplement, 1848. (Library of Congress)

to distinguish the respectable from the unrespectable, as well as citizens from noncitizens, and middle-class moralists often condemned the supposed lack of domesticity among the aristocracy and working classes. To promote his philanthropic work with poor children, for example, the reformer Thomas Barnardo emphasized children's domestic arrangements, rather than their poverty, as the primary cause of their plight, declaring, "*The children must be saved*. To do so they must be rescued from the lodging-houses; from their awful homes, utterly unworthy of the name. . . . They must be transplanted, so to speak, from the wilderness where their existence is every moment in danger, to the fair garden of a Christian Home."[1] This vision of "the fair garden of a Christian Home" stressed the separation of private, domestic spaces from the public worlds of commerce and politics. In practice, however, even as marriage, family, and home life became ever more prominent aspects of women's lives, there was still flexibility in how women of all classes structured their domestic worlds, which remained thoroughly integrated into the fabric of national public life.

## THE FAMILY

Victorian families took many forms and were remarkably malleable. Households could be headed by husband and wife, by adult siblings living together, or by other groupings. Numerous men and women, especially of the working classes, cohabited without being legally married, and visitors who were not kin sometimes lived with families for years at a time. Over the course of the century, however, certain notable trends emerged. While there was a rise in common law marriage in the late 18th and early 19th centuries along with challenges to marriage altogether among select groups of radicals, by the mid-Victorian period, there was again a marked increase in legal marriage. Even as marriage as an institution was challenged and restructured in the second half of the century to recognize the rights of married women, marriage became ever more celebrated as a requirement for female respectability. Illegitimacy rates, which had increased in the 18th and early 19th centuries, declined steadily by the 1850s. In their wills, fathers proved less likely to recognize illegitimate offspring, after the early decades of the century. Furthermore, the role of children changed within families, especially as birth rates among married couples began to decline in the 1860s and 1870s, as did the position of other non-kin groups such as servants.

### Courtship

Among the upper and middle classes, strict social rules surrounding courtship practices allowed parents to oversee the marriage prospects of their children and protect daughters from behaviors deemed dishonorable. Companionate marriage based on love and affection was an expectation for most Victorians, but the middle and upper classes also still drew upon religious, kinship, and commercial networks to form attachments that benefitted the family's interests. Young women from elite families officially marked their "coming out" as marriageable when they were in their late teens or early 20s with a private party or dance. Eligible daughters of the aristocracy and upper gentry were dressed in white and presented to the Queen at court to indicate their introduction to society. These and other events of the London social season—beginning after members of parliament and their families returned to London for the new session in February and extending roughly from late April or early May through July—provided opportunities for youth to meet, though unmarried women under 30 usually attended public occasions with chaperones. Couples generally began courting in their mid to late 20s, and the courtship was in almost all cases initiated by men. The process of formal introductions, however,

Victoria entertains Albert at the piano while the Duchess of Kent and the Duke of Sussex look on with approval. (Mary Evans Picture Library/The Image Works)

ensured that women had some input. For example, initial meetings required the prior permission of both parties being introduced in all settings except for a dance or ball where the introduction did not necessarily lead to a formal acquaintance and could be ignored the next day at the lady's discretion. Women also helped arrange introductions with suitable men through siblings and friends.

If the suitor were unknown to the family, he was to present his prospects and initiate correspondence through the woman's parents, since clandestine letter writing between unmarried couples was considered disreputable. But after parents approved of the connection, couples often developed intense relationships through their letters—a means of communication revolutionized by the creation of the Penny Post in 1840. The postal reforms made letter writing an affordable means of communication for the middle classes. Before the reform, members of parliament were not required to pay postal charges (a privilege extended to family and friends), while members of the middle and working classes—especially in rural areas lacking cheaper local delivery services—paid exorbitant fees to receive a letter: as much as a worker's daily wages. But after 1840, mailing a letter within Britain cost only a penny paid for by the sender rather than the receiver. By the end of the 1840s, almost all English mail traveled long distances by train, so letters arrived remarkably quickly. Couples could also exchange mail more frequently. Beginning in 1857, central London had 12 daily mail deliveries. Greater London districts had six or seven deliveries a day, and other major cities such as Birmingham had three starting at 7:00 A.M. Etiquette guides and novels praised letter writing skills as a sign of good character, and more and more the weekly—sometimes even daily—exchange of love letters served as proof of commitment and affection.

Formal visits in the lady's home, or the residence of friends she might be visiting, followed initial introductions and correspondence. The courting couple would be under the observation of an appointed chaperone, often a female relative or friend, although exceptions were made in many cases to allow for private moments and conversation. Chaperones generally accompanied unmarried women to any outings such as balls, dances, lawn tennis and garden parties, concerts, religious services, and promenades, where they might mingle with suitors. *Manners for Men* (1897) stressed that women should never initiate meetings (suggesting that they sometimes did) and warned against accepting "invitations from a girl to meet her at restaurants, subscription dances, bazaars, or any other place. If a girl so far forgets herself, and is so lacking in modesty and propriety as to make appointments with young men in such ways as these, she cannot be worth much, and may lead the young man into a very serious scrape." Such women, the guide professed, "are usually those who have failed to secure attention in their own circle, and belong, as a rule, to the sort of girl who marries a groom or runs away with a good-looking footman."[2]

**Charlotte Eliza Humphry, *Manners for Men* (London: James Bowden, 1897), 16–17**

It is bad manners to introduce people without permission. Nor must this permission be asked in the hearing of the second party. If Mr. A. wishes to know Miss B., the lady's leave must be obtained before he can be presented to her. The only exception to this rule is at a dance or ball, where introductions need not be regarded as leading to acquaintanceship. They are only for the dance, and may be ignored the next day.

Here, again, it is the lady's privilege to ignore her partner, if she choose. But if she should bow to him he must raise his hat, whether he desires to follow up the acquaintanceship or not. Objections more frequently arise on the woman's side; but should a man prefer to drop the matter he can manage to convey in his manner a disinclination to do so, and yet behave with perfect politeness. A man I knew was once introduced at a ball to a girl, with whom he had danced two or three times. Before he met her again he heard that she had been actively concerned in circulating a slander about another girl whom circumstances had misrepresented. I happened to see the next meeting between the two. The girl bowed, smiled, and showed some sign of an intention to stop and talk. The man raised his hat, looked extremely solemn and unsociable, and passed on. It was enough. The girl understood that he did not wish to resume the ball-room acquaintanceship, and very probably guessed why. He did it beautifully.

When men decided to propose (for in almost all cases, except for Queen Victoria's proposal to Albert because of her sovereign rank, the offer came from the man), they did so either by letter or in person. Except among the very wealthy, it was not considered necessary to ask the lady's father or guardian for permission in advance, but if she accepted, the couple would then seek her family's approval to make the engagement official. The couple exchanged engagement rings, and the expected bride would receive money from her guardian for the goods making up her trousseau (the quality depending on her rank): most notably lingerie, but also dresses (including the wedding dress, which would become part of her wardrobe), ball gowns, and other clothing items traditionally meant to outfit the bride for the year. In the late 1860s, a trousseau of undergarments alone could range from £20 for those with a modest income to £100 for a fashionable bride. A few days before the wedding, the bride's family and friends sent her presents—usually household and ornamental gifts such as jewelry, silver plate, china, card trays, and writing desks—gathered and displayed in the family's drawing room or parlor on the wedding day. It was the bridegroom's responsibility to find and furnish a suitable apartment or house.

Given the substantial financial—not to mention emotional—commitments before marriage, decisions to break off an engagement were not taken lightly. When, however, engagements dissolved, women needed to guard their reputations. Middle-class letter writing guides included instructions and sample letters showing how to end an engagement, advising sympathy and reserve for female writers. In a minority of instances, increasing in number toward the end of the century, jilted women of the lower-middle and working classes turned to the courts for redress by bringing breach-of-promise cases against their former lovers. In trials, judges were most likely to grant women significant monetary damages of on average £100—even when they admitted to having had sex with their fiancés after the promise of marriage—when they stressed their traditionally feminine role as innocent victims betrayed by predatory men and left without future marriage prospects.

More often, after a courtship typically lasting six months to a year, the couple married. The summer months of June, July, and August were the most popular for weddings, and Wednesdays and Thursdays were the preferred days for the ceremony, although any day of the week except for Sunday was acceptable. Morning weddings followed by a breakfast party were the rule until the 1880s, when later weddings celebrated over afternoon tea became fashionable. Whether it was a simple ceremony with only family or an elaborate occasion with many guests, marriage both marked women's legal dependency on their husbands and ironically symbolized a woman's beginning of adulthood.

### Domestic Ideals and Married Life

Marriage provided the foundation for the middle-class domestic ideal of separate spheres. By the 1830s and 1840s, a broad range of middle-class writers promoted the ideal of women's natural mission and characteristics, different from those of men, in secular as well as religious terms by publishing household guides, poems, and novels detailing the intricacies of women's daily domestic life. Such works stressed that women's moral influence stemmed from their roles as wives and mothers.

Sarah Stickney Ellis (1799–1872), daughter of a prosperous Yorkshire farmer and Quaker whose mother died when she was only four years old, emerged as one of the most successful domestic advice writers of her time. Although she herself contributed to her family's income through her writing and teaching, her books advanced the view that women of the middle classes need not work for wages. Increasingly, not having women engage in paid labor became a key attribute of middle-class status. Ellis wrote a series of best-selling conduct manuals aimed at middle-class Englishwomen from the towns as well as the provinces, starting with *The Women of England: Their Social Duties and Domestic Habits* (1839), followed by *The Daughters of England: Their Position in Society, Character, and Responsibilities* (1842), *The Wives of England: Their Relative Duties, Domestic Influence, and Social Obligations* (1843), and *The Mothers of England: Their Influence and Responsibility* (1843). Her titles underscore the primary importance she placed on marriage and motherhood, as well as her belief that women's powers should be expressed through their influence of men. The family unit was the basis of England's political and social harmony, according to Ellis, and within this realm, women should be subordinate to men; women's strength came from willing self-sacrifice as they attended the needs of husbands and children. Idealized representations of the domestic world of women and children proliferated in the mid-Victorian period as Coventry Patmore and John Ruskin extolled the *Angel in the House*. Charles West Cope's painting *A Life Well Spent* (1862), for example, portrays a woman sewing and reading while surrounded by her four young children within a richly furnished interior. Her eyes rest on her eldest boy, offering guidance, while her eldest daughter mimics her mother's actions with a book on her lap and her hand resting on the infant's cradle.

Even as women's leisure emerged as a central characteristic of bourgeois status, the guides written by Ellis and others enumerated the endless domestic duties of housewives. The standards of housekeeping were becoming more elaborate for the expanding middle class. Isabella Beeton's *Book of Household Management* (1861) sold 60,000 copies the first year it was published as a complete volume and sales reached 2 million by 1868. Married to the publisher of *The Englishwoman's Domestic Magazine* (1852–1871), the first monthly magazine of its kind for middle-class women, Beeton (1836–1865) opened her over-1,000-page text by comparing the mistress of the house to an army commander. Her *Book of Household Management* included hundreds of recipes along with all sorts of domestic knowledge from how many servants to hire and the treatment of childhood diseases to the forming of friendships and the legal details of purchasing a house. Like Ellis, whose *Wives of England* contained a chapter titled "Order, Justice, and Benevolence," Beeton envisioned a merging of women's moral guidance with their oversight of daily domestic tasks. Mistresses were to set the household tone for servants and children by rising early and banishing idleness, keeping sewing or needlework close at hand for any free moments. Middle-class women supervised children's training, engaged in philanthropic work, paid social visits, and planned dinners and parties that solidified their husband's business connections. Their duties also included hiring and instructing servants in their work and keeping track of household accounts and supplies. Beeton's detailed guide suggests she was in fact writing not for gentlewomen with many servants, but for women of the new rising middle classes who often did some of their own marketing and lighter domestic chores.

Middle-class Victorians both praised married women's power within the home to create a moral foundation for society and, at the same time, paradoxically described married women's relation to their husbands as one of dependency, like a child to a father. In practice, however, the relatively late average age of first marriage—fluctuating around 25 and 26 for women from 1850 to 1900—meant that many women came to their partners with already formed interests and ambitions and that the ideals of separate spheres and domesticity were always being contested and negotiated. Some women found supportive companions and some pressed to redefine the social as well as the legal subordination of women within marriage. In many more cases, however, women willingly put professional interests or ambitions aside or integrated them into their domestic duties—turning an aptitude for geography, for example, into a child's lesson.

Some wives became intellectual and business partners with their husbands, sharing in professional work, although their contributions generally received little public notice. For instance, Isabella Beeton not only wrote, but also edited and prepared the layout designs for

*The Englishwoman's Domestic Magazine* and *The Queen*, a more elite weekly fashion magazine also initially published by her husband; Agnes Lister (1834–1893) recorded the experiments completed by her husband that led to antiseptic surgery; and the brilliant Mary Catherine Booth (1847–1939) advised her husband in the family business of the Liverpool Booth Steamship Company and contributed directly to his classic 17-volume work of social investigation, *Life and Labour of the People in London* (1902). Perhaps most famously, Harriet Taylor Mill (1807–1858) collaborated with John Stuart Mill on select writings. Her ideas directly influenced many of his works, especially *The Subjection of Women* (1869), published after her death. In these and other more thoroughly hidden lives of wifely companionship, women may have remained primarily within the domestic realm of the family, but this realm also proved to be thoroughly connected with the worlds of business, science, and political reform.

In a minority of cases, couples seeking greater equality directly challenged or reinterpreted the institution of marriage, drawing on the examples of radicals such as Mary Wollstonecraft (1759–1797) and William Godwin from the 1790s. During the 1820s, 1830s, and 1840s, socialists inspired by the reformer Robert Owen stressed the inherent inequalities of marriage and promoted communalism in place of the nuclear family. The Owenite social experiments—most notably the short-lived community of New Harmony in southern Indiana as well as hundreds of smaller collectives in Britain—promoted communal childcare and housekeeping, employment opportunities for women, and free marriage and divorce witnessed by the community rather than being legitimated by the church or state (although Owen himself came to support civil marriage in the 1840s). Owenites envisioned marriage as a flexible, impermanent, equitable institution, although even for most communitarian socialists it continued to be understood as a monogamous, heterosexual coupling. The influence of Owen and other early socialists was perhaps most discernable through the overwhelming defense of traditional marriage circulated in the domestic literature of this period. Marriage as an institution remained at the core of mid-Victorian respectability, and while reformers continued to challenge its inherent inequalities, few women and men of the middle classes risked living together out of wedlock.

In the late 19th century, a handful of prominent radicals once again eschewed marriage—though the pressures for women in particular to marry remained strong. In *The Origins of the Family, Private Property, and the State* (1884), Friedrich Engels argued that legal marriage and the nuclear family served to uphold capitalism by securing the generational passage of property through the male line. He had lived out of wedlock with the factory worker Mary Burns (ca. 1823–1863) for nearly 20 years, and then after her death, cohabited with her sister Lizzie (1827–1878) for almost a decade. But in his personal life, Engels's stance proved less clear-cut than in his writings; he resided with Mary in the suburbs of Manchester tucked away from his family and associates under the names of Mr. and Mrs. Frederick Boardman and married Lizzie on her deathbed. Other leading late-Victorian socialists rejected marriage and created free unions, yet the advantages were often clearer for the men than for the women. For example, Karl Marx's daughter Eleanor Marx (1855–1898) cohabited with Edward Aveling, a married man, for nearly 15 years. Both came to condemn marriage on

George Eliot was the *nom de plume* of Mary Anne (later Mary Ann and then Marian) Evans, one of the leading British novelists of the 19th century. She created a scandal by living openly with the married man George Henry Lewes. (Library of Congress)

principle, but although she remained devoted to Aveling alone until her tragic death by suicide, he had numerous affairs and after the death of his first wife secretly married another woman in 1897. A happier union was formed when the feminist leader Elizabeth Wolstenholme (1833–1918) lived openly with the secularist Ben Elmy for several months (likely after sharing an informal ceremony). They reluctantly married in 1874 when her pregnancy sparked reasonable fear among her cohorts that she would scandalize and discredit the cause of women's rights.

In other cases, circumstances or legal barriers prevented couples from marrying when they would have preferred to do so. Cousins could marry and frequently did, but it was illegal under the Marriage Act of 1835 to marry a deceased wife's sister (or deceased husband's brother, though this arose less often). The strict divorce laws also prevented some couples from marrying. George Eliot (Marian Evans, 1819–1880), for example, was unable to marry the writer George Henry Lewes, whom she met while working at the radical *Westminster Review*. Lewes could not divorce his first wife because he had initially agreed to have an open marriage with her and had registered her illegitimate children as his own and was thus unable to file for divorce on the claim of her adultery. Eliot nonetheless referred to Lewes as "my husband"—publicly dedicating her novel *Adam Bede* to him in 1859. They lived together as companions for almost a quarter of a century after eloping in 1854. Yet Eliot—even more than Lewes—suffered the loss of family and acquaintances unwilling to associate with her with the exception of dedicated friends such as Bessie Parkes (1829–1925) and Barbara Bodichon (1827–1891).

Far more widespread were challenges to legal marriage among the working classes, where cohabitation was a generally recognized and often tolerated part of life. Households headed by unmarried couples were more common in the first half of the century, especially in regions that offered better employment opportunities for women, including areas with strong cottage industries and the Lancashire textile towns, and among itinerant workers such as sailors or street sellers. A young fruit seller told Henry Mayhew, "I dare say there ain't ten out of a hundred gals what's living with men, what's been married Church of England fashion."[3] Most working-class couples who lived together out of wedlock did so not out of ideological opposition to marriage, but for economic reasons. The expenses for the marriage and clergyman's fees remained high. Other, previously married couples cohabited out of wedlock because obtaining a divorce remained prohibitively costly even after the 1857 Divorce

Act (Matrimonial Causes Act). Unlike those who opposed marriage, these couples—comprising roughly 10 percent of working-class unions, significantly fewer than Mayhew suggested—often presented themselves as married and remained together in monogamous relationships.

Working-class marriages—legally sanctioned or not—tended to differ from those of the middle classes in important ways. Most notably, many working-class and even many lower-middle-class wives engaged in some sort of regular paid labor, although by the end of the century this was less common. The close, crowded quarters of much working-class housing made clear gender distinctions of space all the more difficult to navigate, yet the domestic hearths, parlors, and scrubbed front steps were feminine realms cleaned by and identified with women and girls. The gender division of labor also appeared less stark among working-class marriages, where husbands and sons sometimes helped in a pinch with domestic tasks such as cleaning and childcare. At the same time, a wife's failure to provide a meal or to keep children quiet could readily result in her husband's violent enforcement of his privileged position within the home—a position that he perhaps clung to all the more tightly because of precarious economic and class standing. Like their middle-class counterparts, working-class wives oversaw domestic finances, but the limited sums provided after husbands extracted pocket money for pubs and leisure made the task of covering expenses for food, clothing, and children's school fees an arduous one.

While the surviving documentation is limited, there is clear evidence that women in the Victorian period established informal marriages and long-term romantic relationships with other women as well. Women's same-sex marriages were rare, but their existence highlights the centrality of marriage as a cultural (not just a religious or legal) institution that could be reinterpreted and appropriated. The journalist, antivivisectionist, and feminist reformer Frances Power Cobbe (1822–1904), for example, created a conjugal home with the Welsh sculptor Mary Lloyd (1819–1896). Cobbe and Lloyd set up house together in Kensington in 1865. They publicly employed the language of friendship to describe their life partnership, yet members of their social circle—including such luminaries as John Stuart Mill, Charles Darwin, and William Gladstone—treated them as a couple, sending joint invitations and inquiries. In her published writing, Cobbe referred to Lloyd as "my own life-friend," and in private letters to her close married friend Mary Somerville (1780–1872), she called Lloyd her "truant husband" (while Lloyd was away traveling), "my old woman," and "my *wife*."[4] Although the *Times* made no mention of Lloyd in Cobbe's obituary, Lloyd had died in Cobbe's arms, and Cobbe later requested to be buried in Llanelltyd churchyard in northern Wales alongside her.

**Frances Power Cobbe, *Live of Frances Power Cobbe as Told by Herself*, 2nd ed. (London: Swan Sonnenschein & Co., 1904), 709–710**

*Cobbe instructed this poem to be added to the posthumous edition of her autobiography.*

**TO MARY C. LLOYD**

***Written in Hartley Combe, Liss, about 1873.***

Friend of my life! Whene'er my eyes
Rest with sudden, glad surprise
On Nature's scenes of earth and air
Sublimely grand, or sweetly fair,
I want you—Mary.

When men and women, gifted, free,
Speak their fresh thoughts ungrudgingly,
And springing forth, each kindling mind
Streams like a meteor in the wind,
I want you—Mary.

When soft the summer evenings close,
And crimson in the sunset rose,
Our Cader glows, majestic, grand,
The crown of all your lovely land,
I want you—Mary.

And when the winter nights come round,
To our "ain fireside," cheerly bound,
With our dear Rembrandt Girl, so brown,
Smiling serenely on us down,
I want you—Mary . . . .

In joy and grief, in good and ill,
Friend of my heart! I need you still;
My Playmate, Friend, Companion, Love,
To dwell with here, to clasp above,
I want you—Mary.

### Widows, Lone Mothers, and Single Women

While many Victorian women reinterpreted marriage in various ways to create domestic partnerships, still others headed families on their own. High mortality rates contributed to a large number of widows in Victorian society. At mid-century, nearly 20 percent of all marriages ended with the death of husband or wife within 10 years. Some widows eventually remarried, but during the 19th century, widows were more likely than in earlier periods to remain single and care for children on their own. Widows also far outnumbered widowers, who remarried more readily, outnumbering them more than two to one in the second half of the century. Even relatively well-off middle-class widows such as the novelist Margaret Oliphant (1828–1897) struggled with debts and dependent children after a husband's death, leading many to take in paying lodgers for income.

Families headed by lone mothers—whether widowed, deserted, or unmarried—were the most threatened by economic constraints. Under the highly unpopular Bastardy Clauses of the New Poor

*An Infant Orphan Election at the London Tavern, "Polling,"* painted by George Elgar Hicks in 1865. Charitable donors voted on which children most deserved placement in the Infant Orphan Asylum at Wanstead as posters around the room advertised the cause of individual children. (Heritage Images/Corbis)

Law of 1834 (until the clauses were revised in 1844 and again in 1872), unwed mothers became solely financially responsible for their illegitimate children under the age of 16. Mothers of illegitimate children could no longer appeal to the parish for supplemental funds without entering the workhouse or ask parish authorities to seek payments on their behalf from the children's fathers. Over half of children in London poor law schools and charitable institutions were the children of lone mothers struggling to rebuild their households after the death or desertion of their male partner. After the death of her husband from typhoid fever in 1887, for example, one mother began working as a domestic servant and scrambled to find homes and employment for her five children: the daughter also entered service, one son trained for the Navy, another son entered the workhouse, and the remaining two boys were sent to different state and charitable children's institutions. Three years later, the youngest son, then seven years old, returned to live with his mother after she refused to allow the charity to send him to Canada.[5]

Women's household structures took a variety of other forms, and because of their dependent status were even more likely than men's to change frequently over the course of their lives. In addition to living with husbands and children, women shared homes with parents and siblings, siblings-in-law, grandparents, cousins, aunts and uncles, nieces and nephews, distant relatives in need of care, and nonkin such as boarders and visitors. Unmarried women might be pressured to live with relatives and expected to take on an extra share of household duties. The initial household arrangement in Elizabeth Gaskell's domestic novel *Cranford* (1851–1853), where two spinster sisters opened their home to a younger friend, Mary Smith, would have been a familiar one to Victorian readers. Over the course of their lives, women generally experienced several different domestic settings and various degrees of security within each. For example, after leaving her London family home at the age of 16, the future art critic Anna Jameson (1794–1860) worked as a governess for several families before marrying and then separating from her husband. She moved throughout her life, residing with her sisters and mother in Ealing and, after her mother's death, with her sisters in Brighton, but also traveled and stayed for long periods with friends, most notably Robert and Elizabeth Barrett Browning (1806–1861) in Italy and Ottilie von Goethe (1796–1872) in Germany.

**Children and Declining Birth Rates**

One of the most dramatic changes to the Victorian family was the decline in the average number of children born within each family. In the 1860s, English married couples gave birth to on average just over six children. By the 1890s, this had decreased to just over four children. These numbers are averages, so some married couples remained childless, while others had extensive families with 10 or more children, although these "long families" became less common by the late 19th century. High infant mortality rates, miscarriages, and stillbirths at times created significant gaps in age between children. Family size also changed after the death of a mother or father and the surviving parent's subsequent remarriage potentially brought new half-siblings and stepsiblings, who were in some cases closer in age to a new wife than to the youngest children of the family.

The middle classes spearheaded the mid-to-late Victorian decline in fertility rates—as well as the new appreciation of childhood as a time of innocence, joy, and protection that demanded greater resources and attention from parents (see Chapter 5). Those very couples most steeped in the middle-class domestic ideologies of the 1830s and 1840s, men and women who married in the 1860s, were the first to limit their family sizes when faced with the prospect of lowering their newfound standard of living during the economic depression of the 1870s. The gentry were the first to favor fewer numbers of children, followed by the professional classes of military and naval officers, lawyers, doctors, clergymen, journalists, and architects. Then came the business and lower middle classes, such as clerks, civil service workers, teachers, and shop assistants. Among the working classes, textile workers (a group that included many women) were the first to have fewer numbers of children. Miners and agricultural workers continued to have notably large families, but by the 1880s, most working-class families—especially in urban areas—began to decline in size as well, although at slower rates than those of the middle classes.

For the most part, the limitations on family size did not result directly from innovations in birth control. Abstinence and withdrawal remained the most common methods. One working woman who had already had five children and a miscarriage in six years, facing endless housework and her husband's intermittent unemployment, simply "went on strike."[6] Male partners, however, were not always so obliging. Women wary of having more children turned to various "preventatives" or "restoratives" thought to cause miscarriages: folk remedies—pennyroyal, ergot of rye, white hellebore, rue, quinine, mercury, lead, and gunpowder, among others—and various "female pills" purchased from chemists and advertised far and wide by the end of the century. Drinking gin, running up and down steps, and taking hot baths were other popular—often unsuccessful and dangerous—methods used to cause abortions. Victorian women generally did not make a clear distinction between contraception and abortion, despite the efforts of doctors and reformers to the contrary. Women typically perceived the moment when the mother could first feel the fetus move insider her (called "quickening") as the beginning of pregnancy.

Women of the middle and upper classes had greater access to birth control methods that prevented conception. Condoms made from silk and linen and later from animal skins, bladders, and intestines were used in Europe during the early modern period. The first rubber condoms were produced in the mid-19th century, but these still remained too expensive for most workers and, moreover, were mainly associated with prostitutes and the prevention of venereal disease. By the 1880s and 1890s, retailers sold other older contraceptive methods—sponges and douches—as well as the newly invented diaphragm and quinine pessaries. Advertisements touting the benefits of such methods filled the public thoroughfares, appearing in surgical shops, barbershops, pharmacies, street sides, and newspapers.

Groups such as the Malthusian League, founded in 1877, promoted the benefits of family limitation as a means to improve women's health and as a solution to poverty. Two members, Annie Besant (1847–1933) and Charles Bradlaugh, were tried in 1877 under the Obscene Publications Act of 1857 for republishing the American physician Charles Knowlton's earlier birth control pamphlet, *The Fruits of Philosophy or, the Private Companion of Young Married People* (1832; 1877). The courts eventually exonerated Besant and Bradlaugh. Knowlton's pamphlet as well as Besant's own *Law of Population* (1877) went on to sell hundreds of thousands of copies. Besant became a legendary public speaker on the topic and a reformer highly regarded within radical circles, yet she also suffered personally from the trial. Her estranged husband used her views on birth control as evidence that she was no longer morally fit to have custody of their daughter.

Only a minority of Victorian women practiced the artificial contraception methods promoted by Besant and others, but their popularization likely had the much broader effect of raising most women's awareness of the potential to limit their family size through abstinence, coitus interruptus, and extended breastfeeding as a recognized (though not always reliable) method of preventing fertility. Although the methods and motives for family limitation varied by class, region, and individual women, the outcome of reducing the size of families in such a short period of time remains one of the most revolutionary and profound changes in the history of the family.

## THE HOME

The physical structure of the home also changed dramatically during the 19th century. At the beginning of Victoria's reign, most homes contained no running water, no privies, no lighting besides candles and later oil lamps, and no heat besides coal fires generally limited to the kitchen and main room. By the end of the 19th century, most homes had some running water (even if connected only to the ground floor) and indoor flush toilets, and many were likely as well to be equipped with gas lighting and some even with gas heating. The expansion and creation of separate domestic spaces—nurseries, servant quarters, and bathrooms—underscored the use of architecture to demark Victorian ideals of class distinction and separate spheres, as well as changing family roles particularly for servants and children.

Along with these structural changes came the heightened emphasis on domestic settings and furnishings as key signs of respectability. For example, Henry Mayhew claimed that the lack of proper homes made English street sellers comparable to "savage tribes." He wrote:

> They are a part of the Nomades of England, neither knowing nor caring for the enjoyments of home. The hearth, which is so sacred a symbol to all civilized races as being the spot where the virtues of each succeeding generation are taught and encouraged, has no charms to them. The tap-room is the father's chief abiding place; whilst to the mother the house is only a better kind of *tent*. She is away at the stall, or hawking her goods from morning till night, while the children are left to play away the day in the court or alley, and pick their morals out of the gutter.[7]

By the mid-Victorian period, not only Mayhew, but also a broad range of politicians and reformers, including many women, instilled home design with moral meaning, equating a proper "hearth" with English national virtue and identity.

### Aristocratic Homes

For the approximately 3,000–4,000 families of the English aristocracy and landed gentry, the land itself had historically been the source of political and economic power. The aristocratic homes inherited and passed down from generation to generation remained, along with cathedrals, the major English architectural structures of the early 19th century. The great landed families usually rented a city home, but the inherited country estate and surrounding lands of 1,000 acres or more remained their seat of power.

The great Victorian landlords and ladies still held tremendous sway over village life, determining not only rents and living conditions for inhabitants, but also presiding over local political elections, charity and cultural events, and institutions such as hospitals, workhouses, and schools. The country house served as the center for these activities; along with the parish church, it provided a place for the entire community to meet and celebrate at balls and charity events. The mansion itself could contain hundreds of rooms, along with stables, outbuildings, greenhouses, gardens, and parks. Hard hit by the economic depression and poor harvests of the 1870s, many country estates became more famous in the 1880s and 1890s as settings for weekend hunting parties restricted to elite guests, and estate owners were more likely to be absent for long periods during the year or even rent out properties. But for most of the century, the great country houses were places where tenants, villagers, servants, and landowning families mixed regularly, albeit according to strict codes of deference.

Grand estates employed scores of servants, and many employers still attested to earlier, preindustrial understandings of all household workers as being included as interconnected members of the family. As late as 1892, socialite and journalist Lady Mary Jeune (1845–1931) stated, "Our servants and we are all members of a large family, who cannot get on independently of each other."[8] This understanding of the family, however, was one that was increasingly rare particularly among middle-class households that placed greater importance on the privacy of the nuclear family. Even among the aristocracy and landed gentry, the Victorian fondness for adding servants' wings to country houses likely stemmed not from an increase in the number of servants employed, but from a greater desire for privacy, orderliness, and the segregation of servants by gender and class.

### Middle-Class Homes

Unlike the upper classes, the middle and working classes usually rented their homes instead of owning them. Whereas homes of the aristocracy and upper gentry retained many of their essentially public functions with grand reception halls and art galleries, middle-class homes were designed in theory to create separate private domestic spaces distinct from the worlds of politics and business. Historians Leonore Davidoff and Catherine Hall have demonstrated the various ways in which the ideal of separate spheres encouraged middle-class men and women to make clearer distinctions between their domestic homes and places of work. More so than the upper and working classes, the middle classes physically removed the most obvious forms of commercial and productive work from their homes. While it had formerly been common practice for middle-class professionals such as bankers to live with their families in back rooms behind the front banking office, by the early 19th century, this was no longer considered ideal. The practice of having a spinning wheel in the main room became rare, and the productive work of the household was separated as much as possible from the domestic living quarters. The middle classes redesigned homes to move kitchens farther from dining areas (creating extra work for servants), for example, in order to isolate cooking smells. By the 1820s, middle-class renters sought enclaves within urban centers separate from working-class and business areas. By the late 19th century, efficient rail services prompted many more middle-class families to flee city centers altogether for the expanding bourgeois suburbs first developed in the 1830s, where walls, gardens, lawns, and hedges marked off the privacy of individual houses in contrast to the 18th-century practice of sharing a common garden square.

Within individual middle-class homes, there was a greater emphasis on creating separate spaces for men and women, children and adults, and servants and employers. Female maids ideally had their own quarters, often in spare attic rooms, and certainly no longer slept in the same room with daughters as they often did in the 18th century, although in practice many still slept on cots in kitchens in more modest homes. The idea of creating separate day and night nurseries

A Victorian drawing room with pictures in heavy frames and ornately covered furniture, ca. 1860. (Hulton Archive/Getty Images)

for children was also largely a Victorian innovation. In *The Suburban Garden and Villa Companion*, published in 1838, the prominent landscape gardener J.C. Loudon explained the benefits of and defined the very term nursery as a separate space (rather than a stage of life) for children aged four and under, but quickly middle-class Victorians came to view the segregation of children from adult domestic spaces in nurseries and schoolrooms as essential. Women, too, became more thoroughly associated with distinct domestic spaces. After dinners, ladies removed themselves to the drawing room, leaving men in the dining room to converse. Women usually took charge of overseeing the care of family members in the sickroom, a simply furnished extra bedroom reserved for convalescents. While the dining room and library or study were typically associated with men, the drawing room and, in larger homes, the less formal morning room were places primarily for women's activities: receiving visitors, writing letters, engaging in sewing and handiwork, instructing servants, and reviewing accounts. In theory as well as practice, however, such spatial distinctions could be blurred and regularly transgressed.

By the 1830s and 1840s, the elaborate furnishings of Victorian interiors began to replace the sparer 18th-century designs, and Victorian women, more so than their mothers and grandmothers, devoted significant attention to home decoration. Men selected and purchased many household items and were often deeply invested in their domestic worlds, but by the mid-19th century as middle-class incomes rose, women primarily oversaw the increasingly ornate decorating decisions. Household purchases became signs of individual expression, moral character, and status, rather than dangerous examples of sinful materialism, underscoring the public as well as the private meanings of domestic consumption. Making the right choices in terms of taste and income could be tricky decisions to master. In *The Wives of England,* Ellis stressed that women must furnish their homes in a style equal to their station, but also pointed out the precariousness of middle-class incomes by warning that overindulgence led all too many newlywed couples to the pawnbroker's shop. Furthermore, the typical mid-to-late Victorian interior ironically created more work for middle-class women defined by their leisured status. Upholstered furniture and carpets called for cleaning, silver ornaments required polishing, lace curtains needed washing, and vases, pictures, potted plants, writing desks, and other bric-a-brac demanded dusting—altogether tasks too numerous without nominal help from mistresses in those lower-middle-class households employing only one general live-in servant or a daily servant.

### Sarah Stickney Ellis, *The Wives of England: Their Relative Duties, Domestic Influence, and Social Obligations* (New York: D. Appleton & Co., 1843), 51–52

Let us then at least talk common sense; and in doing this, I would advise the newly married woman to look at things in general as they really are, and not as they might be. She will then see that nothing is more difficult to human nature, than to come down even one step from any height it has attained, whether imaginary or real. If, therefore, the appearance of a young couple make on their first outset in life be ever so little beyond their means, so far from their being willing to reduce their appearance or style of living to a lower scale, they will ever afterwards be perplexed by devices, and harassed by endeavours, to maintain in all respects the appearance they have so imprudently assumed. This perpetual straitness and inadequacy of means to effect the end desired, is of itself sufficient to poison the fountain of domestic concord at its source. It is bad enough to have innumerable wants created in our own minds which our utmost efforts are unequal to satisfy; but it is worse, as may thousands can attest, in addition to this, for the husband and the wife to be perpetually disputing at their own fireside, about what expenses can be done without, and what cannot. Yet all these consequences follow, and worse, and more calamitous than tongue or pen can describe, from the simple fact of having begun a new establishment on too expensive a scale.

It may seem like a fanciful indulgence of morbid feeling, but I own my attention has often been arrested in the streets of London, by a spectacle which few ladies would stop to contemplate—a pawnbroker's shop. And I have imagined I could there trace the gradual fall from these high beginnings in the new hearth-rug scarcely worn, the gaudy carpet with its roses scarcely soiled, the flowery tea-tray, and, worst of all, the bride's white veil. What a breaking-up, I have thought, must there have been of some little establishment, before the dust of a single twelve-month had fallen on its hearth!—these articles perhaps disposed of to defray the expenses of illness, or to satisfy the very creditors of whom they were obtained on trust.

### Working-Class Homes

Most working-class homes, often built quickly and cheaply to meet the demands of rapidly expanding industries and cities, were too cramped and overcrowded for the separation of public and private, productive and domestic spheres, as well as the strict classification of spaces touted by the middle classes. By the 1840s, the back-to-back houses common in Yorkshire, Lancashire, and Midland towns were notoriously overcrowded and filthy. Although most cities passed ordinances against their construction by the 1860s, landlords often evaded these and other bylaws against overcrowding, and many working-class families continued to live in older buildings with no through ventilation, crowded together in one- or two-room dwellings. In *The Condition of the Working Class in England* (1845), Engels decried the state of working-class housing. He emphasized the lack of any clear separation of private homes from the smells, refuse, sewage, or even the pigs and other livestock of the streets as well as the close mingling of men and women, children and adults, and family members and lodgers within tenements. Children often slept in the same rooms and beds as parents or on pallets on the floor, leading housing reformers such as the Reverend Andrew Means to raise publicly the issue of incest in his sensational exposé, *The Bitter Cry of Outcast London* (1883). There was no hiding the daily work required from women to maintain their domestic realms or tidy separation of domestic and commercial labor. Women and children regularly engaged in piecework along with their domestic chores, fitting a workstation close beside the bed frame and other meager furniture. Laundry hung from the ceilings or in courtyards to dry, food was prepared within or close to main rooms, and children were nearly always underfoot.

Working-class women often had to change residences. Faced with overdue rents, the poor moved frequently from place to place generally over short distances. In 1884, for instance, when Emma Pimm applied with her two children to the Bethnal Green Board of Guardians in London for poor law relief, her husband had recently deserted her. During the previous year, Emma and her family lived in at least six different residences. Their longest stay in one place was for five months, and their shortest was for a two-week period between the time of her husband's desertion and her application for poor relief.[9] Women also resorted to lodging houses and charities, such as the Salvation Army, for temporary housing. The dangers of such a precarious life were all too present in the drawings of the *Illustrated London News* showing homeless women and children huddled around a fire for warmth, or the last reported words of one of the Jack-the-Ripper victims, Polly Nichols, who when turned away from a lodging house went back into the streets claiming she would soon return with her "doss money."

Yet, even as the very instability, design, and setting of working-class homes made any degree of privacy or spatial segregation by gender and age extremely difficult, working families nonetheless developed their own forms of community and domesticity largely unrecognized by reformers such as Engels, Mayhew, and Mearns. Women more often socialized with friends and neighbors in courtyards or doorways rather than within their homes. During the second half of the century, families of skilled artisans and better-paid workers who could afford larger homes with several rooms often put aside one to use as a parlor for more formal events: Sunday dinners and family entertainment or prayers, holidays, courtship meetings, wedding teas, funeral gatherings, and visits with special guests. Women decorated parlors as feminine spaces, but unlike the middle-class woman's drawing room, the working-class parlor was also a gathering place for the entire family. The careful demarcation by better-off workers of the parlor as a prized domestic space appeared wasteful to many middle- and upper-class housing reformers, who wondered why workers did not use the room more regularly. In 1897, the Duke of Bedford bemoaned of rural cottagers, "If two dwelling-rooms of the same size are provided, one is often kept idle as a parlour, where china dogs, crochet antimacassars, and unused tea-services are maintained in fusty seclusion. This idle parlour adds nothing to the comfort of the cottagers."[10] It might, however, have added a much-needed sanctuary and sense of stability to working women and their families who keenly felt the near constant economic pressures of maintaining their position.

### Food and Drink

Food and drink preparations were primary concerns for women that required constant negotiation between domestic and commercial arenas. Mealtimes varied depending on class and changed over the course of the 19th century. At the beginning of the century, the upper classes generally ate a large late breakfast between 10 in the morning and noon, perhaps followed by a light lunch (or often nothing at all), then the main dinner meal at 5 or 6 P.M., and finally often a late super as well anywhere between 9 at night and 2 in the morning. The dinner hour had gradually moved later for elites during the 18th century and continued to do so in the 19th as lunch—especially for ladies—became a more regular meal. By the 1840s, when elites enjoyed dinner as late as 8 or 9 P.M., it became fashionable for ladies to serve an afternoon tea—biscuits (cookies or savory crackers) and dainty sandwiches along with tea—to visitors in the drawing room or parlor between around 4 and 5 P.M. Lower-middle-class and working-class families had an early breakfast followed by dinner, which remained for most the main midday meal. However, the work schedules of many factory workers and other professionals required that they bring cold pail meals to work instead. For working- and lower-middle-class families, "tea" or "high tea" generally referred to the main evening meal. Most Victorians continued to gather for Sunday dinner, usually served at midday.

The types of food available, as with the mealtimes, depended on class. Working-class diets consisted mostly of bread, potatoes, and limited amounts of protein—fish, eggs, drippings, and meat—often reserved for men. The most common drinks were tea and beer, much safer than unsterilized water. Many working-class women did not have separate kitchens with ranges, relying instead on fireplaces with grates or coal stoves, which made cooking a laborious

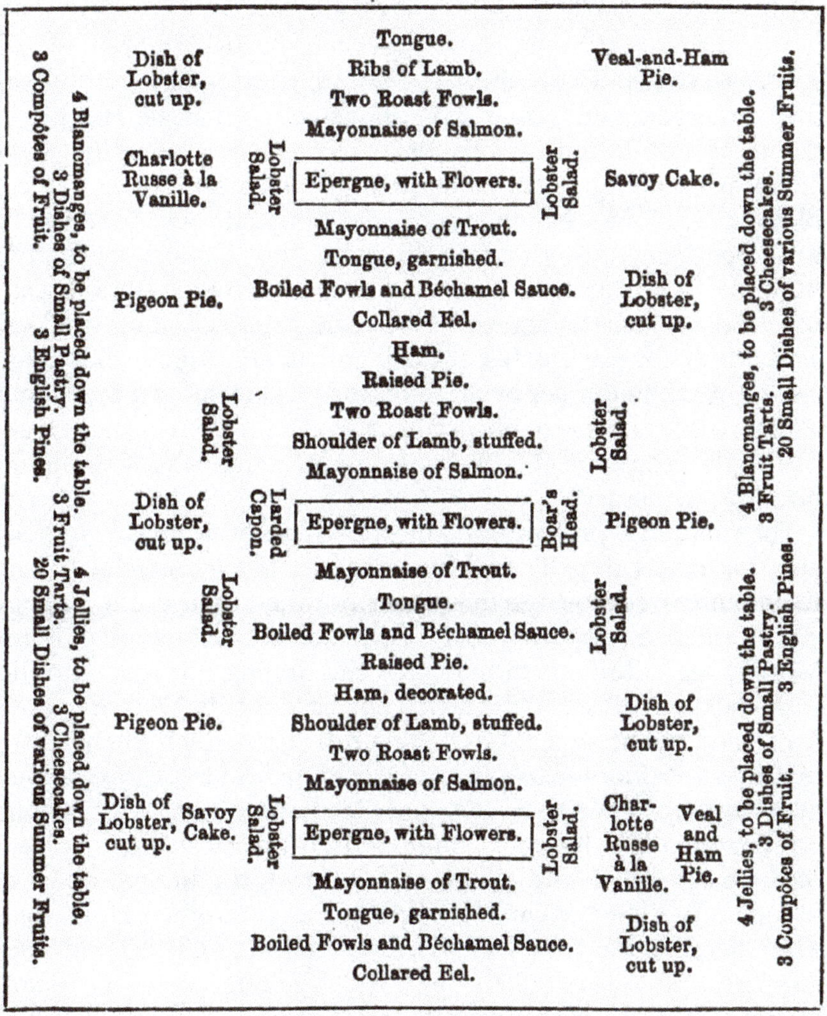

**2143.—BILL OF FARE FOR A BALL SUPPER,**
**Or a Cold Collation for a Summer Entertainment, or Wedding or Christening Breakfast for 70 or 80 Persons (July).**

3 Compôtes of Fruit. 3 English Pines. 20 Small Dishes of various Summer Fruits.
4 Blancmanges, to be placed down the table. 3 Dishes of Small Pastry. 3 Fruit Tarts. 4 Jellies, to be placed down the table. 3 Cheesecakes.

Dish of Lobster, cut up. — Tongue. Ribs of Lamb. Two Roast Fowls. Mayonnaise of Salmon. — Veal-and-Ham Pie.

Charlotte Russe à la Vanille. — Lobster Salad. — Epergne, with Flowers. — Lobster Salad. — Savoy Cake.

Mayonnaise of Trout. Tongue, garnished.

Pigeon Pie. — Boiled Fowls and Béchamel Sauce. Collared Eel. — Dish of Lobster, cut up.

Ham. Raised Pie.

Lobster Salad. — Two Roast Fowls. Shoulder of Lamb, stuffed. Mayonnaise of Salmon. — Lobster Salad.

Dish of Lobster, cut up. — Larded Capon. — Epergne, with Flowers. — Boar's Head. — Pigeon Pie.

Lobster Salad. — Mayonnaise of Trout. Tongue. Boiled Fowls and Béchamel Sauce. — Lobster Salad.

Raised Pie. Ham, decorated.

Pigeon Pie. — Shoulder of Lamb, stuffed. Two Roast Fowls. Mayonnaise of Salmon. — Dish of Lobster, cut up.

Dish of Lobster, cut up. Savoy Cake. — Lobster Salad. — Epergne, with Flowers. — Lobster Salad. — Charlotte Russe à la Vanille. Veal and Ham Pie.

Mayonnaise of Trout. Tongue, garnished. Boiled Fowls and Béchamel Sauce. Collared Eel. — Dish of Lobster, cut up.

4 Blancmanges, to be placed down the table. 3 Fruit Tarts. 3 Cheesecakes. 20 Small Dishes of various Summer Fruits.
4 Jellies, to be placed down the table. 3 Dishes of Small Pastry. 3 English Pines. 3 Compôtes of Fruit.

*The Book of Household Management*: Bill of Fare for a Ball Supper, Or a Cold Collation for a Summer Entertainment, or Wedding or Christening Breakfast for 70 or 80 Persons (July). (Beeton, Isabella Mary. *The Book of Household Management*, 1861) task. Gas stoves became more available in the 1880s, but the cost of gas made them expensive to use. Working-class meals thus tended to be cooked quickly—grilled or fried—rather than baked. A slow-cooked stew would be a special treat. Women could pay a small fee to have food baked at local cook shops, which also sold many prepared foods: fish and chips, smoked and cured fish, sausages and meat pies, and canned goods. Street peddlers also sold a huge assortment of inexpensive fares, such as pickled whelks, oysters, hot eels, fried fish, baked potatoes, meat pies and puddings, sandwiches, coffee, tea, lemonade, and ginger beer.

The middle and upper classes adopted the fashion of dining *à la Russe*, serving food in multiple separate courses brought by footmen or servants with clear separations between sweet and savory dishes. Beeton's guide details the extraordinary array of foods and courses, including remarkable quantities of meat. For example, a plain family Sunday dinner consisted of oxtail soup, followed by roast beef, Yorkshire pudding, broccoli, and potatoes, with plum pudding, apple tart, and cheese for dessert. A more elaborate sample meal for guests suggested vermicelli soup, sole, and fried eels as the first course; entrées of pork cutlets and ragout of mutton; roast goose, boiled leg of mutton, and vegetables for the second course; a third course of pheasants; all followed by whipped cream, meringues, compôte of Normandy pippins, mince pies, and plum pudding for dessert.

The planning, preparation, and purchase of necessary ingredients for meals directly involved women in commercial society. Even many middle-class mistresses outlined their dinner menus, contributed to shopping lists, and purchased a few select items. Most of all, elite women managed the dolling out food supplies from locked pantries to the head cook or servants, who frequently expressed resentment at not having full control over kitchens and materials. Working-class women scrimped and saved, searched and negotiated for bargains, and developed loyal relationships with merchants who might offer credit during a strike or episode of unemployment to make the most out of the limited sums allotted from their husbands' wages for food. Women also keenly evaluated the quality of goods. Especially before the first Food Adulteration Act of 1860, the 1872 Adulteration of Food and Drinks Act, and the significantly more stringent 1875 Sale of Food and Drugs Act, producers and merchants frequently contaminated foods with harmful fillers and chemicals. Dairymen mixed milk with more than the usual amounts of water, and pastry chefs added chalk to flour and lead and mercury to brightly colored confectionaries. The fishmongers at London's Billingsgate Market were said to paint the gills of fish to make them look fresher. What passed as port could be red dye, and what seemed to be cocoa could be mostly dirt. Adulterated food presented serious health risks and constant reminders of the dangers of consumption and commercial exchange in the modern metropolis where appearances could always mislead.

Women's food production also brought them into direct engagement with the global economy as more and more English foodstuffs came from former and existing British colonies. Many of the foods considered quintessentially English originated in the empire. Tea—sipped daily by genteel women to solidify social networks and by working women to cover the pangs of hunger—came from China and India. The sugar to sweeten it was produced on plantations in the Caribbean initially built and worked by slaves. Like tea, sugar evolved from a luxury enjoyed by the few into a mass commodity during the 18th century. By the mid-19th century, English cookbooks contained numerous recipes for curry, showing how through their culinary arts women transformed a foreign South Asian food into a familiar English staple. During the last quarter of the century, a greater variety of inexpensive foods from around the world became available to English shoppers: bananas from the Canary Islands, Cadbury's chocolate produced with cocoa from Trinidad and the Gold Coast, and meat from New Zealand, Australia, and South America. Even the boiled or steamed plum pudding—so often extolled in the 19th century as a symbol of middle-class domesticity, thrift, and Englishness—was partly a product of imperialism featuring spices and dried fruits mixed with flour, bread crumbs, suet, sugar, and milk, brandy, or wine. The round, cake-like puddings were celebrated Christmas desserts, but they also came to signify the bounty of empire. During the 1884–1885 Berlin Conference on Africa that set the policies for European colonization of African territories, the middle-class journal *Punch* presented a cartoon showing the German Chancellor Otto Von Bismark and "The Greedy Boy"—John Bull, the English national figure—fighting over slices of a massive round pudding representing the African continent. As the empire brought new wealth and new foods to the English national population, women played a key role in domesticating these goods, making them a part of English daily life through their roles as purchasers, cooks, and planners of meals.

## LEISURE, HOLIDAYS, AND SOCIAL LIFE

Family remained at the center of most women's social lives, largely determining their social engagements and activities. Among the leisured classes, women spent much of their time at home practicing domestic arts such as sewing and needlework, music, and painting. Women created elaborate scrapbooks and family albums after the invention of photography in the 1830s and 1840s. Some, such as Julia Margaret Cameron (1815–1879) and Lady Clementina Hawarden (1822–1865), became talented photographers in their own right, frequently integrating domestic scenes and children into their images. Lady Hawarden turned the first floor of her Kensington flat into a photographic studio, where she photographed her three eldest daughters in affecting theatrical scenes. Cameron grew to be one of England's most famous portrait photographers, and both she and Hawarden were elected as members to the Photographic Society of London in the 1860s. As a new field, photography created opportunities for female professional and amateur photographers, yet at the same time, the technology prompted the decline of miniature painting, one of the few arts in which women had gained prominence.

Reading and writing were also principle domestic pursuits for women. Literacy rates for both men and women increased during the century. Approximately one-third of all men and one half of all women could not leave a signature mark on English marriage registers in 1840. Nearly all men and women could do so by the end of the century—a clear result of national education after 1870. The number of women who could read likely exceeded those who could write. The expanding publishing industry recognized bourgeois women in particular as an active market of readers, since nearly all Victorian women of the middle and upper classes were literate. Novels, typically first published in multiple volumes ("triple-deckers") or serialized in journals, flourished in the 19th century with plots largely based on domestic scenes of marriage, inheritance, and death. The inexpensive penny dreadfuls—serialized tales such as *Varney the Vampyre* (1845–1847) and *The String of Pearls: A Romance* (1846–1847) featuring Sweeney Todd—proved immensely popular with young working-class readers, but elicited condemnation from the middle classes suspicious of the stories' Gothic sensationalism and criminal exploits. Women novelists and journalists gained national fame, although until the 1880s many, like George Eliot, wrote under male pseudonyms. Especially after the 1840 postal reforms, middle-class women also dedicated large parts of their days to letter writing and social correspondence. Some women may have rarely ventured from their immediate domestic and neighborhood circles, but during the 19th century, developments in literacy made it all the easier for women to engage the wider worlds surrounding them.

### Holidays and Excursions

As middle-class writers such as Sarah Stickney Ellis elevated domesticity into an essential characteristic of England's national strength, major holidays evolved into celebrations of family and home life along beside their religious meanings. Many of the English traditions associated with Christmas, for instance, first became widespread in the 19th century; Victoria and Albert's popularization of the Christmas tree represents a much larger reinterpretation of Christmas that took hold in the 1830s and 1840s. In the 18th century, Christmas gifts were primarily reserved for the poor and household servants, but by the mid-19th century, extended families also gathered to exchange presents. Stories such as Charles Dickens's *A Christmas Carol* (1843) marked the holiday as a time for family reunion and forgiveness in place of the more rollicking, sometimes drunken, festivities formerly associated with Twelfth Night. By the 1880s, Christmas card exchanges, household visits from Father Christmas, and trees loaded with gifts had developed into newly invented commercial traditions of the season.

The constraints of industrial wage labor severely restricted the free time of Victorian workers. In the second half of the century, however, gradually declining daily work hours meant that Victorians enjoyed more leisure time on the whole. Local fairs and horse races such as Derby Day at Epsom Downs continued to draw huge crowds even as the middle classes grew ever more critical of such entertainments. One 1838 London guide condemned the popular fairs as irrational events not fit for the 19th century, claiming that they "engender and foster habits of idleness, frivolity, intemperance, and dissipation of every kind" and ought to be outlawed—as many were during the Victorian period.[11]

By the 1850s, rising standards of living, established rail lines, and the rise of the popular press enabled middle-class women and even many of the better-off working classes to take short trips and excursions of the kind that previously only the upper classes could afford. In the late 19th century, working-class families enjoyed summer holidays or inexpensive day excursions to

Blackpool with its blazing electric lights and other seaside resorts that recreated something of the feel of the summer fairs, featuring music halls, theaters, pleasure gardens, and zoos. The wealthier middle classes preferred southern seaside resorts, such as Brighton and Ramsgate, and as the century progressed, they increasingly planned family trips to the Lake District, the Welsh mountains, the Scottish Highlands, and further abroad to the Alps and other locales. Travel agencies, such as Thomas Cook's, organized trips catering to women. In 1871, *London Society: An Illustrated Magazine of Light and Amusing Literature for the Hours of Relaxation* (itself an example of new forms of middle-class leisure) opened an article on "Ladies' Travel" by noting that women now traveled the world in ways that their mothers never had.

### Visiting and Calls

Closer to home, women of the middle and upper classes spent much of their time making social visits. Ladies regularly walked or, if they could afford to, took carriages for their morning calls—short visits generally of no longer than 30 minutes each to the homes of friends and social acquaintances actually made between 3 and 5 in the afternoon (or until 6 P.M. for close friends) in the hours after lunch and before it was time to dress for dinner. The lady of the highest rank usually initiated the first visit, although in rural areas such social strictures were looser, so established residents might readily welcome newcomers of higher rank. On a first visit, a lady would typically just leave her card with the servant and then return to socialize the following day. If a woman wished to avoid seeing someone, she simply instructed the servant to respond that she was not at home. Ladies returned cards and formal visits within two to three weeks (sometimes taking longer in the countryside) in order to avoid slights. As calling cards first became mass produced in the mid-Victorian period, women turned down corners of the cards to convey various meanings—that there were multiple visitors, a lady and her daughters, for example, or that the card had been delivered in person, not by a servant. By the 1880s, however, the practice of turning down corners was no longer fashionable in most areas. Etiquette guides generally encouraged women to carry simply designed cards bearing their names and perhaps also those of their husbands and young daughters. Yet in practice, many women (and some men) preferred elaborate, colorful cards on glazed or layered paper with symbolic designs, such as hands reaching out in friendship, and even lacework, fringes, and feathers. The intricate rituals of social visitation thus allowed women to form close friendships and connections, while also highlighting the class distinctions, leisure time, and commercial values so central to bourgeois culture.

**_The Etiquette of Modern Society: A Guide to Good Manners in Every Possible Situation_ (London: Ward, Lock, and Co., 1881), 22**

HOUSE-VISITING FRIENDS. A lady is said to have the *entrée* of her friend's when she is allowed or assumes the privilege of entering it familiarly at all times, and without any previous intimation. A familiar visit will always begin more pleasantly if the visitor inquires of the servant at the door if the lady she wishes to see is at home, sends in her name, and ascertains that she can be received. Then, and not till then, let her go to her friend's room, taking care to knock before entering. It is, of course, extremely rude, on being admitted to a private apartment, to look curiously about as if taking an inventory of all that is to be seen. Favourite dogs are never welcome visitors in a drawing-room. Many people have even a dislike to such animals; they require watching lest they should leap upon a chair or sofa, or place themselves on a lady's dress, and attentions of the kind are much out of place. Neither ought a mother, especially when paying a ceremonial visit, to be accompanied by young children. It is frequently difficult to amuse them, and if not particularly well-trained at home, they naturally seize hold of books or those elegant ornaments with which it is fashionable to decorate the drawing-room.

### "At Homes," Dinner, and Dancing Parties

Women of the middle and upper classes found future husbands, developed family business and political networks, and established their role within the social elite through a variety of other domestic entertainments: breakfasts and afternoon teas catering to a few friends or dozens of guests, picnics, afternoon whist parties, dinners, and dances. After coming out in 1846, Lady Dorothy Nevill (1826–1913) experienced an extraordinarily busy social season. "That season I think I went to fifty balls, sixty parties, about thirty dinners, and twenty-five breakfasts," she wrote recalling the gaieties of parties in a period "before the rank and file were admitted!"[12] "At Homes" were informal gatherings in the afternoon or evening featuring dancing, music, theatricals, or simply conversation. Formal dinner parties became more fashionable during the period. The etiquette of dinner parties reinforced distinctions of status, since guests entered the dining room in couples arranged by the hostess starting with the host accompanying the lady of highest rank by the arm. The hostess entered last escorted by the gentleman of highest rank.

Following a dinner party, guests might continue the evening festivities at a public or private ball with a hundred guests or more. Balls typically began late—invitations generally stated 8 or 9 P.M. as the starting time, but many guests did not arrive until 10 o'clock or later—and could last until 3 or 4 the following morning with a light supper usually served around midnight or 1 A.M. Gentlemen asked to dance with ladies for individual dances, and women sometimes kept track of their engagements for the evening with dancing cards that often filled quickly. Unmarried women were to be chaperoned, but amidst the normally strict rules of etiquette, balls offered opportunities for unsupervised interactions: uninvited guests slipped into private parties, the normal rules of introductions loosened, and the very act of dancing quadrilles and dizzying waltzes placed men and women in intimate contact.

### Theatrical and Musical Entertainment

Theatrical and musical performances provided regular entertainments for all women, yet the venues and formats differed by class. In their homes, middle- and upper-class women organized dramatic readings and skits. A gentlewoman's education also typically involved training in voice and the piano—an instrument the Victorians primarily associated with domestic settings and female amateur entertainment. The piano was ubiquitous in elite homes, and by the last decades of the century, declining prices allowed many working-class families to purchase one as well.

Victorian women practiced the musical and dramatic arts mainly within the domestic realm, but an increasing number of female musicians, singers, and actors received acclaim as well as opprobrium for their public performances. In 1872, the Royal Academy of Music admitted its first female violin student, and by the mid-1870s, female musicians gained widespread attention for forming all female ensembles and training in instruments previously limited to men—not only the violin, but also the cello and wind instruments. These new female musicians elicited vexed associations with the New Woman, as the artist George du Maurier highlighted in

"The Fair Sex-tett (Accomplishments of the Rising Female Generation)," *Punch* (1875). George du Maurier's portrayal of the all-female music ensembles that became popular in the 1870s. (Vassar College Library)

his 1875 *Punch* cartoon, "The Fair Sex-tett (Accomplishments of the Rising Female Generation)," in which he portrayed an audience of admiring men gazing up at the strong, confident, sexually provocative female musicians on the stage. By the late 1870s, women such as Ellen Terry (1847–1928) and the internationally famous Sarah Bernhardt (1844–1923) captivated London and national audiences with their spectacular dramatic talents, providing models of successful women actors even as they flaunted bourgeois codes of respectability with their extramarital affairs and out-of-wedlock children.

The popular entertainments for working-class audiences—in the less reputable theaters, the music halls, and the streets—prompted widespread criticism from middle-class reformers who often viewed such leisure activities as immoral. The Evangelical writer Ellen Barlee (b. 1825/1826), for example, compared the wildly popular pantomime performances using young child actors to cock fighting and bull baiting, condemning what she understood as pleasure-seeking amusements based on the pain of others. Barlee declared the "pantomime waifs"—a group she extended to include child actors, scantily dressed ballet dancers, acrobats, and girls performing on stage dressed in men's clothing as "mashers," or effeminate young men living the "fast life"—were "sacrificed on the altar of public amusement," "making shipwreck of their Innocence and Purity," "everything that is happy and good in a Woman's existence," and left "unsexed" with "every feminine instinct crushed out of them, while too young to appreciate the value of God's gift of womanhood."[13] Nonetheless, the pantomimes and *tableaux vivants*—live reproductions of famous paintings and events that sometimes included female nudes—remained immensely popular, especially for Christmas and holiday pageants, along with a rich assortment of street theatricals and music.

Chief among urban working-class places of entertainment were the music halls, which developed from the coffee houses and taverns of the 18th century that first began including small stages for variety performances—song and music, dance, comedy, and short skits. By the 1850s, innovative publicans in London's East End and in northern and midland industrial cities expanded their businesses and built large halls where hundreds of people came to see shows and enjoy the food and drink. There were some 375 music halls in Greater London by 1875, including the magnificent Alhambra and the Empire in Leicester Square. Despite the success of music halls in the wealthier West End London districts, the audiences—primarily from the working classes and aristocracy—and the shows continued to receive widespread censure from middle-class reformers. The content of the songs and skits often celebrated a rough masculinity—domestic violence, drink, and womanizing—along with a potentially subversive blurring of class distinctions. Some music hall owners, such as Charles Morton, tried to make the halls respectable by enticing more women to attend the shows with weekly "Ladies' Nights." The end result, however, was that music halls became widely viewed as places frequented by prostitutes. By the 1860s, the halls provided greater opportunities for working-class female performers, and by the end of the century, women such as Jenny Hill (1848–1896) and Marie Lloyd (1870–1922) emerged as beloved stars renown for their ability to engage audiences, recount the comedies and trials of working-class life, and imbue seemingly innocent lyrics about love and work with *double entendres* to create an art form that publicly recognized female desire.

**"Buy Me Some Almond Rock" (1893), sung by Marie Lloyd, written and composed by Joseph Tabrar, reprinted in John M. Garrett, *Sixty Years of British Music Hall* (London: Chappell & Company, 1976)**

1

I feel so glad, I never had
Such joy within my heart;
I've been asked out, and without doubt
I'm dying to make a start.
I've never seen a ball, nor been
Allowed out after dark,
I'll mash the men, nine out of ten,
Oh! wont it be a lark.

CHORUS.

Only fancy if Gladstone's there,
And falls in love with me,
If I run across Labouchere,
I'll ask him home to tea.
I shall say to a young man gay,
If he treads upon my frock,
Randy pandy, sugardy candy,
Buy me some Almond Rock.

2

I heard in truth that General Booth
Is going to be M.C.,
And if he is, 'twill be good "biz,"
No end of fun there'll be.
Ma said last week, I'm not to speak
To even one young man,
But just you wait, in spite of fate,
I'll speak to all I can.
(*Chorus.*) Only fancy, &c.

3

If Sir Charles Dilke sees me in silk,
To dance with me he'll try,
I'll sing "Tral la" Ha! "There you are"
Then "Wink the other eye."
If by a "fluke" I meet a Duke,
A Marquis or an Earl,
I'll win all three, in fact I'll be
A regular "Giddy girl."
(*Chorus.*) Only fancy, &c.

**Galleries, Museums, and Exhibits**

The middle-class emphasis on moral, instructional entertainments promoted the creation and expansion of museum and gallery exhibits during the 19th century. For women in particular, galleries offered new public settings in which they could both see and be seen; elite women's leisured wanderings through exhibits allowed them freedoms in public spaces typically reserved for men, while at the same time, Victorian depictions of female patrons suggest that they, much like the paintings and collections from around the world, were also on display. An 1889 article on the Grosvenor Gallery (1877–1890) in the *Scots Observer*, for example, said nothing of the paintings, yet wrote in detail about the dress of female patrons, surmising "Perhaps it is due to this worst of London winters, perhaps to some strange but momentary indifference to dress; but certain it is that women are this year unnaturally careless of their looks," although a "mother and her two daughters, all three dressed in copper-brown cloth coats—tight-fitting, and adorned with a series of tiny capes on the shoulders—formed a pleasant enough spectacle."[14]

Visiting museums and exhibits developed into a regular part of elite women's social activities. The annual May exhibition at the Royal Academy of Arts celebrated the opening of the London social season with private viewings for the upper classes before the official public showing of the selected paintings. By the mid-Victorian period, reformers' pressure to use museums as educational sites, free and open to the public, outweighed earlier understandings of museums as private collections for the elite, and middle-class women and their families increasingly visited older galleries, such as the British Museum (founded in 1753), as well as newer ones, such as the National Gallery (founded by parliament in 1824 and moved to the enlarged site at Trafalgar Square in 1837) and the South Kensington Museum (originally opened in 1852 as the Museum of Ornamental Art and moved to South Kensington in 1857). In 1899, The South Kensington Museum was renamed the Victoria and Albert Museum. As her last public act, Queen Victoria laid the cornerstone for the new building.

More than anything else, the 1851 Great Exhibition of the Works of Industry of All Nations inspired the Victorian interest in museums—and later provided the bulk of the initial collection for the Victoria and Albert Museum. Held in Hyde Park, London, at the Crystal Palace—a spectacular modern construction made from iron, wood, and glass enclosing an area six times the size of St. Paul's

Cathedral—the Great Exhibition promised to bring the benefits of free trade, manufacturing, internationalism, consumerism, and artistic taste (not always without conflict) before the British public. Between May and October 1851, 6 million people visited the Crystal Palace to view a huge array of materials—everything from a 24-ton hunk of coal and model English textile looms to a pocketknife with 80 blades and the exquisite Medieval Court designed by A.W.N. Pugin. The exhibits included select lacework and other crafts produced by Englishwomen, but for the most part, women engaged with the event not as exhibitors, but as spectators and visitors. The displays and arrangement of the Great Exhibition inundated women with messages about their role in the world. In the India Court, for example, they walked through a truncated narrative of imperial power told by the raw materials, luxury goods, stuffed elephant, and representations of Indian workers on display that situated Britain as the leader of the world's largest empire. The Great Exhibition reaffirmed Englishwomen's roles as imperial consumers. Women left the Crystal Palace praising the beautiful Indian silks and cashmere shawls, which became all the rage in the 1850s. The thousands of pieces of furniture and other domestic goods—cutlery, clothes, and curtains—on show provided models and inspiration for home design. Prince Albert even erected a building next to the Crystal Palace promoting model working-class housing in which each flat contained running water, a separate kitchen, and three bedrooms. In 1852, workers took apart the Crystal Palace and moved it to Sydenham in south London, where it reopened in 1854 as a site for public events and colonial displays.

The Great Exhibition demonstrated that the home and the family never existed solely in private, but also shaped the core of England's national and imperial identity. Working-class housing and women's overall domestic prosperity arose as readily understood signs of the condition of England. In turn, women's basic domestic decisions about leisure, food, design, marriage, and even about how many children to bear directly related to the economic and political conditions within England and the empire.

## NOTES

1. *Barnardo's Annual Reports, 1883–1884*, 9, D239/A3/16, University of Liverpool Library Special Collections and Archive, emphasis in original.
2. C.E. Humphry, *Manners for Men* (London: James Bowden, 1897), 23–25.
3. Henry Mayhew, *London Labour and the London Poor*, Vol. 1 (New York: Dover Publications, Inc., 1968; 1861–1862), 45.

4. Frances Power Cobbe, as quoted in Sharon Marcus, *Between Women: Friendship, Desire, and Marriage in Victorian England* (Princeton, NJ: Princeton University Press, 2007), 52 and see also Martha Vicinus, *Intimate Friends: Women Who Loved Women, 1778–1928* (Chicago, IL: University of Chicago Press, 2004), 33.

5. Lydia Murdoch, *Imagined Orphans: Poor Families, Child Welfare, and Contested Citizenship in London* (New Brunswick, NJ: Rutgers University Press, 2006), 2.

6. Letter 24, "Utterly Overdone," in *Maternity: Letters from Working Women*, ed. by Margaret Llewelyn Davies (New York: W. W. Norton & Co., 1978; 1915), 50.

7. Mayhew, *London Labour and the London Poor*, 43, emphasis in original.

8. Lady Jeune, as quoted in Jessica Gerard, *Country House Life, Family and Servants, 1815–1914* (Oxford: Blackwell, 1994), 4.

9. Application of Emma Pimm (July 15, 1884), 131, Bethnal Green Board of Guardians, Settlement Records and Records Relating to Relief Examinations (rough), February 19, 1884–February 10, 1885, Be.BG.267/35, London Metropolitan Archives.

10. Duke of Bedford, as quoted in F.M.L. Thompson, *The Rise of Respectable Society: A Social History of Victorian Britain, 1830–1900* (Cambridge, MA: Harvard University Press, 1988), 195.

11. James Grant, *Sketches in London* (1838), reprinted in *Unknown London: Early Modernist Visions of the Metropolis, 1815–45*, Vol. 6 (London: Pickering and Chatto, 2000), 319.

12. Lady Dorothy Nevill, *The Reminiscences of Lady Dorothy Nevill* (London: Edward Arnold, 1906), 52–53.

13. Ellen Barlee, *Pantomime Waifs: Or, a Plea for Our City Children* (London: S. W. Partridge & Co., 1884), 70, 8, xiv, ix, 116, 117.

14. "Dress at the Grosvenor," *The Scots Observer* 1.11 (February 2, 1889): 295.

# 4

# HEALTH AND SEXUALITY

The Victorians, we are often told, epitomized prudery and sexual propriety to the extreme. They supposedly covered piano legs with skirts so as not to draw attention to a bare limb of any kind. To prepare her daughter for her wedding night, Queen Victoria is said to have advised, "lie back and think of England." Such myths, though often repeated, have little basis in historical fact. There is no record connecting Victoria or anyone else from the period to the "lie back" counsel, and the reference to skirted piano legs likely started in the late 1830s as a satire of American women's excessive refinement placed in unfavorable comparison with British women's sensibility. Victorian women no doubt had to negotiate codes of decorum and modesty that restricted their physical experiences. However, in their daily lives, they also dealt with bodily issues in ways that may seem surprisingly frank to modern readers. Focus on the body—particularly on issues of women's dress, hygiene, medical care, and sexuality—reveals both how Victorians imposed ideals of femininity through physical regulation and how individual women experienced the embodied pleasures and pains of life.

Historians have examined the various ways in which health itself is socially constructed rather than simply an objective state of being, so that discussions about individual physical well-being become intertwined with parallel understandings of moral vigor and the strength of the nation. The health and condition of Victorian female bodies—above all the ability of these bodies to reproduce—emerged as main topics in debates about women factory workers in the 1830s and 1840s, women's education in the 1860s and 1870s, and increasing infant mortality rates in the last decades of the century. Understandings of physical fitness varied by class, so that what Victorians considered to be healthy for a working-class woman might be construed as dangerous for an elite woman. Doctors, policy makers, and reformers discussed women's physical conditions—everything from menstruation and reproduction to beauty and dress. Women's most personal bodily and mental states provided rich material for public debates on the "Condition of Woman" question.

## BEAUTY AND DRESS

Feminine ideals of beauty connoted respectability, class standing, and morality. For example, the middle classes viewed obvious applications of cosmetics as vulgar demonstrations of vanity. Many elite women certainly wore face powder with discretion to achieve a "naturally" glowing complexion, but rouge and lipstick were associated with actresses and licentious women. Still, by the late 1860s, enough middle-class women must have experimented with cosmetics and hair dye to inspire the journalist Eliza Lynn Linton (1822–1898) to condemn such practices as signs of how the "Girl of the Period" rejected all womanly ideals of English domesticity and blurred the lines of class, race, and respectability. Women generally grew their hair long and wore it up in public—the tighter, simpler styles suggesting spinsterhood, advanced age, religious austerity, or professional authority. In their late teens, girls from the middle and upper classes began wearing longer, ankle length skirts and their hair up to signify the transition to adulthood. Working-class girls generally did so earlier, when they commenced regular waged work around the age of 12 or 13. Short, cropped hair on a working-class girl was a telltale indication that she was one of the "unfeminine masses" recently released from the workhouse, poor law school, or reformatory, where officials cut girls' hair short to prevent the spread of lice.

**Eliza Lynn Linton, "The Girl of the Period,"**
***The Saturday Review* (March 14, 1868): 340**

The girl of the period is a creature who dyes her hair and paints her face, as the first articles of her personal religion; whose sole idea of life is plenty of fun and luxury; and whose dress is the object of such thought and intellect as she possesses. Her main endeavour in this is to outvie her neighbours in the extravagance of fashion. No matter whether, as in the time of crinolines, she sacrificed decency, or, as now, in the time of trains, she sacrifices cleanliness; no matter either, whether she makes herself a nuisance and an inconvenience to every one she meets. The girl of the period has done away with such moral muffishness as consideration for others, or regard for counsel and rebuke. It was all very well in old-fashioned times, when fathers and mothers had some authority and were treated with respect, to be tutored and made to obey, but she is far too fast and flourishing to be stopped in mid-career by these slow old morals; and as she dresses to please herself, she does not care if she displeases every one else. Nothing is too extraordinary and nothing too exaggerated for her vitiated taste; and things which in themselves would be useful reforms if let alone become monstrosities worse than those which they have displaced so soon as she begins to manipulate and improve. If a sensible fashion lifts the gown out of the mud, she raises hers midway to her knee. If the absurd structure of wire and buckram, once called a bonnet, is modified to something that shall protect the wearer's face without putting out the eyes of her companion, she cuts hers down to four straws and a rosebud, or a tag of lace and a bunch of glass beads. If there is a reaction against an excess of Rowland's Macassar, and hair shiny and sticky with grease is thought less nice than if left clean and healthily crisp, she dries and frizzes and sticks hers out on end like certain savages in Africa, or lets it wander down her back like Madge Wildfire's, and thinks herself all the more beautiful the nearer she approaches in look to a maniac or a negress. With purity of taste she has lost also that far more precious purity and delicacy of perception which sometimes mean more than appears on the surface. What the *demi-monde* does in its frantic efforts to excite attention, she also does in imitation. If some fashionable *dévergondée en evidence* [obviously loose woman] is reported to have come out with her dress below her shoulder-blades, and a gold strap for all the sleeve thought necessary, the girl of the period follows suit next day; and then wonders that men sometimes mistake her for her prototype, or that mothers of girls not quite so far gone as herself refuse her as a companion for their daughters. She has blunted the fine edges of feeling so much that she cannot understand why she should be condemned for an imitation of form which does not include imitation of fact; she cannot be made to see that modesty of appearance and virtue ought to be inseparable, and that no good girl can afford to appear bad, under penalty of receiving the contempt awarded to the bad.

Women's daily dress also varied significantly depending on class. English ladies were expected to expend great amounts of time, money, and effort in selecting appropriate attire for specific settings. A gentlewoman's bonnet for walking in the park, for example, would be completely inappropriate for church. Elite ladies changed dresses several times a day, beginning with a day dress, then perhaps putting on a carriage dress for outings or tweeds for outdoor events at country house parties, a tea gown for afternoon socializing, and finally a more formal evening dress for dinner. Ball and opera gowns were the most exquisite dresses—typically low cut and made from expensive materials such as silk, satin, velvet, and tulle. Middle-class women rotated several woolen dresses each season. They, too, changed into a morning or walking dress to make visits and then into a finer dress for dinner. By the end of the century, clothing styles for specific activities—not only horseback riding, but also tennis, gymnastics, skating, garden parties, boating, and seaside outings—became popular for women.

Vegetable dyes and chemical aniline dyes, after their invention in 1859, provided a rich array of colors with poetic names marking fine distinctions between "London dust," "London mud," and "London smoke," or "the flame of Mount Vesuvius" and "the flame of burnt brandy."[1] Bold contrasts of bright colors became fashionable after the Crimean War (1854–1856), suggesting the influences of Orientalism on English fashion. White remained a popular color, especially for summer dresses, symbolizing purity and social standing among the leisured classes. A young lady wore white for her first ball gown, but not necessarily for her wedding dress, which might be cream, grey, pastel, or even more richly colored, although white wedding dresses became more fashionable after Queen Victoria chose a white silk gown for her wedding. Black was associated with mourning, but the black silk dress remained a respectable option for ceremonial occasions.

By the end of the period, women made more extensive use of undergarments, although these tended to be plainly made compared to the elaborate frills, ribbons, and lacework ornamenting outer attire. Underclothing was most often made from wool, flannel, or silk and generally white until colors became more fashionable in the 1870s and 1880s. Drawers or knickerbockers came in vogue for aristocratic women in the early 19th century, for middle-class women in the mid-Victorian period with the introduction of the crinoline, and for working-class women generally later in the 1880s. Combinations—a camisole top attached to drawers—also became popular, along with multiple petticoats—the number and material depending on the style of dress and season. Most women put on some sort of stockings made from wool, cotton, or silk. Throughout the century, women and older girls from all classes generally wore corsets, also called stays. Made from whalebone, metal, or wood frames covered in padded fabric, corsets could be tightly laced to accentuate the waist or left loose to allow for physical movement and manual labor.

**Gwen Raverat, *Period Piece* (Ann Arbor: The University of Michigan Press, 1991; 1952), 264.**

This is what a young lady wore, with whom I shared a room one night—beginning at the bottom, or scratch:

1. Thick, long-legged, long-sleeved woolen combinations.
2. Over them, white cotton combinations, with plenty of buttons and frills.
3. Very serious, bony, grey stays, with suspenders.
4. Black woolen stockings.
5. White cotton drawers, with buttons and frills.
6. White cotton "petticoat-bodice," with embroidery, buttons and frills.
7. Rather short, white flannel, petticoat.
8. Long alpaca petticoat, with a flounce round the bottom.
9. Pink flannel blouse.
10. High, starched, white collar, fastened on with studs.
11. Navy-blue tie.
12. Blue skirt, touching the ground, and fastened tightly to the blouse with a safety-pin behind.
13. Leather belt, very tight.
14. High button boots.

I watched her under my eyelashes as I lay in bed. She would have been horrified if she had known that I was awake.

Fashion accessories marked women's social status and engagement with consumer culture. When outside, women always wore hats or bonnets, which ranged in shapes, styles, and designs from simple lace and ribbon trimmings to fancy feathers, artificial flowers, and veils. In the 1830s and 1840s, women usually wore mobcaps while inside, but by mid-century younger women ceased to do so. By the 1880s, caps were generally used inside only by older women, servants, nurses, or widows, who wore a special mourning cap for two years or longer. Elite women wore gloves whenever they ventured outside (failure to do so could spark a stern rebuke) and in the evening. Like gloves, parasols were important accessories signifying upper- and middle-class femininity. They protected women from the elements, thereby reinforcing the association of pale skin with leisure and privilege, while allowing women to screen themselves from unwanted views. Women similarly adorned outfits with painted and decorated fans, hand bouquets or scent bottles, and jewelry. In the 1850s, the choice of shawl was said to be a true test of a gentlewoman's taste. The expensive, highly coveted Indian cashmere signified bourgeois domesticity as well as erotic intrigue, demonstrating how the growth of western imperialism influenced women's fashion.

The popularization of the sewing machine in the 1850s gradually led to the availability of inexpensive, mass-produced ready-made clothing during the last quarter of the century. Working-class women could buy fashionable clothes similar in style to those worn by elite women. At the same time, however, fine distinctions of color, material, and cut took on even greater significance as signs of social standing. By the late-Victorian period, the bright colors once fashionable among the elite became more associated with female factory workers. Poor women bought clothing from secondhand shops or reworked clothes handed down from employers to fit. Bourgeois employers and leaders of the Metropolitan Association for Befriending Young Servants, a philanthropic organization that worked with poor law authorities to find domestic service positions for girls, openly criticized servants for wearing fancy dress deemed inappropriate for their station. Clothing, in sum, had long served as a most visible sign of class, and any attempt to subvert class distinctions could entail a moral affront.

Crime reports also suggest the meaning imbued in fine sartorial distinctions. In the *Times* reports of the 1888 Whitechapel or Jack-the-Ripper murders, for example, the paper described the intimate details of a victim's dress: the "redish ulster, somewhat the worse for wear, a new brown linsey dress, two flannel petticoats, having the marks of the Lambeth Workhouse on them, and a pair of stays." Another female victim dressed in a "black cloth jacket, with imitation fur collar and three large metal buttons." The *Times* even described the pattern of her dress—dark green with Michaelmas daisies and golden lilies. "She also wore a thin white vest, a drab linsey skirt, and a very old dark green alpaca petticoat, white chemise, and brown ribbed stockings, mended at the feet with white material. Her bonnet was black straw, trimmed with black beads and green and black velvet. She wore a pair of men's laced-boots; and a piece of old white coarse apron and a piece of riband

"Mr. Punch's Designs After Nature. Might Not Wasp-Waisted Young Ladies Adopt This Costume With Advantage?" *Punch* (1869). (Vassar College Library)

were tied loosely round the neck."[2] Such details helped identify the women among family and friends, yet also served to indicate for the wider public the victims' status as prostitutes who struggled between stints in the workhouse and visions of a higher, illusionary life suggested by imitation furs and cheap sateens.

Women and girls from all classes experienced the restrictions of feminine dress. Insufficient clothing likely caused the worst health effects among working women suffering from cold and exposure, but public attention focused on how high fashion for elite women constricted and damaged the female form. Dresses alone could weigh over 15 pounds. The crinoline, a wire cage worn under skirts, could encompass a circumference of four to five yards even for a less formal day dress. When they were the height of fashion in the mid-to-late 1850s and early 1860s, women stumbled to move through narrow spaces, and newspapers reported cases of crinoline wearers burnt to death from their extended dresses catching fire. Some women, however, preferred the freedom of movement crinolines allowed their legs in comparison with the heavy weight of multiple petticoats. Crinolines were outmoded by the late 1860s, but in the following two decades, the bustle—a cloth pad or wire frame attached to the waist and wrapped with fabric to enlarge the back of skirts—grew in size and popularity. *Punch* ran a long series of Linley Sambourne cartoons in the late 1860s and 1870s mocking women's fashions—the off-kilter gaits caused by high heels, the Medussa-like heads covered in heavy artificial hair, and the "wasp-waisted" forms from tightly laced corsets. But most disturbing was the inhuman nature of women implied by Sambourne's depiction of them as beetles, birds, sea creatures, and other animals.

*Punch* was not alone in its critique of women's fashion. Many Victorians supported various dress reform movements throughout the period. The American suffragist and temperance reformer Amelia Bloomer (1818–1894) visited England in 1851 attempting to promote trousers paired with short dresses for women. "Bloomerism" became popular among a handful of women, but primarily sparked ridicule from public journals including *Punch* and prominent women such as Caroline Norton (1808–1877), who cited her sister-in-law's penchant for short hair and trousers as proof that she was ill-suited for society. Later, more widespread movements focused pointedly on questions of women's health and beauty, rather than their political rights. Beginning in the 1860s, the Artistic Dress movement—a forerunner of Aesthetic trends of the 1880s

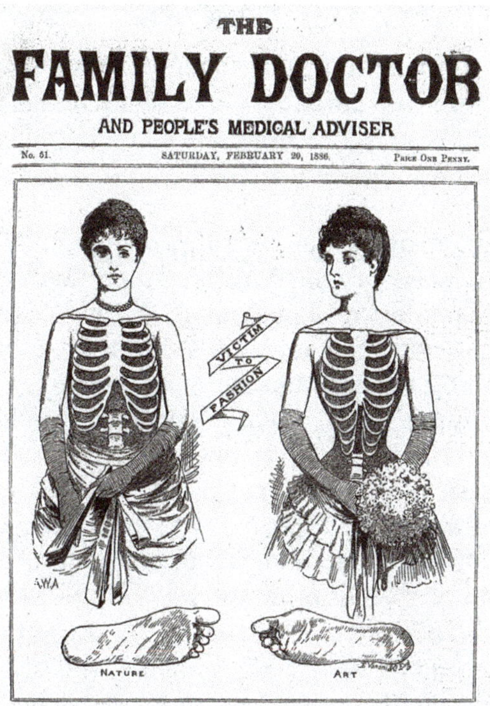


*The Family Doctor*, first published in 1885, highlighted the dangers of women's corsets and tightlacing. (National Library of Medicine)

and 1890s—drew support from great artists such as William Morris, who designed free-flowing dresses in the Pre-Raphaelite style without hoops, bustles, or corseted waists. The more moralistic Rational Dress Reform Society, founded in 1881, railed against the dangers of tightly laced corsets and other restrictive fashions for women. Doctors and dress reformers argued that tightlacing in particular caused numerous health problems and diseases ranging from indigestion and poor muscle development to curved spines, severed livers, prolapsed uteruses, and hardened ovaries. It is difficult to gauge whether reformers exaggerated the effects of corsets. However, many women—including those who did not practice extreme tightlacing—described the torture and constraint of wearing their first stays or "corselets" at the age of 10 to 12 and full corsets by 16.

## HYGIENE, ILLNESS, AND MEDICINE

Women's general health improved significantly by the end of the 19th century, especially after the 1870s. The average life expectancy at birth for women in 1838 was 42 years (compared to 40 for men)—an average lowered by the inclusion of the large numbers of children who died under the age of 5. By the 1890s, life expectancy for women in England and Wales was approximately 47 (44 for men)—a significant increase in longevity given that in many areas infant mortality rates remained high through the end of the century. Life expectancy varied by region, with women in London and other parts of southern England living longest on average and women in the northern counties and Midlands dying at younger ages.

Urban death rates began to decline only in the 1870s as an understanding of germ theory became more widespread and city and national governments supported urban reform movements to improve sanitation, water, and sewages supplies. Early studies of sanitary conditions such as James Kay-Shuttleworth's *The Moral and Physical Condition of the Working Classes Employed in the Cotton Manufacture in Manchester* (1832), Edwin Chadwick's *Report on the Sanitary Condition of the Labouring Population* (1842), and Friedrich Engels's *The Condition of the Working Class in England* (1845) brought national attention to widespread overcrowding, horrific sanitary conditions, and the devastating effects of shock diseases such as cholera, which killed up to 60 percent of those infected, sometimes within hours. In 1837, the state initiated the registration of births and deaths—a process not made compulsory until 1874. By the 1840s, local and national statistical societies formed to track the effects of poor sanitation on public health. Men dominated these organizations, but in 1858, Florence Nightingale (1820–1910) became the first elected woman fellow to the Statistical Society. Women also joined the Ladies' Sanitary Association, founded in 1856, to work for improved hygiene, infant care, and nutrition. By the 1860s and 1870s, statistical studies of health and sanitation translated into the very first efforts by municipal and state governments to improve water supplies, sewage systems, housing conditions, and air and food quality—the environmental aspects of modern life that had until that point been almost entirely left to private enterprise and the free market.

The general sanitary conditions for most of the period, however, remained appalling. Dense black coal smoke filled the air above industrial towns. Many neighborhoods had no access to pumped water or effective sewage systems until after the 1870s. For much of the Victorian period, crowded tenements that could house hundreds shared a single privy, and human waste often drained directly into local water sources—or simply into the streets. Queen Victoria is said to have asked, "What are all those pieces of paper floating down the river?" when visiting Trinity College, Cambridge, where until the mid-1890s sewage flowed directly into the waterway. Her mindful guide replied, "Those, ma'am, are notices that bathing is forbidden."[3]

Washing practices changed significantly during the Victorian period and varied by class. When Queen Victoria began her residence at Buckingham Palace in 1837, there were no bathrooms; she used a portable tub filled and drained by servants. Elite women likewise washed regularly in their dressing rooms or chambers using a tub, washstand, or shower bath. By the 1840s, the most expensive homes included hot water pumped upstairs. Middle-class houses began to include hot running water upstairs by the 1870s, as well as separate bathrooms either designed for new homes or converted from dressing rooms. Most urban homes, however, did not include internal plumbing until the mid-1880s, and indoor plumbing became an expectation in rural homes only in the 1890s. At the end of the century, many women still relied on outdoor communal pumps for water.

As access to pumped water differed by class and region, cleanliness took on greater moral significance as a sign of respectability in the 1850s and 1860s, differentiating the elite from the "great unwashed." Soap production and consumption increased dramatically during these decades, especially after the removal of the soap tax in 1853. Although most working-class women did not have ready access to full baths, they did their best to clean their bodies regularly—particularly their faces, necks, and hands. From her late-Victorian childhood in rural Oxfordshire, Flora Thompson (1876–1947) recalled that "women would lock their cottage doors for a whole afternoon once a week to have what they called 'a good clean up.' This consisted of a stripping to the waist and washing downward; then stepping into a footbath and washing upward. 'Well, I feels all the better for that,' some woman would say complacently. 'I've washed up as far as possible and down as far as possible,' and the ribald would inquire what poor 'possible' had done that that should not be included."[4]

Women from all classes took a leading role in promoting hygiene and sanitary reforms as an extension of their religious and domestic duties. Catherine Wilkinson (1786–1860)—a former servant, mill worker, and nail maker—responded to the cholera epidemic of the early 1830s by washing and disinfecting linens in her home with chloride of lime, saving countless lives. In 1842, Wilkinson encouraged the Liverpool municipal authorities to open the first public washhouse where people could take a bath or wash their clothes for a small charge. Philanthropists and municipal governments built public bathhouses throughout England during the 1850s. By the early 1860s, gentlewomen had also formed branches of the Ladies' Sanitary Association in London, Manchester, Salford, and other major cities. The society organized lectures on health practices directed toward working-class audiences and published tracts with titles such as "The Worth of Fresh Air," "The Use of Pure Water," "How to Save Infant Life," and the "Power of Soap and Water" for door-to-door distribution. They advised poor families on matters of health and budgeting, organized day trips to parks for urban children, and set up funds to support struggling dressmakers (while also encouraging ladies to pay their milliners' bills on time).

During the first half of the century, only the most expensive homes had water closets or flush toilets, first developed in the 18th century. The Great Exhibition of 1851 provided many people with their first introduction to the flush toilet. Thousands of people a day paid a small fee to use the Crystal Palace public lavatories displaying the latest technologies. Many remained wary, however, of modern plumbing, distrusting the smells and blockages caused by insufficient water pressure. The gradual introduction of plumbing within elite homes to replace chamber pots or external privies at first overwhelmed inadequate drainage systems. The Thames became so polluted that in the unusually hot summer of 1858, all of London suffered from what was called the Great Stink, during which even Queen Victoria had to cover her face with a bouquet against the noxious odor as she traveled downriver. Parliament rushed through funding for an extensive sewage works leading to the 1868 completion of the marvelous Abbey Mills Pumping Station in East London. The art critic John Ruskin pronounced that "a good sewer" is a "far nobler and a far holier thing . . . than the most admired Madonna ever painted."[5]

Such environmental conditions, combined with extreme overcrowding in many urban as well as rural areas, provided the perfect conditions for the spread of contagious disease. Women, like other members of the population, suffered from major sanitation-related illnesses of the period and in many cases were at greater risk because of poor nutrition and exposure to infection through their role as caretakers. With the exception of the smallpox vaccination developed by Edward Jenner in 1798, there were few medical discoveries that stemmed the spread of infectious diseases. Tens of thousands of women, men, and children died in the major cholera epidemics that struck England in 1831–1832, 1848–1849, 1853–1854, and 1866–1867. Women also struggled and often died from the other chief contagious diseases of the period: typhus, typhoid, influenza, scarlet fever, and diphtheria (or croup). Tuberculosis or phthisis (also known as consumption in its chronic form and as scrofula when the illness affected the glands) was by far the greatest killer and notable along with some other infectious diseases in that it generally affected women more than men. The sickness likely caused one-third of all Victorian fatalities from disease and one half of all deaths among women between the ages of 15 and 35. The illness could destroy whole families. The elder Brontë sisters Mary and Elizabeth died six weeks apart from tuberculosis in 1825, as did their brother Bromwell and younger sister Emily in 1848, Anne in 1849, and perhaps Charlotte as well in 1855 (though the cause of her death is disputed and was likely related to her pregnancy).

While the major contagious diseases attacked men as well as women, certain other illnesses and conditions remained unique to women. Death during childbirth (see Chapter 5) was a significant cause of women's fatalities. Over 1 out of every 200 women died during childbirth from complications such as excessive bleeding or infection. Though often not publicly discussed, many women also suffered from breast cancer, which caused the deaths of countless unknown as well as prominent Victorians, including the social reformer and writer Charlotte Elizabeth Tonna (1790–1846), the paleontologist Mary Anning (1799–1847), the Salvation Army leader Catherine Booth (1829–1890), and the illustrator Kate Greenaway (1846–1901). More widespread and difficult to trace were the effects of general malnutrition among women. In many working-class families, women rarely if ever ate meat, saving the best food for men and boys, and thus suffered from chronic anemia and malnourishment that made them more susceptible to disease.

When family members became ill, women and older girls served as caretakers. Mrs. Beeton's *Book of Household Management* (1861) proclaimed that "All women are likely, at some period of their lives, to be called on to perform the duties of a sick-nurse. . . . The main requirements are good temper, compassion for suffering, sympathy with sufferers, which most women worthy of the name possess, neat-handedness, quiet manners, love of order, and cleanliness."[6] Women and girls did their best to provide comfort for family members. They oversaw the maintenance of fires, proper ventilation, and daily cleaning in the sick room. Women also provided their patients with special foods, such as spoonfuls of beef tea or wine mixed with arrowroot offered every hour. As caretakers, women protected the sick from all unpleasant household or external noises. Beeton even advised her readers to wear dresses made from material that did not rustle. Through such acts as silent prayer and reading aloud, women and girls offered comfort and sympathy to the sick in addition to medical assistance.

When serious conditions required more care than family members could provide, women called upon and received medical attention from a wide array of services. In cases of long-term illness, families who could afford to do so might employ a professional nurse. Doctors also made house visits to their middle-class and aristocratic patients. There were distinct types of medical practitioners. The highest in status were physicians who were licensed university-educated men (until women gained access to the profession in 1877). The lowest in status were apothecaries, who distributed medical advice along with drugs to the general population. Surgeons who performed operations, set bones, and attended to skin diseases and some gynecological disorders fit somewhere in between, often combining their services with apothecary. Hospitalization in one of the growing number of charity hospitals was typically only for the working classes who could not afford private doctor fees. After the creation of the medical register in 1858 set standards for recognizing qualified practitioners, major teaching hospitals in urban centers and cottage hospitals in rural areas expanded their free or inexpensive inpatient and outpatient services. The very poor resorted to workhouse infirmaries and, much more often, visited local dispensaries and outpatient clinics. Poor women also routinely relied on informal medical services from neighbors.

In the 1860s and 1870s, women such as Florence Nightingale, Ellen Ranyard (1810–1879), Florence Lees Craven (1840–1922), and Mary Catherine Booth (1847–1939) established organizations of volunteer nurses to visit impoverished communities. Called district nurses because they served specific urban districts, these middle-class, educated women set out to "civilize" and provide basic medical services to the poor. Along with much-needed medical assistance, district nurses brought religion and housekeeping advice. For many working-class women, the district nurse may have been a key example of class condescension, but she also offered invaluable services by coming daily during times of illness to supervise children, clean houses, bring in clean water and coal, provide nourishing food, cook meals, and wash and care for patients. What began as localized volunteer organizations in Liverpool, Manchester, Salford, London, and other cities developed into a major source of medical care for the working classes.

**Florence S. Lees, "District Nursing in a Large Town,"**
***Good Words* 16 (December 1875): 318, 320**

It is now rather more than twelve years since the first Training School for District Nurses was started at Liverpool. These nurses were to receive a year's training in the Nurses' Home attached to the Royal Infirmary, and were then to be sent out into a district under one or more ladies who undertook to superintend their work and provide the necessary medical stores, appliances, and comforts, for the sick under their charge. It would be impossible to overestimate the amount of good done by the visits of these nurses. . . .

I felt that I should like to visit some of these districts myself, to judge better the class of patients helped and the nature of the help given. . . .

We went to many cases of diseased or burnt limbs, and in every case the nurse who was with me washed and dressed the wound or sores. The services of the nurse in dressing wounds of this description saves the patient from the separation from home, and loss of time necessary for hospital treatment. Each nurse carried with her a small bag, containing lint, ointment, gutta percha, &c., in addition to any "medical comforts" and old linen that she might be taking to special cases. I cannot refrain from quoting a few examples from one of the reports, relating to the work of the nurse, which show the mitigation effected of much unnecessary suffering among the sick poor, arising from lack of attention, ignorance of proper remedies, and want of cleanliness.

*Example No.* 1.— "Afflicted with asthma and other diseases. Found lying on the floor, covered with bed-sores, and so thin that she had to be lifted on a sheet. Her husband is a porter; they have two children, and are unable to pay for nursing. She was attended by the dispensary doctor, but in other respects was left to the mercy of the world, in a low neighbourhood, in dirt and bad air, wretched in body and mind; causing her husband to feel wretched also on coming home and finding his house in such a condition. To use the man's own expression, he 'thought he was forsaken both by God and man.' Our nurse comes in, washes her, and lends bedstead and bedding, and shows how to use an air-cushion, changes her linen, &c., cleans the house, persuades the husband to whitewash the apartments; suitable nourishment is sent, and she and her household are now in comparative comfort. She is able to get up. The man is now helpful and hopeful, and has added, by his own exertions and savings, to the comfort of his home."

When women and girls suffered from long-term serious physical or mental conditions that could not be treated within the home, they sometimes resorted to care within one of the growing number of asylums or homes for the disabled. These institutions, like most in the Victorian period, varied widely depending on the class of patients. The very poor turned to poor law and charitable establishments in times of crises, when they could not find sufficient support from friends and relatives. Whereas in the 18th century most asylums treating mental illnesses were private, there was a movement beginning in the early 19th century to provide public asylums for the poor. Parliament passed legislation in 1808 and 1845 creating funds through the poor rates for the pauper insane, and in the second half of the century, there were many more asylums created for women suffering from mental illness and depression. Reformers also sought to regulate and make the care of patients more humane—a reaction to the publicized atrocities at Bethlem Hospital ("Bedlam") where reformers found naked patients chained to walls and confined in cages. By the 1820s, the *Times* celebrated how women suffering from mental illness were more likely to be given needlework than placed in a straightjacket, and by 1860, the *Illustrated London News* remarked that the former prison cells of Bethlem had evolved into cheerful domestic spaces.

Victorians only gradually and unevenly distinguished individuals experiencing mental and physical disabilities from birth from the "mad" or "insane." Earlswood Asylum in Surrey, England's first home for mentally impaired children and adults, was founded in 1847 and opened the following year. It treated mostly charity patients from the "respectable" poor, but also a number of middle-class paying patients, with the goal of teaching them basic skills—particularly housework for females—so that they might gain a greater degree of independence and integration with society. The Victorian focus on philanthropy also contributed to an upsurge in specialized hospitals, asylums, and schools for women and girls suffering from a wide array of physical disabilities. By 1865, London alone had scores of charities for women and girls who were "crippled," blind, deaf, or mute.

An *Illustrated London News* engraving from 1860 portrays a patient rushing to the dining room in the women's wing of Bethlem Royal Hospital for mental illness (also known as the Royal Hospital of Bethlehem or Bedlam), while a woman at the table sews in what the journal described as a "cheery, domestic room." The majority of female patients were former governesses or servants. (Mary Evans/The Image Works)

Yet the medical treatments for physical and mental infirmities remained limited, at times extremely painful, and in many cases counterproductive. Working-class women combined advice from medical practitioners with folk medicines and home remedies—spiritual healings, herbal mixtures, and other concoctions including rarefied ingredients such as crushed snails. By the end of the century, such methods had declined in popularity, but remained in use. Medical professionals also integrated herbal and homeopathic remedies in their practices, along with alcohol and opiates to relieve pain. Many women became dependent on opiates to manage chronic illness and suffering. Mrs. Beeton's *Book of Household Management* instructed middle-class wives to keep a long list of medicines on hand, including liniments (a mixture of limewater and linseed oil), fever mixture (powdered niter, carbonate of potash, antimonial wine, sweet spirits of niter, and water), iron tablets, and myrrh and aloe pills. Professional care and home advice most often involved regulation of the diet and rest. Purges from rhubarb, castor oil, and other substances remained widespread treatments, as did bleeding during the first half of the century with leeches, cupping, or the lancing of a vein.

Elite families also took ailing family members to the seaside or other warm environments to promote recovery. Bath, in Somerset, the scene of Jane Austen's later novels, became a fashionable spa town in the 18th century and remained a popular site in the 19th where the leisured classes enjoyed the healing properties of its hot springs and lively social life. Doctors also advised elite Victorian women suffering from consumption and other chronic illnesses to travel abroad to warm climates in places such as Spain, Portugal, Egypt, Morocco, and Algeria—though they warned patients to avoid the more fashionable destinations where picnics, sketching parties, and evening soirées might overwhelm recovery.

Over the course of the century, major developments in surgery made invasive procedures more common—not always for the benefit of female patients. After the novelist Fanny Burney (1752–1840) was discovered to have breast cancer in 1811, she left a vivid account of her mastectomy performed without anesthesia by Napoleon's military surgeon. Burney wrote to her sister that the pain was "most torturing." She recalled, "when the dreadful steel was plunged into the breast—cutting through veins—arteries—flesh—nerves—I needed no injunctions not to restrain my cries. I began a scream that lasted unintermittingly during the whole time of the incision—& I almost marvel that it rings not in my Ears still! So excruciating was the agony."[7] Burney luckily survived and lived another three decades following her operation. By the early Victorian period, however, doctors tended no longer to recommend surgery for breast cancer patients, because of the painful procedure and high death rates from infection. This changed with the discovery of anesthesia in the mid-1840s, Joseph Lister's development of antiseptic surgical methods in the 1860s, and the gradual acceptance of these methods in the following decades. Doctors such as James Paget, famous for detecting the external signs of a particular form of breast cancer, began to favor once again breast surgery—a procedure that remained unavailable, however, for most working-class women.

Often the distinctions between women's physical and mental illnesses became blurred, and it was equally unclear whether conditions arose from causes intrinsic to individuals or in response to the larger constraints imposed on women and girls by Victorian society. Hysteria was a classic example of an illness, primarily affecting women though also men in rare cases, largely instigated by social factors for which the treatments caused more harm than good. In *The English Malady* (1733), the Scottish physician George Cheyne argued that nervous disorders such as hysteria developed primarily among the leisured and wealthy classes of modern society. By the 19th century, the classic "English malady" evolved into the "female malady," since by then the vast majority of sufferers from hysteria were upper-class women—typically young and unmarried. Characteristic symptoms included shortness of breath, fainting spells, convulsions, heart palpitations, insomnia, depression, muteness, loss of appetite, as well as fits of crying, laughter, and screams. Denied body and mind, female sufferers experienced suffocation and speechlessness. A broad range of nonmedical factors contributed to a woman's diagnosis: a dissatisfaction with marriage, a failure to follow strict rules of decorum, even a notable fondness for reading.

The treatments for hysteria varied, but most often doctors prescribed bed rest and advised women to refrain from all mental and physical exertion. Many male doctors engaged in a battle of wills with their female patients, whom they charged with falsely mimicking the signs of illness. These doctors sternly refused to recognize women's complaints as real. Other physicians interpreted hysteria as proof of woman's supposedly inferior physical and mental composition rooted in her reproductive organs. English doctors reported on experiments with hysterics at the Salpêtrière Hospital in Paris by the French neurologist Jean-Martin Charcot. He claimed to relieve convulsions, fainting episodes, and other symptoms in patients such as Blanche Wittman (1863–1913), the "queen of hysterics," by placing external pressure on the area surrounding the uterus. Other English doctors sought to cure their patients with mesmerism, faradism (an early form of electric shock therapy), and drugs.

The English gynecologist Isaac Baker Brown took the most extreme approach in recommending the surgical removal of the clitoris as a cure for female hysterics. Brown theorized that hysteria resulted from an excess sexuality (often evidenced by masturbation) that drained women's vital energies. He claimed that removal of the clitoris would return his patients' health, enabling them once again to take up their expected domestic roles as wives and mothers. During the late 1850s and 1860s, Brown performed clitoridectomies on elite women at his London hospital, The London Home for Surgical Diseases of Women, and published his findings in his controversial study *On the Curability of Certain Forms of Insanity, Epilepsy, Catalepsy, and Hysteria in Females* (1866). Although previously a highly regarded physician, Brown was expelled in 1867 by the Obstetrical Society. His demise likely stemmed from his breech of professionalism in seeking self-promotion and public advertising as well as from his explicit focus on female sexuality, rather than from any sense of harm his services caused to female patients. Other English medical practitioners continued to experiment with surgery for women suffering from mental illness. In the last decades of the century, the surgeon Lawson Tait of Birmingham conducted several hundred ovariotomies on women who came to him seeking relief from tumors and cysts as well as from nervous conditions.

**Baker Brown, F.R.C.S., *On the Curability of Certain Forms of Insanity, Epilepsy, Catalepsy, and Hysteria in Females* (London: Robert Hardwicke, 1866), 84**

**CASE XLVIII. INCIPIENT MANIA—ONE YEAR'S DURATION—OPERATION—CURE—SUBSEQUENT PREGNANCY.**

In 1863, Mrs. S.M., married, mother of three children, aet. 30, came under my care, because she had been suffering for more than a year from menorrhagia, which had gradually affected her mind, causing her to have a great distaste for her husband; so much so, that he and his friends were induced seriously to contemplate a separation. On the first examination, her face indicated mental disturbance, eyes restless, pupils dilated, and manner generally excitable. She told me that she could not sleep at night, complained of constant weary uneasiness in her womb, pain in her back, great pain on defecation, constant desire to micturate. She said she was glad to be away from home, as she made every one around her unhappy. Believed that she would be a permanently insane patient, and never expected to return to her family again. . . .

I pursued the usual surgical treatment [clitoridectomy], which was followed by uninterrupted success; and after two months' treatment, she returned to her husband, resumed cohabitation, and stated that all her distaste had disappeared; soon became pregnant, resumed her place at the head of her table, and became a happy and healthy wife and mother. She was in due time safely delivered, and has ever since remained in perfect health.

*Remarks.*—From observations of this case, one feels compelled to say, may not it be typical of many others where there is a judicial separation of husband and wife, with all the attendant domestic miseries, and where, if medical and surgical treatment were brought to bear, all such unhappy measures would be obviated?

Some doctors estimated that as many as a quarter of all women suffered from hysteria, but even beyond these exaggerated calculations it is clear that the cultural construction of the illness influenced the expectations and limits placed on all women. During second half of the century, as middle-class women pressed for access to higher education, medical professionals warned that serious mental exertion would ruin women's health—particularly their reproductive capabilities—and spoil them for domestic life. In 1863, the supporter of women's higher education and suffragist Emily Davies (1830–1921) publicly rejected claims that serious mental work would make a woman "mad," "wholly unfit" for domestic life, "cold, calculating, masculine, fast, strongminded, and in a word, generally unpleasing." Responding to fears that educated women would end up in asylums suffering from hysteria and other nervous ailments, Davies pointed out that "a physician at the head of a large lunatic asylum near London, having under his charge a considerable number of female patients of the middle-class," stressed "that the majority of these cases were the result of mental idleness."[8] Ten years later in *Sex in Education: Or, a Fair Chance for the Girls* (1873), the Harvard physician Dr. Edward Clarke asserted that the education at Vassar College and other American colleges for women permanently damaged female reproductive organs, caused a variety of nervous disorders, and created immoral "unsexed" women—a position taken up by the leading English medical psychologist Dr. Henry Maudsley in his 1874 article for the *Fortnightly Review*.

Women responded on both sides of the Atlantic. With her characteristic dry wit and forcefulness, the physician Elizabeth Garrett Anderson (1836–1917) replied to Maudsely in the *Fortnightly Review* that women suffered far more from restrictive clothing and a lack of fresh air. In fact, she argued, physical exercise and mental engagement contributed to good health. Speaking in plain language for a literary journal, Anderson stressed that women's reproductive organs and menstrual cycles did not affect their aptitude for higher education and careers any more than they disrupted a domestic servant's ability to complete her daily work.

**Elizabeth Garrett Anderson, "Sex in Mind and Education: A Reply," *Fortnightly Review* 21 (May 1874): 585, 590**

Is it true, or is it a great exaggeration, to say that the physiological difference between men and women seriously interferes with the chances of success a woman would otherwise possess? We believe it to be very far indeed from the truth. When we are told that in the labour of life women cannot disregard their special physiological functions without danger to health, it is difficult to understand what is meant, considering that in adult life healthy women do as a rule disregard them almost completely. It is, we are convinced, a great exaggeration to imply that women of average health are periodically incapacitated from serious work by the facts of their organization. Among poor women, where all the available strength is spent upon manual labour, the daily work goes on without intermission, and, as a rule, without ill effects. For example, do domestic servants, either as young girls or in mature life, show by experience that a marked change in the amount of work expected from them must be made at these times unless their health is to be injured? It is well known that they do not. . . .

The cases that Dr. Clarke brings forward in support of his opinion against continuous mental work during the period of development could be outnumbered many times over even in our own limited experience, by those in which the break-down of nervous and physical health seems at any rate to be distinctly traceable to want of adequate mental interest and occupation in the years immediately succeeding school life. Thousands of young women, strong and blooming at eighteen, become gradually languid and feeble under the depressing influence of dulness [sic], not only in the special functions of womanhood, but in the entire cycle of the processes of nutrition and innervation, till in a few years they are morbid and self-absorbed, or even hysterical.

## SEXUALITY AND INTIMATE DESIRE

Victorian attitudes of class and domesticity similarly structured understandings of female sexuality and desire. The Victorian ideal of womanhood envisioned the bourgeois, Anglo-Saxon woman as chaste, pure, innocent, and uncorrupted by worldly and material desires. However, women from all backgrounds clearly explored their sexuality in thoughts and actions far less restrictive than what popular etiquette and training guides prescribed. Communal responses to women's sexuality at times proved flexible and contradictory. Yet Victorian women, much more so than heterosexual men, always remained in danger of public censure and social ostracism for sexual acts or desires that challenged their status within the home and family.

Victorian ideals of sexuality accepted heterosexual desire as natural for men (at least until the rise of the social purity movement in the 1880s and 1890s), but this was not the case for women. Moralists, preachers, educators, and reformers hailed women as symbols of moral and physical purity. Stereotypical women fell into two extremes: they either lacked all sexual desire or were fully "fallen" and corrupted by their sexuality. For example, the highly regarded mid-Victorian doctor and author of *Prostitution* (1857), William Acton, claimed in his study of the reproductive functions that "the majority of women (happily for them) are not very much troubled with sexual feeling of any kind. . . . There are many females who never feel any sexual excitement whatever." "The best wives, mothers, and managers of households," according to Acton, "know little or nothing of sexual indulgences. Love of home, children, and domestic duties, are the only passions they feel." He believed "a modest woman seldom desires any sexual gratification for herself," but would submit to her husband's attentions only to please him and to fulfill her maternal role.[9] Views such as Acton's construed active sexual desire in women as pathological. Female sexuality, according to this understanding, could lead to hysteria and other illnesses as Baker Brown suggested. Acton went so far as to theorize that nymphomaniacs filled the lunatic asylums.

Such beliefs contributed to a widespread disregard for female education on issues of sexuality and reproduction. Aristocratic and upper-class women were more likely to receive some basic instruction, however limited, from female relatives, but working-class women in particular often noted their complete ignorance on sexual matters. Women recalled being shocked and frightened when they began menstruation. They were simply handed towels to use and wash clean or given nothing at all, left to hope that their layers of petticoats would protect external clothing. Many women remained ignorant about the details of pregnancy and birth until after their first child, often later regretting that their mothers had not provided them with the necessary knowledge. Some did not realize they were pregnant until the final months, and even then did not understand how the baby would exit their bodies.

**"Eight to Keep on Eleven Shillings and Threepence," in *Maternity: Letters from Working Women*, ed. by Margaret Llewelyn Davies (New York: W.W. Norton & Co., 1978; 1915), 187–188**

I should tell you I was twenty-eight years old when I was married, and I had been married eleven months when my first baby was born, and I can truthfully say I was ignorant of anything concerning married life or motherhood when I was married. In fact, when the midwife came to me when I was in such pain, I had not the slightest idea where or how the child would come into the world. And another thing, I was not even told what to expect when I was leaving girlhood—I mean the monthly courses. I often wonder I got along as well as I have. I will say here that I do not intend my daughters to be so innocent of natural courses. I feel it is unkind of parents to leave girls to find these things out. It causes unnecessary suffering.

During the last decades of the century, women such as Elizabeth Blackwell (1821–1910), the first female doctor admitted to the medical register, and Edith Lees Ellis (1861–1916), wife of the sexologist Havelock Ellis, argued for basic sex education for girls and boys. As part of her campaign for women's rights, including the right to consent to sexual relations, the feminist Elizabeth Wolstenholme Elmy (1833–1918) also coauthored with her husband Ben Elmy several works on sex education: *The Human Flower* (1894) for adolescents, *Baby Buds* (1895) for young children, and *Life to Woman* (1896) for adults. Writing popular works on sex education had political meaning for these authors, even if the information they provided at times proved inaccurate—as was much of the existing medical and scientific thought regarding reproduction. Proponents of sex education stressed that sexual ignorance should not be misconstrued for innocence, as many Victorian parents had assumed.

The general lack of sex education and prevalence of assumptions like Acton's that modest women had no interest in sex did not mean that middle-class women led lives of sexual repression. An elite woman's reputation would be ruined if she had sex before marriage or extramarital affairs, but courtship practices among couples remained flexible enough to allow for intimate moments. The remarkably frank sexual correspondence between the Reverend Charles Kingsley and Frances (Fanny) Grenfell (1814–1891) during their courtship provides rich evidence of women's physical intimacy with men. After a short visit in 1843 at the home of Fanny's sister in Dorset, Charles recalled their walks together: "my hands are perfumed," he wrote to her, with your "delicious limbs, and I cannot wash off the scent, and every moment the thought comes across me of those mysterious recesses of beauty where my hands have been wandering, and my heart sinks with a sweet faintness and my blood tingles through every limb."[10] A humorous *Punch* cartoon from 1871 suggests that respectable families generally acknowledged physical contact—within bounds—as a part of courtship. The caption queried: "Cousin Guy and Mary are looking very innocent, and sitting very far apart, when Emily comes into the room. But how comes Guy to have an ear-ring hanging to his whisker?" Certainly, many Victorians condemned physical intimacy before marriage, but in these and other examples, Victorians recognized sexual desire as a natural part of life that could reinforce, rather than degrade, emotional and spiritual bonds.

Many working-class communities also accepted a degree of sexual intimacy before marriage, although responses varied by the individual family's outlook and religious background. Along with the overall growth in the birth rate, illegitimacy rates increased from the 18th century through the first half of the 19th century. During the 18th century, working-class communities maintained more permissive attitudes toward premarital sex if the couple had vowed to

"Cousin Guy and Mary are looking very innocent, and sitting very far apart, when Emily comes into the room. But how comes Guy to have an ear-ring hanging to his whisker?" *Punch* (1871) poking fun at the courtship practices of a young middle-class couple. (Vassar College Library)

marry. When women became pregnant before marriage, communal and religious structures generally succeeded in pressuring couples to marry. By around 1800, at least half of all firstborn children had been conceived out of wedlock primarily by couples that subsequently married. During the first half of the 19th century, however, fewer of such couples eventually married—likely as a result of disrupted family and communal networks caused by industrialization and migration. Still, even as late as the 1870s, Flora Thompson claimed that it remained common and "little thought of" in rural Oxfordshire for working-class couples to marry after the birth of their first child.[11] But such practices became far more rare and controversial in rural as well as in urban areas by the 1880s.

While working-class communities could be accepting at times of unmarried mothers, adulterers—male as well as female—provoked widespread scandal by the last quarter of the century. Thompson recalled that villagers shunned a hamlet woman caught sleeping with her male lodger. Before running the woman and her husband out of the village, they shamed them with the ritual of "rough music." Men and women from the community arrived at night banging pots, blowing whistles, yelling, jeering, and carrying effigies of the adulterous pair outside the couple's house.[12] Women accused of adultery had always been in danger of social ostracism, but by the late Victorian period, male adulterers, too, increasingly risked public and professional censure as the Regency characteristics of manliness—love of drink, sport, gambling, swearing, and women—gradually became replaced by the self-restraint, control, domesticity, and Christian piety characteristic of Victorian masculinity.

Women also expressed physical closeness in their relationships with other women. Victorians did not consider such feelings and expressions of intimacy as unusual or necessarily threatening to heterosexual marriage. Physical intimacy was a recognized, even celebrated aspect of sisterly love and female friendship. For example, in her renowned poem frequently anthologized for Victorian schoolgirls, "The Goblin Market" (1862), Christina Rossetti (1830–1894) praised the sisterly devotion of Lizzie who risks her own life to retrieve the forbidden fruit for her dying sister. On Lizzie's return from the goblins, she calls on her sister to taste the fruit juices dripping from her face: "She clung about her sister,/ Kissed and kissed and kissed her." "She kissed and kissed her with a hungry mouth."[13] Scholars have interpreted the poem as a critique of heterosexual marriage, consumer culture, and women's exclusion from the world of professional art, among other things, but what is remarkable here is that the sensual intimacy among women—sisters in this case—was not striking for Victorians. Women's lifelong friendships with other women could be characterized by emotionally stirring correspondences containing passionate expressions of love and devotion. They exchanged jewelry and locks of hair, wrote poems for one another, kissed, and slept together in the same bed during visits, all with the understanding that intense physical and emotional attachments need not be limited to husbands.

In some cases, the connections between women did become explicitly erotic and sexual. Women sometimes framed their lifelong partnerships with other women by vows of celibacy, but their relationships could also involve sexual pleasures along with the many other social and economic ties of marriage. Most of the more overt Victorian references to women's same-sex erotic relationships appeared in professional discourses. Doctors and moralists warned

Cover illustration by D. G. Rossetti of Christina Rossetti's *Goblin Market*, 1862. (Rossetti, Christina. *Goblin Market*, 1862)

that girls might learn dangerous sexual practices from boarding schools and governesses. However, the Yorkshire gentlewoman Anne Lister (1791–1840) left a remarkably detailed diary account of her sexual encounters with women—complete with a coded record of orgasms that she and her lovers experienced. Lister proclaimed in her writings, "I love and only love the fairer sex and thus, beloved by them in turn my heart revolts from any other love but theirs."[14] She lived and traveled openly with female companions and eventually formed a union in the 1830s with the Yorkshire heiress Anne Walker.

Lister's elite social standing allowed her certain freedoms, but by the end of the century, the overall context had changed. Male homosexuality among consenting adults was made illegal under the Labouchère Amendment to the Criminal Law Amendment Act of 1885—the law that resulted in the 1895 trials against Oscar Wilde ending with his imprisonment and death soon thereafter. Women

"Willful Waste Makes Woeful Want." *Punch*'s 1901 critical fascination with female intimacy and the New Woman. (Vassar College Library)

did not receive the same persecution under the law, but the rise of eugenics and public reactions to sexologists' writings on lesbianism or "female inversion" in the 1890s presented women's same-sex desire as increasingly pathological and threatening to heterosexual marriage. For example, a turn-of-the-century full-page *Punch* image showed two women about to kiss. The woman on the left preparing to leave the domestic setting represented the typical New Woman professional in a shirtwaist and skirt, carrying a black bag of the sort a district nurse might use. A man in the image's background looks on leeringly at the women with the caption: "Wilful [sic] Waste Makes Woeful Want." "'It is very delightful to see young ladies so fond of each other,' thinks young Jones; 'but I do dislike having to watch such pitiful waste!'" Female same-sex desire could still be represented in a popular middle-class journal, but coupled with the challenge of the New Woman's professional ambitions, women's intimate affection for each other became viewed as a "waste" detracting from, rather than supporting, heterosexual marriage and reproduction.

## NOTES

1. C. Willett Cunnington, *English Women's Clothing in the Nineteenth Century* (London: Faber and Faber, 1948), 14, 440.
2. "The Whitechapel Murder," *Times*, September 4, 1888: 8 and "More Murders at the East-End," *Times*, October 1, 1888: 6.
3. Gwen Ravarat, *Period Piece* (Ann Arbor: University of Michigan Press, 1991; 1952), 34.
4. Flora Thompson, *Lark Rise to Candleford* (London: Penguin Books, 1973; 1939), 137.
5. John Ruskin, as quoted in Anthony Wohl, *Endangered Lives: Public Health in Victorian Britain* (Cambridge, MA: Harvard University Press, 1983), 101.
6. Isabella Beeton, *Mrs. Beeton's Book of Household Management* (London: Cassell & Co., 2000; S. O. Beeton, 1861), 1017.
7. Letter from Frances Burney to Esther Burney, "A Mastectomy," September 30, 1811, in Joyce Hemlow, ed., *The Journals and Letters of Fanny Burney*, Vol. 6 (Oxford: Clarendon Press, 1975), 612.
8. Emily Davies, "The Influence of University Degrees on the Education of Women," *The Victoria Magazine* (1863), reprinted in *Thoughts on Some Questions Relating to Women, 1860–1908* (Cambridge, U.K.: Bowes and Bowes, 1910; New York: Kraus Reprint Co., 1971), 48, 55, 58–59.
9. William Acton, *The Functions and Disorders of the Reproductive Organs in Childhood, Youth, Adult Age, and Advanced Life, Considered in Their Physiological, Social, and Moral Relations*, 3rd ed. (London: John Churchill, 1862), 101–102.

10. Charles Kingsley to Frances Grenfell, October 1843, as quoted in M. Jeanne Peterson, *Family, Love, and Work in the Lives of Victorian Gentlewomen* (Bloomington: Indiana University Press, 1989), 76.

11. Thompson, *Lark Rise to Candleford*, 138.

12. Thompson, *Lark Rise to Candleford*, 140.

13. Christina Georgina Rossetti, *The Goblin Market and Other Poems*, 2nd ed. (London: Macmillan, 1865), 26.

14. Anne Lister, *I Know My Own Heart: The Diaries of Anne Lister, 1791–1840*, ed. by Helena Whitbread (London: Virago, 1988), 145, as quoted in Anna Clark, "Anne Lister's Construction of Lesbian Identity," *Journal of the History of Sexuality* 7 (1996): 23.

# 5

# CHILDREARING, YOUTH, AND EDUCATION

In his *Divine Songs* written for children in the early 18th century, Isaac Watts urged children to offer "Praise to God for learning to read." The child student of the Bible gave thanks "That I am brought to know/The Danger I was in,/By Nature and by Practice too/A wretched Slave to Sin." By the late 19th century, however, Victorians offered a very different understanding of childhood. An 1886 essay coauthored by Benjamin Waugh, founder of the National Society for the Prevention of Cruelty to Children, claimed, "A child is not only made in the image of God, but of all His creatures it is the most like to Himself in its early purity, beauty, brightness, and innocence." Waugh characterized the Victorian child—by then more often represented by girls than boys—as full of "joy and bliss," but also "helpless and defenceless." This understanding positioned children not as slaves to sin, but as innocents in need of protection from "fiendish" adults and the "brutal," "licentious cities" of modern society.[1] The Victorian ideal of childhood, like the ideal of womanhood, celebrated purity and innocence while associating these values with the private domestic sphere. Yet, from infancy and youth to education and work, the lives of Victorian children revealed sharp distinctions of class, gender, and region. So, too, did the experiences of their mothers, who approached the work of mothering in very different ways.

## PREGNANCY AND CHILDBIRTH

Victorian women typically first became pregnant in their late 20s during the year or two after marriage, but their pregnancies and childbirths varied dramatically depending on class. Middle-class families hired a nursemaid—or, in upper-middle-class and aristocratic families, an upper nurse aided by several under nursemaids—to oversee the washing, dressing, feeding, and general care of young children. Well-off families also engaged a monthly nurse to assist with delivery and attend to the needs of mother and baby, day and night, for the month immediately after birth, although in some cases families hired monthly nurses well before the birth to help with preparations. The monthly nurse could be called on for general cleaning, diapering, and caring for the newborn.

Working-class women of some means hired a midwife, nurse, or neighborhood woman to care for the baby and, for an extra fee, do household washing and other chores for two or three weeks after the baby's birth. Many working-class women, however, could not afford paid help during their pregnancies, births, and recovery period, relying instead on help from older children and visits from family and neighbors. Women who worked for wages tended to continue working until just before the birth, sometimes taking on extra jobs to save for the added expense of a new child. Many working-class women remembered going without adequate food while pregnant in order to provide for husbands and children, and scrimping on necessities to save for doctors' fees.

With little rest, insufficient nourishment, and frequent pregnancies, it was not uncommon for women to suffer miscarriages or stillbirths. A 1915 Women's Cooperative Guild study found that 42 percent of the mothers responding had at one point in their lives endured miscarriages or stillbirths—traumas that many women recalled as more painful and physically debilitating than normal childbirth. Elite women experienced similarly high rates of miscarriage and stillbirth in the 18th and early 19th centuries, but by the mid- and late 19th century they had significantly fewer unsuccessful pregnancies. The change likely stemmed from the more marked decline in fertility rates among elite women and their improved prenatal care and resources. For upper- and middle-class women with a history of miscarrying, male doctors or male midwives, known by the 19th century as "accoucheurs," recommended regimens similar to the treatments for infertility: vegetarian or bland diets, limited alcohol, bathing, and bed rest.

Except for the very poor who resorted to workhouse infirmaries or charity hospitals, most women gave birth in their homes. Accoucheurs typically assisted aristocratic and middle-class women throughout the Victorian period. Among aristocratic families, it was not uncommon to have the accoucheur, a gentleman in manner and background, live with the family for months before the birth. Such men relied on a system of patronage and could be handsomely paid. At the highest level, the accoucheur Sir Charles Locock reportedly received £1,000 for the delivery of Queen Victoria's first child in 1840. By comparison, the female midwives who attended working-class women typically charged 5–10s. for their services by the 1890s. London's extensive network of maternity charities, poor law medical dispensaries, and teaching hospitals also provided trained assistants who helped with home births. By the late Victorian period, working-class women who could afford other options increasingly called on private physicians. Often, however, even in large cities there was only one doctor serving an area covering many miles, so doctors relied on midwives or trained medical personnel for assistance. Even when working-class women showed a preference for doctors over midwives, women often complained that male doctors arrived late, unprepared, or drunk.

With labor and childbirth, women began what was called their confinement or lying-in: the period during which they were in bed and removed from normal domestic routines. Many aristocratic families continued the earlier practice of renting a house in London for a child's birth, demonstrating the public and political importance of these births for elite society. On the whole, childbirth among the aristocracy gradually became a more domestic, less public event as, for example, the tradition of receiving many social visitors during the lying-in period declined during the 19th century. By the Victorian period, many upper-class husbands joined their wives in the birth room. Prince Albert remained by Queen Victoria's side, offering comfort and assistance by reading and singing to her. It would have been rare, however, for a working-class man to be present during a woman's confinement. Even in one-room tenements, midwives did their best to create a sense of privacy for women, sending older children to neighbors or into the streets on errands. In one case, professional midwives from the London Hospital built a makeshift tent using chairs and nurses' cloaks in which young children could play, while their mother gave birth only feet away. When the newborn cried out, the adults saw "3 or 4 little curious faces poke through the curtains," asking, "Whatever was that?"[2]

**"A Half-Starved Pregnancy," in *Maternity: Letters from Working Women*, ed. by Margaret Llewelyn Davies (New York: W.W. Norton & Co., 1978; 1915), 24**

The first confinement I managed to get through very well, having some money left from what I had saved before marriage. But how I managed to get through my second confinement I cannot tell anyone. I had to work at laundry work from morning to night, nurse a sick husband, and take care of my child three and a half years old. In addition I had to provide for my coming confinement, which meant that I had to do without common necessaries to provide doctor's fees, which so undermined my health that when my baby was born I nearly lost my life, the doctor said through want of nourishment. I had suffered intensely with neuralgia, and when I inquired among my neighbors if there was anything I could take to relieve the pain, I was told that whatever I took would do no good; it was quite usual for people to suffer from neuralgia, and I should not get rid of it till my baby was born.

I had to depend on my neighbours for what help they could give during labour and the lying-in period. They did their best, but from the second day I had to have my other child with me, undress him and see to all his wants, and was often left six hours without a bite of food, the fire out and no light, the time January, and snow had lain on the ground two weeks.

When I got up after ten days my life was a perfect burden to me. I lost my milk and ultimately lost my baby. My interest in life seemed lost. I was nervous and hysterical; when I walked along the streets I felt that the houses were falling on me, so I took to staying at home, which of course added to the trouble.

Beginning in the 1820s, obstetric doctors intervened more directly in childbirth—an approach influenced by the tragic 1817 death of Princess Charlotte Augusta, the only child of Queen Caroline and George, Prince of Wales (later Prince Regent and George IV), and her stillborn son after she suffered through 50 hours of painful labor. Victorian doctors explored various methods to reduce the pain and speed the process of labor. The Scottish physician James Simpson experimented with chloroform in 1847 and promoted it as a popular option for elite women during childbirth. Queen Victoria received what she termed "that blessed chloroform" with the birth of her eighth child, Prince Leopold, on April 7, 1853, later praising the effects as "soothing, quieting and delightful beyond measure."[3] Many women shared the Queen's enthusiasm, but there were also moral fears concerning the use of chloroform. Some religious critics claimed that relieving women's pain in childbirth undermined the biblical punishment of Eve for tasting the fruit in the Garden of Eden. Others feared the abuse of chloroform for dissolute doings, such as those listed in the typically detailed mid-Victorian pamphlet title: *Seduction by Chloroform . . . as Applied in the Most Artful Manner for Seducing Females! Whereby They Have No Power to Resist the Wicked Desires or Inclinations of Their Seducers; Also the Tricks Played to Stupify the Senses and Overcome Virtuous Female Servants, and Afterwards Dragging Them into Secret Places, or Private Closets; and, finally, the Art Practiced by Unfortunate Women in Stupifying the Male Sex, by the Use of Chloroform, to Rob and Plunder Them* (ca. 1850).

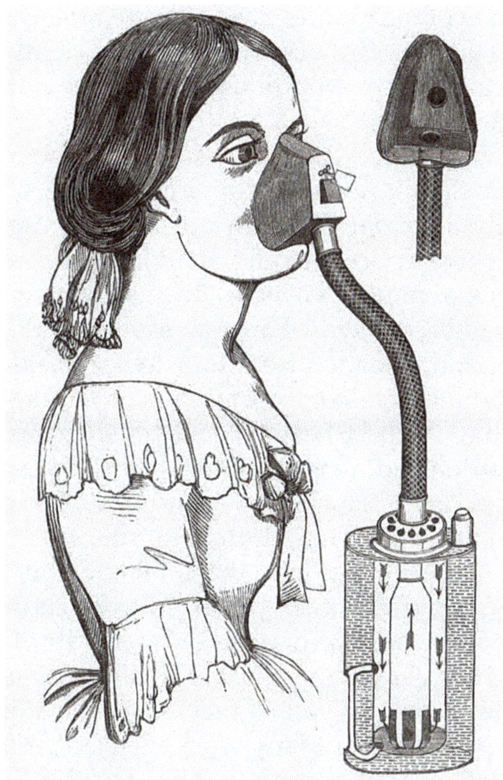

Illustration of a woman using a chloroform inhaler from John Snow's *On Chloroform and Other Anaesthetics*, published in 1858. (Snow, John. *On Chloroform and Other Anaesthetics*, 1858)

For all women, childbirth brought great risks of maternal death and injury. As chloroform became more widely administered in the 1870s, Victorian doctors used forceps more often to aid in difficult births and hasten delivery. In expert hands, forceps could save the lives of mother and child, but when used by the many physicians with little obstetrics training, forceps and other instruments left women suffering from tears and internal wounds and contributed to the spread of disease. In the days following childbirth, many women died from puerperal fever, a streptococcal infection in part transmitted by doctors who served many patients and even in some cases went directly from dissections to childbirth without proper sterilization. Female midwives rarely used instruments or chloroform, and in the latter part of the century, the maternal death rates for the working-class women they assisted were notably lower than those for women of the middle classes despite the vast discrepancy in resources. The minority of women who gave birth not in their homes but in hospitals or workhouse infirmaries suffered the highest maternal death rates.

Following childbirth, women's period of recovery depended largely on their class status and economic resources. Working-class women usually anticipated 10 days of rest—a respite that many could not take out of necessity and often later yearned for, looking back on the lack of proper recovery time as the main cause of their subsequent health problems. For new mothers of the aristocracy, the lying-in period extended from four to six weeks. Elite women followed a gradual process of resuming their normal roles, first letting the light into their darkened chambers, then moving from bed to sofa, and gradually downstairs into the public areas of the house. The more ritualized aristocratic period of confinement traditionally ended with the mother's "churching," her first trip away from home to attend church and give thanks for the birth. By the 19th century, many wealthy women preferred to be churched at home, signifying the increasing secularization of childbirth and growing importance of the domestic sphere. For elite women, the child's christening more often served as their first formal public appearance and return to society. Many working-class women, however, continued the practice of visiting the local parish priest for churching, even if they were not regular church attendees.

For the first three days after birth, mothers ate a basic diet of gruel, toast, broth, and tea. This was followed by more substantial fare including meat and a half-pint or more of stout each day for those with means. Midwives typically washed the child immediately after birth, but until the late 19th century, folk practice warned against extensive washing of the mother. Writing in 1915, a leader of the Women's Cooperative Guild praised reforms in cleanliness, recalling how during her own confinement caregivers washed only her face, neck, and hands, "and it was thought certain death to change the underclothes under a week. For a whole week we were obliged to lie on clothes stiff and stained, and the stench under the clothes was abominable, and added to this we were commanded to keep the babies under the clothes."[4] Only the frequent breaths of fresh air brought by a mother's adoration, she surmised, allowed infants to survive under such conditions.

## EARLY CHILDREARING

The successful birth of a new child brought joy as well as new worries to families with limited resources, and in almost all cases among the rich as well as the poor, caring for children was a collective undertaking. Remembering her late-Victorian childhood, Flora Thompson (1876–1947) described how the first news of a village birth came from seeing a young girl of 10 to 13 pushing toward her home a borrowed perambulator carrying "the box"—a collection of newborn clothes and cloth diapers maintained and lent out for each new village baby by the clergyman's daughter, along with gifts of tea, sugar, and commercial packets of porridge. Whether assisted by neighbors, older children, or servants, the mothers of new children rarely undertook the vast demands of feeding, clothing, and caring for babies entirely on their own. When forced to do so, many women found themselves overwhelmed.

Nursing the newborn was the first priority. Hiring a wet nurse to breast-feed had been a widespread practice among elite families in the 18th century. Wet-nursing remained a common option for wealthy Victorian mothers and single fathers unable or unwilling to nurse their own children, though one increasingly criticized by doctors and reformers as a selfish rejection of women's maternal and domestic duties. Recruited from the poorer classes, wet nurses tended to be single women who found employment through connections at workhouses, lying-in hospitals, and other charities. Subject to intimate physical examination and regulation in ways that underscored how Victorian rules of propriety did not apply across class lines, wet nurses typically lived with their employers for the infant's first year or longer. They were separated from their own children (if still living), who were much more likely to suffer early death or malnourishment. Some wealthy women preferred wet nurses because of the physical strains and social disruptions of breast-feeding as well as the widespread belief that nursing was unflattering for the figure. Other elite women seeking more children, particularly a male heir, wished to avoid the unpredictable limitation on conception associated with breast-feeding. Many more, such as Catherine Gladstone (1812–1900), young wife of the future prime minister, hired a wet nurse out of necessity after being unable to breast-feed themselves.

**"The Wet-Nurse," in Isabella Beeton, *Mrs. Beeton's Book of Household Management* (London: S. O. Beeton, 1861; Cassell and Co., 2000), 1022–1024**

When from illness, suppression of the milk, accident, or some natural process, the mother is deprived of the pleasure of rearing her infant, it becomes necessary at once to look around for a fitting substitute, so that the child may not suffer, by any needless delay, a physical loss by the deprivation of its natural food. The first consideration should be as regards age, state of health, and temper.

The age, if possible, should not be less than twenty nor exceed thirty years, with the health sound in every respect, and the body free from all eruptive disease or local blemish. The best evidence of a sound state of health will be found in the woman's clear open countenance, the ruddy tone of the skin, the full, round, and elastic state of the breasts, and especially in the erectile, firm condition of the nipple, which, in all unhealthy states of the body, is pendulous, flabby, and relaxed; in which case the milk is sure to be imperfect in its organization, and, consequently, deficient in its nutrient qualities. . . .

Besides her health, the moral state of the nurse is to be taken into account, or that mental discipline or principle of conduct which would deter the nurse from at any time gratifying her own pleasures and appetites at the cost or suffering of her infant charge. . . .

Respecting the diet of the wet-nurse, the first point of importance is to fix early and definite hours for every meal; and the mother should see that no cause is ever allowed to interfere with their punctuality. The food itself should be light, easy of digestion, and simple. Boiled or roast meat, with bread and potatoes, with occasionally a piece of sago, rice, or tapioca pudding, should constitute the dinner, the only meal that requires special comment; broths, green vegetables, and all acid or salt foods, must be avoided. . . . Half a pint of stout, with a Reading biscuit, at eleven o'clock, will be abundantly sufficient between breakfast at eight and a good dinner, with a pint of porter at one o'clock. About eight o'clock in the evening, half a pint of stout, with another biscuit, may be taken; and for supper, at ten or half-past, a pint of porter, with a slice of toast or a small amount of bread and cheese, may conclude the feeding for the day.

Nursing typically continued until the baby's first year. The monthly nurse assisted those upper- and middle-class women who were willing and able to breast-feed, even helping them to express excess milk with a breast pump or by hand if necessary. In her popular domestic advice book, Mrs. Beeton warned the new mother not to sleep with "her baby vampire" or nurse a child with teeth and old enough to ask for the "breast."[5] Working-class women did more often hold babies close through night and day, nursing frequently, contrary to the strict schedule advised by domestic guides, to keep them quiet in cramped quarters.

In the late 1860s, the first commercial baby formula, Liebig's, was marketed to all but the very poor, and in the following decades, there were many brands available made most often from cereals or dried milk. After 1870, improved sterilization methods promoted bottle-feeding as a supplement or replacement to breast-feeding. Bottle-feeding remained rare in many rural districts, but became common by the end of the century in urban areas. While bottle-feeding was generally safe for middle-class infants, it was associated with higher infant mortality rates in working-class families without access to clean water for washing bottles or fresh, unadulterated cow's milk. By the end of the century, many working-class babies drank canned condensed milk, which had little nutritional value. Bottle-fed babies were much more likely to suffer from diarrhea, the leading cause of infant deaths.

With deaths of infants under one year comprising one quarter of all deaths in the nation, child illness was a major concern for parents and caretakers. Working-class mothers could rarely afford a private doctor's fees except in emergencies and thus served as their children's primary medical caretakers, but middle-class mothers also regularly supervised children's medical care. Mothers' guides gave instructions for dealing with common problems such as teething, thrush, and more serious childhood diseases—measles, smallpox, scarlet fever, whooping cough, croup, and diarrhea. Guides also included detailed directions for emergency intervention on how to bleed a patient, set a broken bone, or revive a child from a coma. In an era before antibiotics, parents and medical professionals relied on a range of home treatments, including warm baths, blisters, and wine, port, and watered-down brandy. The 19th-century growth of empire made opium more available to the British public. Adults frequently gave children medicines with opium or laudanum, which was unregulated until the end of the century and widely sold by druggists and in patent medicines such as Godfrey's Cordial to serve as infant "quieteners," sleeping aids, and teething remedies.

Mothers from the upper classes generally took an active role in nursing children through illnesses, but their day-to-day interactions with healthy children remained limited. The heightened Victorian emphasis on women's maternal, domestic role did not always imply intimacy with children's daily care. Upper- and middle-class mothers expressed their maternal love through moral and religious instruction, rather than routine physical care or comforting. Queen Victoria claimed to have no great affection for newborns, for example, finding them frog-like in appearance for the first several months. In 1858, she advised her eldest daughter Victoria, then Princess Frederick William and expectant mother to the future Kaiser Wilhelm II, not to neglect her royal and wifely duties by becoming too enchanted with the baby. In aristocratic and upper-middle-class homes, servants usually cared for young children. In many cases, mothers simply made a daily visit to the nursery as part of their general oversight of the household. Gwen Raverat (1885–1957), one of Charles Darwin's granddaughters, recalled, "I can never remember being bathed by my mother, or even having my hair brushed by her, and I should not at all have liked it if she had done anything of the kind. We did not feel it was her place to do such things."[6]

Working-class mothers, however, typically did all these things, ensuring that young children were cleaned, dressed, and fed as well as possible. Infants and young children rarely left their mother's side, accompanying her on errands and into courtyards for conversation with neighbors. When working-class women needed to leave the home to work for wages or were occupied with household chores, they usually left young children under the care of older siblings. Even after the introduction of national education in 1870, girls and less often, though not infrequently, boys as young as 10 would be kept home from school and left solely in charge of babies and younger children. Mothers needing childcare also regularly turned to relatives or paid a neighbor, typically a widow or older woman. Charity crèches or infant nurseries were rare blessings for working mothers. When, after 1870, there was growing pressure for state-funded nurseries, local governments usually rejected these proposals as too socialistic until the heightened demand for women factory workers during World War I prompted significant, though largely temporary, state funding for nurseries.

Single mothers and the very poor thus had limited options if they could not provide for infant children. In the most extreme cases, parents pressed to part with children could bring them to charitable foundling homes. Since the 18th century, Thomas Coram's Foundling Hospital accepted London babies delivered with nothing at all, simple letters marking a name, or keepsake pieces of ribbon, cloth, or embroidery. Most of the children in Victorian orphanages were not in fact true orphans. They were most likely the children of single women, widowed or deserted by their partners, or the children of parents struggling with unemployment, illness, and the high cost of housing. When parents, usually only as a last resort, turned to a charity such as Thomas Barnardo's Homes or the parish workhouse, they were more likely to send away older children and keep younger children and infants in greater need of parental care at home. Many parents retrieved their children from workhouses or other poor law institutions after several weeks or visited them regularly during longer stays.

Although adoption was not officially legal in England until 1926, 19th-century parents arranged for informal adoptions with neighbors or through the local poor law parish. Most of these arrangements involved adoptive parents who deeply cared for their children. "Baby farmers," women paid to keep laudanum-dosed infants at starvation levels and even kill them, were by no means as common as the public scandals focused on the issue in the 1860s and early 1870s suggested. However, particularly in London and other large cities, they did exist. The sisters Margaret Walters and Sarah Ellis were convicted of killing infants under their care in 1870. Doctors, religious leaders, and philanthropic men responded by organizing the passage of the Infant Life Protection Act of 1872, which required anyone who took in more than one child under the age of one to register the names of all children under their care with local authorities and report all deaths. Women suffragists opposed the act for failing to address the underlying causes of infanticide: continued financial burden placed on mothers under the bastardy laws, amended later that year, and social prejudices against hiring unwed mothers. In the 1880s and 1890s, charities and poor law authorities created foster home programs for children (a practice referred to as "boarding out"), though even with improved state and philanthropic supervision the mortality rates for foster children could be tragically high.

## VICTORIAN GIRLHOOD

The Victorian ideal of the child, and particularly of the female child, took on great importance, becoming by the middle of the century a cornerstone in major debates ranging from national identity and imperialism to liberalism and social welfare. Childhood was by no means a wholly modern concept. As many historians writing in response to Philippe Ariès's classic work *Centuries of Childhood* (1962) have argued, medieval and early modern societies understood childhood as a life stage, and parents in these earlier periods expressed deep love for children despite high rates of child mortality. In comparison to earlier periods, Victorians increasingly described childhood as a time of innocence and protection distinct from adulthood. Children, like women, became more thoroughly associated with the domestic sphere. It is thus no surprise that so many of the most popular children from Victorian fiction, such as Jane Eyre, Little Dorrit, and Alice, were girls. The first child labor laws in the 1830s and 1840s and the gradual movement toward national education by the last decades of the century established childhood as a period of education rather than work. And yet, these transitions occurred unevenly. Ideals of childhood often contrasted sharply with the lives of real children, highlighting differences of region, ethnicity, gender, and most of all class.

The Victorian ideal of childhood innocence questioned the earlier Christian emphasis on children's innate sinfulness, a belief that nonetheless continued to have great influence throughout the 19th century. By the late 18th and early 19th centuries, English parenting guides began reiterating Jean Jacques Rousseau's landmark writings on childhood. In *Émile* (1762), Rousseau asserted there "is no original perversity in the human heart," calling on parents and educators to allow children—"little innocents"—to develop naturally and learn from the consequences of their actions without strict religious or social disciplining.[7] Critics such as Mary Wollstonecraft (1759–1797) pointed out that Rousseau was much more consistent in applying these ideals to boys than girls, but by the 19th century, Romantic poets such as William Wordsworth and Elizabeth Barrett Browning (1806–1861) equally celebrated the female child's innate goodness and purity.

Certainly, the religious emphasis on children's original sin persisted alongside ideals of childhood innocence, but these Puritan-inspired approaches to childhood became much less prominent by the end of the century. Watts's *Divine Songs* stressing children's innate sinfulness and corruption continued to be the most popular hymns sung by Victorian children. Between 1715 and 1901, publishers printed over 650 new editions. However, in *Alice in Wonderland* (1865), Lewis Carroll rewrote Watts's moralistic piece "Against

Idleness and Mischief," which his readers would have known by heart, as the parody "How Doth the Little Crocodile"—a celebration of childlike playfulness and fantasy. In *Jane Eyre* (1847), Charlotte Brontë (1816–1855) drew from her own childhood experiences to critique society's misrepresentation of Jane as a wicked girl, whose willfulness should be broken. The vicar gives Jane the *Child's Guide*, a religious pamphlet detailing the painful death of a girl "addicted to falsehood and deceit," and arranges for her admission to Lowood School, where she might learn Christian humility and subservience.[8] By revealing the many injustices Jane suffers as a child, including the stark routine, meager nourishment, and drab clothing (all examples of Christian discipline that did not, however, apply to Jane's

Frontispiece of an 1889 edition of Charlotte Brontë's *Jane Eyre*, first published in 1847. (British Library/Robana/Getty Images)

wealthy counterparts), Brontë ultimately reaffirmed and expanded upon Rousseau's views. In this innovative novel written from a young girl's first person perspective, Brontë suggested that girls as well as boys should be given the freedom—and love—to develop naturally. By the 1870s and 1880s, most reformers and writers of parenting guides emphasized children's innocence, rather than their sinfulness, and encouraged their protection, rather than harsh discipline.

While the protection of children, especially girls, became a major concern of the Victorian period, childrearing practices differed depending upon the context. In colonial settings, middle-class children were often not as thoroughly associated with the domestic or as separated from adult society as their counterparts in England. Harriet Tytler (1828–1907), for example, described her childhood in India as a time when she roamed the countryside on her own, mixed freely with adult society, and regularly interacted with Indian servants. Like most elite British children growing up in India, Tytler returned to England for her education. For girls especially, this education tended to involve a more guarded domestic training. From age 11 to 18, Tytler lived a life evoking Jane Eyre's time at Lowood under the close eye of an overbearing English aunt in Birmingham. Here, in contrast to her perhaps idealized Indian childhood, Tytler was forbidden to talk with servants, served a bland diet of cold mutton, and forced to practice piano and follow a daily exercise routine running circles within the enclosed walls of the garden. The local cemetery provided the only "safe place for children" beyond the home for unchecked play.[9]

In contrast to Tytler's strict early-Victorian English upbringing, childrearing practices in the mid- and late Victorian periods stressed domestic leisure and play as key markers of bourgeois status. Play for girls took many forms, yet often mirrored their future roles as wives and mothers. Many girls developed maternal skills by pretending with dolls, in some cases through their late teens. They also practiced sewing by making dolls' clothing. For some girls, however, dolls became actors in creative play that defied these feminine expectations. The Brontë sisters, for example, used theirs to recreate military conflicts, and Darwin's granddaughter Gwen Raverat incorporated dolls in her play only when they could "be sailors in a shipwreck, or human sacrifices."[10] Girls in elite families enjoyed dollhouses and other popular handcrafted toys, such as Noah's ark sets with wooden animals, rocking horses, alphabet blocks, jack-in-the-boxes, and jigsaw puzzles. Card games such as Happy Families (a matching game first introduced at the Great Exhibition with family members representing different occupations), National Gallery (a picture-matching game), and Muggins (a domino game), as well as word games remained popular family entertainments throughout the Victorian period. Girls and boys enjoyed acting games such as charades and produced their own plays, often with elaborate scripts, sets, and costumes, for family members. At least until the spread of national education in the 1880s, girls of the rural, working poor similarly played a rich repertoire of games on village greens—hopscotch and marbles, jump rope and blind man's bluff, as well as scores of rhyming and dancing games that heralded the girls' future lives as wives and mothers.

Sport and physical exercise gradually came to be understood as important for girls as well as for boys, though parents, teachers, and reformers warned that girls should be guarded from physical activity that might promote unfeminine attributes. In the early Victorian period, some writers encouraged physical exercise for girls and outdoors games such as battledore and shuttlecock (an early form of badminton), and play with wooden hoops. However, through the 1830s and 1840s, most writers stressed that girls should play sports only within safely enclosed domestic spaces—gardens and courtyards—and never on the streets or in public. When, in the 1850s and 1860s, girls' primary schools began introducing gymnastics and drill exercises, some critics proclaimed the physical exertion would be too draining and hardening. However, supporters such as Edwin Chadwick successfully campaigned to make drill and calisthenics a part of the curriculum for girls in most poor law and national board schools by the 1880s by promoting what they understood to be the health and disciplinary benefits, including self-restraint and feminine grace.

There was much greater resistance to girls playing team sports, which critics believed encouraged girls to become overly competitive, rowdy, unrestrained—in essence, unfeminine. Many girls growing up in the 1880s and 1890s, however, did participate in active physical sport alongside boys—swimming, boating, skating, running, climbing, hide-and-seek, lawn tennis, and croquet. Elite girls took hiking tours through Wales, the Swiss Alps, and other locales with their families. By the 1890s, girls joined the national bicycling craze and, in select schools, were able to join team sports playing hockey, golf, tennis, and cricket. While there were many more options for female physical sport by the end of the century, the girls and young women who engaged competitively in such activities risked censure or open ridicule as examples of the modern New Woman who ventured into public spaces and vied with men for physical superiority. The etiquette writer Charlotte Eliza Humphry (1843–1925), for example, warned that bicycling too often led to the formation of promiscuous acquaintanceships. Despite such cautionary advice, many respectable girls and women adopted bicycles for their visiting rounds. By the century's end, some also formed their own cycling clubs.

**"The Ladies at Lord's," in *Mr. Punch's Book of Sports* (London: The Amalgamated Press, Ltd., 1898), 20**

**THE LADIES AT LORD'S**

**OLD STYLE—EARLY SIXTIES.**

**SCENE**—*The Ground and its Accessories.*

| | |
|---|---|
| *Superior Creature.* | Really very pleasant. |
| *Weaker Sex.* | Oh! charming. So delightful having luncheon *al fresco*. The lobster salad was capital. |
| *S.C.* | Very good. And the champagne really drinkable. |
| *W.S.* | And our chat has been so interesting, Captain SMORLTORK. |
| *S.C.* | So pleased. And now, what do you think of the cricket? |
| *W.S.* | Oh! I haven't time to think of the cricket. |

**NEW STYLE—LATE NINETIES.**

**SCENE**—*The Same.*

| | |
|---|---|
| *Mere Man.* | Really rather nice. |
| *Stronger Sex.* | Quite nice. Capital game, too. Up to county form. That last over was perfect bowling. |

While middle-class girls experienced greater opportunities for sport and domestic leisure, this was generally not true for working-class girls until the very end of the century. Mid-Victorian reformers portrayed working-class children as children without childhoods, children who lacked the ever more valued protection, dependency, and vulnerability of middle-class childhood. Until the late 19th century, the lives of most working-class children remained structured by work, rather than play or education. Urban, working girls developed their own street games, such as hopscotch or makeshift swings made from rope tied to lampposts. Yet they also often described being too tired to play after hours of labor and caring for younger siblings. In his account of London street life, the journalist Henry Mayhew lamented how the eight-year-old "watercress girl" who sold her wares on the streets had "entirely lost all childish ways, and was, indeed, in thoughts and manner, a woman." She could tell Mayhew little about toys and games, and when asked about the parks, she replied, "where are they?"[11]

**"Watercress Girl," in Henry Mayhew, *London Labour and the London Poor*, Vol. 1 (New York: Dover Publications, Inc., 1968; reprint of 1861–1862 edition), 151–152**

The little watercress girl who gave me the following statement, although only eight years of age, had entirely lost all childish ways, and was, indeed, in thoughts and manner, a woman. There was something cruelly pathetic in hearing this infant, so young that her features had scarcely formed themselves, talking of the bitterest struggles of life, with the calm earnestness of one who had endured them all. I did not know how to talk with her. At first I treated her as a child, speaking on childish subjects; so that I might, by being familiar with her, remove all shyness, and get her to narrate her life freely. I asked her about her toys and her games with her companions; but the look of amazement that answered me soon put an end to any attempt at fun on my part. I then talked to her about the parks, and whether she ever went to them. "The parks!" she replied in wonder, "where are they?". . .

"I go about the streets with water-creases, crying, 'Four bunches a penny, water-creases.' I am just eight years old—that's all, and I've a big sister, and a brother and a sister younger than I am. On and off, I've been very near a twelvemonth in the streets. Before that, I had to take care of a baby for my aunt. No, it wasn't heavy—it was only two months old; but I minded it for ever such a time—till it could walk. It was a very nice little baby, not a very pretty one; but, if I touched it under the chin, it would laugh. Before I had the baby, I used to help mother, who was in the fur trade; and, if there was any slits in the fur, I'd sew them up. My mother learned me to needle-work and to knit when I was about five. I used to go to school, too; but I wasn't there long. . . ."

"All my money I earns I puts in a club and draws it out to buy clothes with. It's better than spending it in sweet-stuff, for them as has a living to earn. Besides it's like a child to care for sugar-sticks, and not like one who's got a living and vittals to earn. I aint a child, and I shan't be a woman till I'm twenty, but I'm past eight, I am."

Mayhew presented the watercress girl with pathos and sympathy, but in other cases, his accounts of girls who eschewed middle-class visions of childhood came across as much more threatening. His portrayal of urban childhood in *London Labour and the London Poor* highlighted the supposed lack of domesticity among working-class children. Mayhew described girls without recognized homes or any supervision, who lived lives of debauchery and who in some cases willfully chose prison over life in the streets. When Mayhew depicted working-class girls at leisure, it was often to stress their immorality stemming from a lack of adult supervision as well as the unclear boundaries between adult and childlike behaviors. For example, in his sketch of the "penny gaffs" or variety show theaters offering admission for one penny, Mayhew wrote that the girls "stood laughing and joking with the lads, in an unconcerned, impudent manner, that was almost appalling." Seeing "Lads jumping on girls' shoulders, and girls laughing hysterically from being tickled by the youths behind them, every one shouting and jumping, presented a mad scene of frightful enjoyment." Even worse, in London's lodging houses supposedly swarming with unsupervised children, Mayhew suggested that "whatever could take place in words or acts between boys and girls did take place."[12] The penny gaff entertainments were likely much more wholesome than Mayhew suggested, and most children who worked as street vendors lived in homes with their parents, not alone in lodging houses. Overall, Mayhew's comments highlighted changes in middle-class ideals of childhood and growing anxiety about the independence and alleged immorality of working-class girls.

The condition of working-class youth became a major focus for urban reformers, who established England's leading child welfare organizations between the late 1860s and the 1880s. Thomas Bowman Stephenson founded the National Children's Home in 1869, and Thomas Barnardo opened the East End Juvenile Mission in 1868, followed by his Boys' Stepney Home in 1870 and the Girls' Village Home in Ilford, Essex, in 1876. Edward de Montjoie Rudolf created the Church of England Waifs and Strays Society (now the Children's Society) in 1881. Reverend Benjamin Waugh specifically addressed issues of child abuse through the National Society for the Prevention of Cruelty to Children, founded in 1889, five years after the local London society. Reformers applied ideals of childhood innocence to working-class girls, claiming that all children needed adult protection and should have recognized rights. However, this approach to reform, like Mayhew's earlier account, also stressed that the relative independence of working-class girls—their lack of recognizable middle-class domestic homes, their waged labor, their public presence, and their interactions with adult society—threatened middle-class values.

By the last decades of the 19th century, child welfare reformers campaigned against the sexual abuse and exploitation of girls. These child advocates built upon the earlier child labor laws of the 1830s and 1840s as well as upon national education policies and medical reforms to authorize state intervention in family life, but focused much more directly on regulating sexuality in an effort to secure girlhood as a recognized state of dependency, protection, and innocence for all classes. In 1875, parliament raised the age of consent for girls from 12 to 13. Then, in 1885, the sensational journalist William T. Stead, editor of the *Pall Mall Gazette*, shocked the Victorian public with his account of child prostitution in London, "The Maiden Tribute of Modern Babylon." Stead's four-part exposé presented a horrifying narrative of the allegedly growing, international "white slave trade" of young girls tricked, sold, and trapped into lives of prostitution, including the details of how he purchased 13-year-old Eliza Armstrong for £5. Stead's portrayal included many exaggerations, yet "The Maiden Tribute" gained such popularity likely because the public understood juvenile prostitution to be at least partly a euphemism for the much more common issue of child sexual abuse.

"The Maiden Tribute" and subsequent rallies brought attention to women's inadequate wages and limited employment opportunities as root causes of prostitution, but the legislative response primarily focused on regulating sexuality. Stead's exposé resulted in the passage of the Criminal Law Amendment Act of 1885, which raised the age of consent for girls from 13 to 16. In addition, the Labouchère Amendment made any act of "gross indecency" among consenting adult men illegal. Despite similar public scandals involving male juvenile prostitutes and the sexual abuse of boys, age of consent legislation remained explicitly limited to girls. The 1908 Punishment of Incest Act also failed to recognize that boys too were victims of sexual abuse, by making sexual intercourse between a man and a female relative under 13, regardless of consent, a felony. Thus, while late-Victorian reformers brought much-needed attention to issues of child abuse, they often framed the issue so as to promote increased regulation of sexuality. Moreover, reformers supporting such legislation stressed the overall goal of protecting girlhood innocence. Those groups who fell beyond this ideal—both boys as well as girls whose prior actions brought to light through the trial process might raise questions about their status as innocent children—could be deemed unworthy of the state's protection.

## FEMALE EDUCATION

Education for girls as well as for boys changed radically during the Victorian period. At the beginning of Queen Victoria's reign, most boys and girls did not regularly attend school of any kind. By Victoria's death, there was a national system of education in place for elementary school children. There were more day and boarding school opportunities for girls from the rising middle classes and several major colleges for women. Access to education nonetheless continued to vary drastically depending on gender and class. As late as 1929, Virginia Woolf contrasted the wealth and resources of men's and women's universities. The men enjoyed "libraries and laboratories," "observatories," "splendid equipment of costly and delicate instruments," as well as elaborate meals contributing to the sense that there was "No need to hurry," "No need to sparkle," and "No need to be anybody but oneself." At the women's universities, however, "Not a penny could be spared for 'amenities'; for partridges and wine, beadles and turf, books and cigars, libraries and leisure. To raise bare walls out of the bare earth was the utmost they could do."[13]

### Elite Female Education

For girls from the aristocracy and upper-middle classes, education primarily took place at home, typically within a designated schoolroom. The quality of gentlewomen's education varied widely, but for the most part was a serious and structured undertaking. Mothers guided daughters in their lessons, though fathers also often provided specialized instruction. Governesses typically took charge of educating girls older than six or seven. Some women recalled their childhood governesses with great fondness, while others critiqued governesses' harsh discipline and shoddy academic training. Most aristocratic and upper-middle-class girls studied the basics of scripture, reading, writing, and arithmetic. Many also had lessons in literature, history, geography, and botany, along with training in French, German, Italian, and possibly Latin and Greek. Although many educational writers warned against training girls in classical languages, gentlewomen often had enough knowledge of Latin and Greek to instruct their own children in the fundamentals. Hired tutors—often highly esteemed experts in their fields—taught girls special classes in music, painting, drawing, dancing, and poetry. The education of most Victorian gentlewomen was deep and sustained, if somewhat idiosyncratic. Elite women's pursuit of knowledge remained central to their lives as wives and mothers.

In comparison to girls from the aristocracy and upper-middle classes, middle-class girls received instruction that was notoriously uneven and often superficial—a smattering of piano, embroidery, watercolors, and poor French meant to make them enticing wives. If not educated at home, girls from middle-class commercial families attended private day schools or, after they reached adolescence, secondary boarding schools. The number of day and boarding schools for middle-class children increased dramatically during the 19th century. However, the quality of girls' schools generally lagged far behind those for boys, so that the gap in academic training for boys and girls remained greatest among middle-class children. Girls' schools typically gained prominence for their social networks and emphasis on cultivating female respectability, rather than for their academic programs. In the 1870s and 1880s, reformers established more secondary schools for middle-class girls with curriculums similar to those in boys' public schools (schools for elite boys that were, despite the designation, privately funded). Even with these improvements, many women from the middle classes later regretted what they viewed as insufficient educations in comparison to what their brothers received. For example, the women's suffrage leader Emmeline Pankhurst (1858–1928) recalled:

> The education of the English boy, then as now, was considered a much more serious matter than the education of the English boy's sister. My parents, especially my father, discussed the question of my brothers' education as a matter of real importance. My education and that of my sister were scarcely discussed at all. Of course we went to a carefully selected girls' school, but beyond the facts that the head mistress was a gentlewoman and that all the pupils were girls of my own class, nobody seemed concerned. A girl's education at that time seemed to have for its prime object the art of "making home attractive"—presumably to migratory male relatives.[14]

Middle-class girls' education continued to encourage the ideal that women's primary role was domestic, and thus female learning had value not in and of itself but as a means to promote the accomplishments of men.

### Schools for Working-Class Girls

Working-class children experienced the most extensive changes in education over the course of the 19th century. Before the creation of national education in 1870, most working-class children did not regularly attend schools of any kind. When parents could afford to send children to school, they were more likely to send boys than girls. Those girls who received formal education before 1870 would have attended religious or charity schools or small private schools. Sunday schools, started in 1785, provided the first model for mass education by offering weekly classes in Bible study and reading, along with free meals and recreational activities, such as magic lantern slide shows and religious-based youth groups. The Sunday schools became immensely popular, claiming some 1,800,000 children in regular attendance by 1851. During the week, young girls between three and eight years old from better-off working-class families might also attend private dame schools, typically offered by a single main teacher in her home for a few pence a week. Immensely varied, dame schools ranged from early nursery schools that provided little instruction to industrial schools where girls practiced lace-making, knitting, glove-making, embroidery, and other crafts to academic schools teaching the basics of reading, writing, and arithmetic. Other voluntary religious organizations, such as the Church of England National Society and the Nonconformist British and Foreign School Society, set out with the support of government grants to make working-class elementary education available for a small fee. These schools provided a basis for national education in 1870, though the quality varied tremendously. The worst classes contained hundreds of children, poorly qualified teachers, extensive use of corporal punishment, and the rote style of learning satirized by Charles Dickens in *Hard Times* (1854).

Girls from families of the working poor who could not afford any school fees might attend charity day schools, also known as "ragged schools." The Ragged School Union was founded in 1844 to educate poor children. By 1870, there were some 350 ragged schools in Britain. The schools offered basic instruction in reading scripture and writing along with essential economic support for families through such associated programs as children's teas, soup kitchens, and clothing donations. Mary Carpenter (1807–1877), the Unitarian prison reformer, emerged as a leader of the ragged school movement and a fierce advocate for equal education for girls. She

The girls' classroom at Marlesford Lodge, the Kensington and Chelsea branch poor law school. Note that many of the girls have cropped hair to prevent the spread of lice. *The Sixth Report of the Managers of the Kensington and Chelsea School District,* 1899. (City of London, London Metropolitan Archives)

founded the first ragged school for children in Bristol in 1846 and wrote many books on education in which she argued that delinquent children were not by nature corrupt, but that they, like all children, required love and reformation, rather than punishment.

In times of extreme poverty, children attended residential philanthropic or state poor law schools. Initially, after the passage of the New Poor Law of 1834, children whose parents entered the workhouse were schooled in individual workhouse schools. By the 1850s and 1860s, however, most parishes—especially in urban areas—sent children away to separate schools in order to educate them more efficiently (i.e., in greater numbers) and remove them from what was understood to be the corrupt influence of adult paupers in the workhouse. The large separate schools—known as district schools when they combined children from more than one poor law union—could contain hundreds of children. In the 1870s, a new group of reformers, many of them women inspired by Carpenter, condemned these large, "barrack" schools for applying a military, rather than a domestic model for raising children. Gradually, many state poor law authorities and philanthropists developed residential schools for poor children that adopted cottage-style living spaces and domestic training for girls. Until the 1890s, the primary instruction in poor law schools aimed at training girls to become servants.

The 1870 Education Act, known as Forster's Act, established a national system of elementary board schools in England so that by the turn of the century the lives of children from all classes chiefly focused on education rather than wage labor. Still, the initial legislation was neither comprehensive nor mandatory. School age attendance requirements varied by locality until, in 1880, parliament made full-time school attendance compulsory until the age of 10, and then raised the minimum age to 11 in 1893 and to 12 in 1899 (excluding agricultural workers). Girls and their parents found ways to evade these requirements—indeed, truancy cases appeared frequently in the newspaper police reports. Parents more often kept girls home from school to work or care for younger siblings, and officials treated girls' truancy with more leniency. However, those working-class girls who could attend school regularly were more likely than girls from the middle class to receive a comparable education to boys. After the age of seven, students in larger schools were segregated by sex—an arrangement generally unfeasible in smaller, rural schools. Yet, even when schools separated boys and girls, their curriculums remained remarkably similar with classes in reading, writing, arithmetic, and religion, along with some history, geography, and limited offerings in science. Even with the roughly similar curriculums, girls' additional required classes in needlework and other domestic tasks took time away from their advancement in core academic areas.

### Universities and Higher Education for Women

Women of all classes seeking university or specialized higher education had extremely limited opportunities—particularly before the creation of the first women's colleges in the mid-Victorian period. Most women who continued their studies and became experts in their fields did so mainly through self-education and chance opportunities. This was true for the working-class paleontologist Mary Anning (1799–1847), who without any formal education as a child growing up along the coast of Lyme Regis, Dorset, supported her family by selling the fossils she discovered to tourists. At the age of 12, Anning unearthed an ichthyosaur, identified as the first extinct creature known to science. She later discovered the first complete plesiosaurus along with many other fossils and was key to the discovery that coprolites were fossilized feces. Anning corresponded with eminent natural scientists of the day, though some like Georges Cuvier failed to recognize her work and decried her as a fraud. In the year just before her death, Anning ultimately received recognition and financial support from the Geological Society in London, though not membership, which continued to be barred to women until 1904. Anning's profound contributions to paleontology were largely forgotten, her memory reduced to the anonymous tongue-twister that she likely inspired: "She sells sea shells on the sea shore."

Even elite women who sought training in traditionally male fields faced incalculable obstacles. Women were excluded from the universities as well as from most professional and learned societies where members presented and discussed research, such as the Royal Geographical Society (until 1913), the Society of Antiquaries of London (until 1920), the Royal Chemical Society (until 1920), the Royal Academy of the Arts (which had two women among its founders in 1768, but no other women members until 1922), and the Royal Society of London for Improving Natural Knowledge (known as the Royal Society, it was the oldest, most esteemed society, founded in 1660). The Royal Society did not admit women fellows until 1945 with one exception: Queen Victoria.

Victorians justified women's exclusion with claims that women's nature ill-suited them for original intellectual work. Even the celebrated, widely published and influential Scottish scientist and mathematician Mary Somerville (1780–1872) claimed in her *Personal Recollections*, "I was conscious that I had never made a discovery myself, I had no originality. I have perseverance and intelligence, but no genius. That spark from heaven is not granted to [my] sex." In response to this line of argument, the American Maria Mitchell (1818–1889), Somerville's great admirer and the first professor of astronomy at Vassar College, told her female students: "The laws of nature are not discovered by accident; theories do not come by chance, even to the greatest minds, they are not born in the hurry and worry of daily toil, they are diligently sought . . . and until able women have given their lives to investigation, it is idle to discuss their capacity for original work."[15]

In the second half of the 19th century, many women shared Mitchell's commitment to female education and dedicated their lives to establishing women's colleges and opportunities for higher learning. However, some of the first female colleges were not created in order to provide women with the same opportunities as men, but rather to enhance what educators understood to be women's appropriately feminine areas of expertise. Thus, Queen's College, London, opened in 1848 primarily as a training school for governesses. Other reformers, such as the abolitionist Elisabeth Reid (1789–1866) and the suffragist Emily Davies (1830–1921), promoted women's colleges out of the belief that women should study the same subjects as men. In 1849, Reid established Bedford College, London, the first such college for women significant also in that women took on official positions as directors. Even Reid's close friends dismissed Bedford as an example of how she applied "radicalism to a romantic excess."[16] Working with Barbara Bodichon (1827–1891), who had taken art classes at Bedford College, Emily Davies sought even greater educational opportunities for middle-class women and eventually founded Girton College, Cambridge, in 1869, after numerous financial setbacks. (Girton moved from the original site in Hitchin to Cambridge in 1873.) Davies firmly believed in women's equality, yet she nonetheless framed her public appeal in the *Times* for scholarships by stressing that female graduates would become teachers—a respectable profession for women—and knowingly signed her letter "yours obediently." Still, Davies argued that women university students should take the same examinations as male students—a controversial stance at the time even among supporters of women's education.

**Emily Davies, "Letter to the Editor: Girton College," *Times* (August 21, 1873): 8.**

The young women who, as destined to become teachers, most need systematic training are in a large proportion of cases hindered from obtaining it by want of money. They cannot afford to pay 100 guineas a year for three years after they have left school. . . . How are such cases to be met? Those who know anything of the cost of a University education for men, or even of the cost of good schools for girls, will not suppose it to be possible to reduce the College fees, and at the same time to retain its character of being self-supporting. If we look at the corresponding class of men, the remedy appears obvious enough. Of all the large number of men who year by year are prepared at the Universities for high positions as tutors and schoolmasters, it may safely be asserted that there is not one who in some form or other has not received substantial assistance towards the cost of his education. In many cases such assistance begins at an early stage of school life, and is continued to the end of the University course. Any boy with good abilities and fair industry may rely upon being helped forward at every step of his educational career. It would scarcely be too much to say that no girl, however able, however industrious and eager to learn, can safely rely upon any help at all. . . . One cannot help fancying that if rich men and women only knew the facts, and could be brought directly into contact with them, they would be glad to gratify aspirations honourable in themselves and the satisfaction of which would be not only an individual gain but a benefit to society. Those who have themselves enjoyed the advantage of liberal culture must surely be willing to extend it; those who have not can, perhaps, sympathize all the more keenly with the desire for it. If mental cultivation is of real worth, why should women be shut out from it? If it is worthless, or a mere luxury to be enjoyed by those who can pay for it, why are such earnest and persistent efforts put forth to give more and more of it to boys and men? These are questions which women cannot help asking, and which wait for an answer.

I am, Sir, yours obediently,
EMILY DAVIES.

Other reforms in women's education followed. In 1871, what became Newnham College, Cambridge, opened for women. Sophia Jex-Blake (1840–1912), previously denied the opportunity to pursue her medical training at the University of Edinburgh, created the London School of Medicine for Women in 1874. Similarly, Emily Davies joined her father and close friend Elizabeth Garrett Anderson (1836–1917) to demand the University of London offer degrees to women. In 1878, the University of London became the first university in the United Kingdom to admit women for all degrees, including medicine. Somerville (named for Mary Somerville) and Lady Margaret colleges for women in Oxford University were founded in 1879. That same year, Louisa Twining (1820–1912) and the heiress philanthropist Angela Burdett-Coutts (1814–1906) established a home for female art students, the first of its kind in London. Unsurprisingly, many of these early advocates for women's education emerged as leaders of the women's suffrage movement.

## NOTES

1. Isaac Watts, *Divine Songs* (London: M. Lawrence, 1715), 11–12 and Henry Edward and Benjamin Waugh, "The Child of the English Savage," *Contemporary Review* 49 (1886): 688–689.

2. E. J. Morris, "Report of a Visit to the District Maternity Charity with Miss Nicholls, District Midwife" (1922), as quoted in Ellen Ross, *Love and Toil: Motherhood in Outcast London, 1870–1918* (New York: Oxford University Press, 1993), 112.

3. Journal of Queen Victoria (April 22, 1853), *Queen Victoria in Her Letters and Journals*, ed. by Christopher Hibbert (New York: Viking Penguin, 1984), 97.

4. "I Was Awfully Poor," in *Maternity Letters from Working-Women Collected by the Women's Co-Operative Guild*, ed. by Margaret Llewelyn Davies (New York: W. W. Norton, 1978; 1915), 32.

5. Isabella Beeton, *Mrs. Beeton's Book of Household Management* (London: Cassell & Co., 2000; S. O. Beeton, 1861), 1034, 1038.

6. Gwen Raverat, *Period Piece* (Ann Arbor: University of Michigan Press, 1991; 1952), 76.

7. Jean Jacques Rousseau, *The Émile of Jean Jacques Rousseau*, trans. William Boyd (New York: Teachers College Press, 1956; 1762), 40, 33.

8. Charlotte Brontë, *Jane Eyre* (New York: W. W. Norton, 2001; 1847), 29.

9. Harriet Tytler, *An Englishwoman in India: The Memoirs of Harriet Tytler, 1828–1858*, ed. by Anthony Sattin (Oxford: Oxford University Press, 1988), 38.

10. Raverat, *Period Piece*, 248.

11. Henry Mayhew, *London Labour and the London Poor*, Vol. 1 (New York: Dover Publications, Inc., 1968; 1861–1862), 151.

12. Mayhew, *London Labour and the London Poor*, 40, 41, 413.

13. Virginia Woolf, *A Room of One's Own* (London: Harcourt, Inc., 1981; 1929), 10–11, 23.

14. Emmeline Pankhurst, *My Own Story* (London: Virago, 1979; 1914), 5–6.

15. Mary Somerville and Maria Mitchell, as quoted in Richard Holmes, "The Royal Society's Lost Women Scientists," *The Observer*, November 20, 2010.

16. Henry Crabb Robinson, as quoted in Sybil Oldfield, "Reid, Elisabeth Jesser (1789–1866)," in *Oxford Dictionary of National Biography* (Oxford: Oxford University Press, 2004).

# 6

# WAGE LABOR AND PROFESSIONAL WORK

For millions of women in the Victorian period, work was a central fact of life. The 1861 census listed women employed as prison officers and workhouse matrons, publicans and innkeepers, capitalist shareholders, pawnbrokers, toll collectors and turnpike keepers, artificial tooth makers, wheelwrights, stay-makers, hair merchant dealers, rag gatherers, chimney sweeps, stone quarriers, and fishmongers. Out of a total population of over 10 million women and girls, there were 18 private literary secretaries, 213 telegraph service workers, and 259,074 cotton manufacturers. The most exclusive occupational category included only one person, Her Majesty the Queen Victoria, while the largest single group listed 644,271 general domestic servants. Women made up just over 34 percent of the total working population, yet this calculation did not include women employed as itinerant workers or as paid pieceworkers in their homes. Women also earned incomes by informally taking in lodgers, caring for neighborhood children or mothers who had recently given birth, doing laundry and ironing, and working as charwomen paid for daily household work. Even married women of the lower-middle classes sometimes earned extra wages by, for instance, tending to sick neighbors. During the second half of the century, middle-class women increasingly entered the workforce as they campaigned for greater employment opportunities beyond the limiting option of serving as governesses.

No matter what the job, women faced a set of common obstacles in the workplace. The wages for female workers varied tremendously, as did the nature of their work, but in practically all professions, women earned less than men. In 1883, for example, the School Board of London specified that the salaries of female teachers should be three-quarters of those for male teachers of equal qualifications and experience. In 1890, male assistant teachers had an average annual salary of £117, while women earned £88 for the same work. In addition to their subordinate status in relation to men of their profession, all women workers shared the experience of being judged by the evolving, contradictory Victorian gender ideal of femininity, which held that women should not work outside the home and that women's paid labor was unnatural. In the face of these pressures, women drew upon understandings of feminine domesticity and separate spheres to justify their work in new areas—as teachers, as local politicians, and as nurses headed to the battlefront to care for soldiers.

## AGRICULTURAL WORK

Britain was the first industrial nation, but agriculture continued to be central to the British economy. In 1851, agriculture remained the largest general area of employment for all workers. Just over 8 percent of all British female laborers worked in agriculture, the fourth largest category of female workers after domestic service, textile production, and clothing manufacture. Women and girls worked as hired laborers during the hay and wheat harvests and at other tasks, such as planting and digging potatoes, weeding, hoeing turnips, and milking and cheese-making on dairy farms. They also contributed to the family food supply by gleaning or collecting fallen grain from the harvested fields—a practice still regarded as a customary right in some early Victorian rural communities, although one that was steadily restricted along with the privatization of land resulting from the rapid enclosures and loss of common lands after 1750. Even among those who professed that women's proper role was in the home, there was recognition in the 1840s that paid agricultural work remained an important source of employment for women that allowed them to improve the overall health of their families by earning incomes of approximately 3–5s. per week (compared with 8–10s. for male agricultural laborers).

Women testifying for the parliamentary report *On the Employment of Women and Children in Agriculture* (1843) gave accounts of long hours during harvests, difficult conditions, and meager diets based mainly on potatoes, but also expressed a sense of pride in their physical strength as well as an appreciation for outdoor work. Older female agricultural workers noted a decrease in the range of tasks made available to women, who were, for example, generally no longer given work leading plough horses as they had been in their youth. While women struggled to find childcare solutions for young children, they acknowledged the opportunities agricultural labor offered them to work alongside older children. At times, women also carried nursing infants with them as they worked.

By the late-Victorian period, agriculture had ceased to be a popular source of employment for women in most parts of England. The number of female agricultural workers declined significantly between 1851 and 1871. During this same period, the cultural reputation of female farmworkers fundamentally changed. No longer praised for their strength and physical health, they became a source of concern as parliamentary reports and popular lore cast them as slatternly, rough, undomestic women. Agricultural gangs of young women and children hired out for day work sparked a public reform movement, even though such forms of agricultural work proved rare. In 1867, parliament passed the Gangs Act, which banned children under eight and the mixing of males and females in gangs. Moreover, the developing agricultural trade union movement opposed cheaper female agricultural workers in the 1870s. By the 1880s, women and girls in the fields were most likely to engage intermittently in weeding, hoeing, and clearing the ground of rocks or seasonal work such as hop-picking. The tasks were in many cases the same as earlier in the century, but female wages had declined significantly, and women tended to work in sex segregated fields rather than alongside male workers as had often been the case in the early 19th century.

While there was certainly no "golden age" when employers compensated female agricultural laborers on par with men, over the course of the Victorian period, heavy farmwork was increasingly presented as an inappropriate occupation for women. From the mid-18th to the mid-19th centuries, attacks on women's customary agricultural rights—not only gleaning, but also the collection of wood and grazing rights on commons—along with limitations on women's wage earning work reinforced the ideal of the male breadwinner and female dependent. Given these conditions, rural women of all ages and especially younger women tended to find other options for work in towns as domestic servants or factory hands at rates even faster than men.

***Report of Special Assistant Poor Law Commissioners on the Employment of Women and Children in Agriculture* (London: W. Clowes and Sons, 1843), House of Commons Sessional Papers, 68**

*Mary Hunt,* Wife of—*Hunt, Studley, Wiltshire,* Agricultural Labourer, examined.

I am in my fiftieth year. I have had 12 children, and, if it please God, I shall very soon have my 13th. I was left early without father and mother, with a crippled brother, whom I had to help support. I began to work in the fields at 16. I had to work very hard, and got a good deal of lump-work. I have earned as much as 2*s*. 6*d*. a-day at digging, but I was always considered a very hard worker. I married at 22, and had to put up with a good deal with a young family; and have often had only salt and potatoes for days together. I was always better when out at work in the fields: and as for hard work I never was hurt by it. I have carried half a sack of peas to Chippenham, four miles, when I have been large in the family way. I have known what it is to work hard.

I think it a much better thing for mothers to be at home with their children; they are much better taken care of, and other things go on better. I have always left my children to themselves, and, God be praised! nothing has ever happened to them, though I have thought it dangerous. I have many a time come home, and have thought it a mercy to find nothing has happened to them. It would be much better if mothers could be at home, but they must work. Bad accidents often happen. I always hold to it to put children out early, and to bring them up to work: they do better. Families are better altogether when children go out regularly: the children are better than when kept at home getting into all sorts of mischief.

## FACTORY WORK

Over the course of the 19th century, the industrial sector became one of the chief sources of jobs, particularly in textile manufacture. When the first factories developed in England in the 1770s and 1780s, they resembled large communal workshops more than any image of modern industrial factories employing hundreds of workers. The greater efficiency of early factories came from centralizing all stages of production under one roof. The invention in 1785 of the Boulton and Watt steam engine prompted owners to move factories from waterpower sources in rural areas to urban centers, where they could draw on a greater workforce. With innovations in spinning and weaving, textile factories producing silk, wool, linen, and

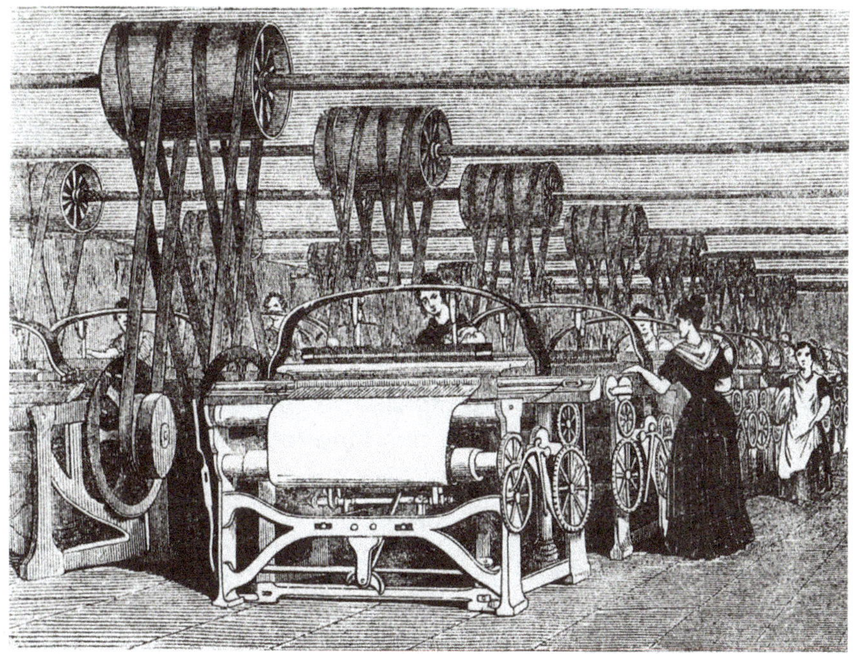

Textile mills during the 1800s employed power looms, machines that greatly increased the efficiency of weaving cloth. Many textile workers, like those depicted here in *The Illustrated London News* of 1844, were women. (Hulton Archive/Getty Images)

most of all cotton emerged as leading producers. In the 18th century, when most Britons still wore clothes made from wool or linen, the British cotton trade was insignificant. By 1831, however, cotton manufacture led the country's industrial revolution, accounting for 22 percent of Britain's national production.

From the beginning, industrial production depended heavily on child and female labor. In cotton textile factories, primarily based in Lancashire, the number of female laborers increased rapidly as employers relied more and more on cheaper female labor. In 1835, female employees made up 54 percent of the cotton industry workforce in the United Kingdom. By 1901, the proportion of female workers increased to 63 percent. In other textile industries, women were an even greater presence. Female silk and flax workers, respectively, represented 68 and 70 percent of all workers in each industry in 1835, and 70 and 72 percent of workers in 1901.

Work in early factories was notoriously harsh and dangerous. The parliamentary investigations led by the Tory Michael Sadler in 1831 and 1833 produced hundreds of interviews with child and adult factory workers detailing abusive conditions. Children as young as 6 would rise before dawn to walk several miles to factories where they worked for 14 hours or longer with only an hour break at noon for the midday meal. If they were late, or if they became drowsy at their work set to the pace of machines, girls as well as boys could be fined or beaten by the factory overseers. In textile factories, workers breathed in dust-filled air that contributed to lung diseases ranging from asthma to consumption. In flax mills, where water was sprayed on the spindles as part of the process of spinning linen, the children and women who dominated this work carried on for hours wearing thoroughly soaked clothing. Without safety or environmental regulations of any kind for much of the century, workers also suffered from lead poisoning from the glazes used in pottery factories, from "phossy jaw" caused by the phosphorus used in matchmaking, and various other industrial illnesses. Youths who grew up working in factories displayed growth deformities caused by sitting in the same position, repeating the same motions hour after hour, day after day. In the 1840s, the *Manchester Guardian* and other local papers in industrial districts regularly reported on factory accidents—instances of girls killed after falling into the machinery, of women scalped when their hair got caught, and, most common of all, of fingers or limbs crushed by factory equipment.

In response to these conditions, a surprising mix of reformers, including Tory paternalists such as Michael Sadler and socialists such as Friedrich Engels, drew on the rhetoric and methods of the most popular reform movement of the time—the movement for the abolition of slavery—to condemn industrial capitalism by describing factory workers as the "white slaves of England." Parliament had outlawed the British slave trade in 1807 and slavery in British colonies in 1833. Labor reformers directly applied the strategies of abolitionists by first gathering information, then publishing moving accounts detailing the dangers of factory work with the goal of spurring parliamentary regulation. Most often, reformers singled out female and child workers as in special need of government protection so as not to challenge the belief that the government should not interfere with the right of adult men to form individual contracts as free agents—an approach that even the most liberal thinkers, such as the Member of Parliament Thomas Macaulay, eventually came to support.

The 1833 Factory Regulation Act, the first factory act with any real enforcement powers, banned all children under 9 from working in textile mills and limited the working hours of youths between the ages of 9 and 13 to 48 hours a week and those between 13 and 18 to 69 hours a week. Since children comprised a significant proportion of the workforce in the textile industries, attempts to control their hours were understood to have the effect of limiting the hours of adult workers as well. The Factory Act of 1844 set additional restrictions on young children and, for the first time, limited adult female textile workers to the same hours as youths between the age of 13 and 18. The Factory Act of 1847 (called the Ten Hour Act) further limited hours of employment to 10 hours a day for women and youths between 13 and 18 in textile factory mills—a reform that, as with the previous laws, many employers managed to evade.

Thus from its very origins, the movement to improve working conditions presented women and children as unnatural industrial wage earners who were defying their proper roles in the domestic sphere. Even Engels, who would soon join Karl Marx in calling on all workers of the world to unite in *The Communist Manifesto* (1848), revealed his own bourgeois upbringing in his representation of women factory workers from Manchester. In *The Condition of the Working Class in England* (1845), Engels not only condemned the dangerous conditions, long hours, and poor wages associated with factory work, but also asserted that by providing paid employment for women when many men remained unemployed, the factory system "turned [the family] upside down," creating a situation that "unsexes the man and takes from the woman all womanliness" by undermining the middle-class ideals of the male family breadwinner and the female Angel in the House.[1]

Female factory workers became notorious figures in Victorian reform literature, portrayed as boisterous, aggressive, even violent. Middle-class reformers linked women's work in factories with rising rates of illegitimacy and infant mortality. Rather than simply dismissing cheaper female workers, some factory owners such as the Cadbury chocolate makers of Birmingham responded to reformers' pressures and workers' protests by increasing paternalistic practices within the workplace—segregating male and female workers, building cottages for workers on factory grounds, and creating playgrounds for children—in an attempt to replicate ideal gendered domestic structures.

Despite the often unhealthy, abusive working conditions, many Victorian women continued to demonstrate a preference for factory work over other sorts of employment. Many female factory laborers appreciated the relative independence of factory work in comparison to domestic service. In some cases, women preferred even awful factory conditions to their cramped, unsanitary homes. Factories also offered women and girls a sense of community and a social network to help with childcare and domestic chores. This was especially the case in cotton districts where at mid-century, approximately a fourth to over a third of all married women were employed. In response to the needs of working mothers, Lancashire, for example, was the first area to develop fish and chip shops that sold prepared meals at a relatively inexpensive price for women without time to cook. Wages varied tremendously, so a woman worker in a London jam factory in the 1880s earned a meager 5–8s. a week, while a Preston weaver in the early 1900s made 21–27s. weekly. On the whole, however, female factory workers, particularly weavers in the cotton factories of Lancashire, had better wages than women in most other occupations. The economic pull, greater independence, and female support largely explain why, in spite of the dangers and drudgery, many women chose factory work when given the option.

## COAL MINING

Mining was not one of the top areas of employment for women, but the trade nonetheless sparked some of the most important debates about female labor. Women and children had worked with men in England's earliest coal mines dating back to the 14th century. Not all mines employed women and children, who, if they worked in underground pits, were most likely by the early Victorian period to work in Lancashire and Cheshire, the West Riding, parts of eastern Scotland, and south Wales. Although men most often did the work of hewing the coal from the rock face, women sometimes did this as well. Women and youths usually worked as "hurriers" (also called "putters" and "drawers"), who transported the hewn coal in carts along the underground paths to the bottom of the mine shaft. In larger mines, horses might pull the carts along rails, but in most cases, children and women hurriers did this work. In smaller or poorly built mines, the drawer moved through wet, narrow seams on all fours, pulling the cart attached to her by a belt around her waist and a chain between her legs. Girls and boys as young as six also worked as "trappers" in charge of opening and closing the air vents. Reporting before Lord Ashley's Mines Commission of 1842, the eight-year-old trapper Sarah Gooder testified, "I have to trap without a light and I'm scared. I go at four and sometimes half past

Illustration from a plate in the *Westminster Review* of two children being lowered down into a coalmine, ca. 1840. (Hulton Archive/ Getty Images)

three in the morning, and come out at five and half past. I never go to sleep. Sometimes I sing when I've light, but not in the dark; I dare not sing then."[2]

Following the precedent of the 1833 Factory Act, reformers sought to improve working conditions for miners by highlighting the particular dangers to women and children and the ways in which their work challenged middle-class gender and domestic ideals. To that end, the 1842 parliamentary investigation underscored issues of morality and gender roles as much as the actual working conditions. Images of women and girls pulling carts like beasts of burden roused the Victorian public. Furthermore, the investigators emphasized the intermingling of male and female workers in the pits as well as the practice in some mines of men working partially or even fully naked because of the heat. Women and girls wearing trousers and working without a shirt also shocked the public. Most female witnesses testified that male coworkers treated them well, but some gave accounts of being sexually assaulted, raped, or beaten. Reformers also argued that mining interfered with children's religious instruction—a point highlighted in the final report by witnesses' repeated statements of ignorance about fundamental aspects of Christianity. Most of all, Lord Ashley and other supporters of the bill argued that employment in the mines caused women to ignore their domestic duties and thus posed a threat not only to mining families, but also to the well-being of the entire country.

**Children's Employment Commission, *First Report of the Commissioners—Mines* (London: William Clowes and Sons, 1842), House of Commons Sessional Papers, 84**

Betty Harris, aged thirty-seven, drawer, in a coal-pit at Little Bolton: "I have a belt round my waist, and a chain passing between my legs, and I go on my hands and feet. The road is very steep, and we have to hold by a rope; and, when there is no rope, by anything we can catch hold of. There are six women and about six boys and girls in the pit I work in: it is very hard work for a woman. The pit is very wet where I work, and the water comes over our clog-tops always, and I have seen it up to my thighs: it rains in at the roof terribly; my clothes are wet through almost all day long. I never was ill in my life but when I was lying-in. My cousin looks after my children in the day-time. I am very tired when I get home at night; I fall asleep sometimes before I get washed. I am not so strong as I was, and cannot stand my work so well as I used to do. I have drawn till I have had the skin off me: the belt and chain is worse when we are in the family way. My feller [husband] has beaten me many a time for not being ready. I were not used to it at first, and he had little patience: I have known many a man beat his drawer. I have known men take liberty with the drawers, and some of the women have bastards."

The passage of the 1842 Mines and Collieries Act anticipated changing Victorian attitudes about childhood as a life stage increasingly associated with education rather than work. The law banned all female workers along with boys under 10 from working underground. By outlawing all female employees, adult women as well as girls, the 1842 Mines Act also set the precedent for protective legislation for women and reinforced women's status as secondary workers without full rights to form individual contracts. The state thus recognized and reproduced patriarchal structures in the very formation of labor legislation meant to improve working conditions. Women left the underground pits after 1842, but according to the 1851 census, approximately 11,000 women in England and Wales continued to work aboveground in mines and quarries. Women miners mostly served as "pit brow lasses" who pushed the carts (sometimes called "corves") of coal brought up from the mine shaft to the central sorting pit and as "screen lasses" who sorted the coal from waste materials either by hand using a "riddle" or hand-held sieve, or later by picking the coal from mechanized conveyor belts.

In the following decades, representatives from the Miners' Union as well as Liberal and Conservative politicians sought to ban all women from mining—again using fears of sexual immorality, accounts of the "unfeminine" nature of the work, and provocative images of female miners dressed in trousers to inspire public support. Whereas in the 1840s, however, middle-class reformers were largely unified in their support of banning female underground miners, in the 1880s, prominent feminist leaders such as Frances Power Cobbe (1822–1904) and Lydia Becker (1827–1890) defended women miners' right to work, arguing that banning them from better-paying mining jobs—work that they described as arduous yet honorable—would lead women into more dangerous employment or, worse, the workhouse. When, in 1887, a group of 22 female miners from Wigan marched through the streets of London to present their case to the home secretary, they dressed in their work trousers as an act of protest. Even the writer of an article opposing further restrictions on women workers could not help but remark on the miners' "peculiar" appearance. The report noted, "Their nether garments are not very womanly. A few wear men's coats and waistcoats as well as breeches, so that . . . we have determined their sex only by the earrings, as well as perhaps by the bunch of hair done up in a kerchief, and half drooping from under an ordinary man's cap."[3] The protesters won the Home Office's assurance not to interfere further with the work of women miners. Over the course of the 20th century, however, as government reforms and union agitation addressed some of the worst abuses in the mining industry, women were effectively excluded from the profession.

## OUTWORK OR "SWEATED" LABOR

Outwork—also sometimes called homework, domestic industry, piecework, the putting-out system, or sweated labor—refers to work typically done in workers' homes or small unregulated workshops. For women, especially those with children, outwork was among the most common and least documented form of paid labor. Some trades developed out of older cottage industries associated with local economies, such as the 18th-century clothing production in Halifax praised by Daniel Defoe, a system that involved entire families working together during agricultural down times. Over the course of the 19th century, however, outwork production came to rely more heavily on the exploitative work of women and children. As the factory reform movement increasingly sought to legislate for better working conditions, some sweated home industries expanded in an effort to evade regulation of hours, conditions, and wages. In some cases, factory or small workshop owners shifted part of the production process to outworkers or simply had workers take home additional work in order to evade paying overtime. Employers generally paid outworkers by the amount of goods produced, rather than by the hours of their labor, and the earnings were notoriously low. In the 1890s, outworkers earned as little as 7d. for pulling 60 rabbit skins (foul work for cramped quarters) or 3d. for finishing a pair of boys' trousers—sums that required long hours of labor with few breaks and still did not provide a living wage.

The many different kinds of outwork varied depending on the locality. In agricultural areas, lace-making and plaiting straw for hats and baskets were popular sources of piecework for women and girls. In the 1840s, children in central and southwestern England as young as four or five would attend lace schools, more accurately described as workshops, where they learned the trade before its decline by the 1880s. Women and girls also often worked at sewing gloves, a craft that by the 19th century followed industrial labor practices and was divided into simple, repetitive tasks distributed to different workers for greater efficiency. In Birmingham and surrounding areas in the West Midlands, female workers—frequently the wives and daughters of miners—produced nails and chains as well as other small metal goods. London was home to an extensive range of sweated industries manufacturing materials for the domestic and colonial markets. Women and children worked in homes making artificial flowers, brushes, and boxes for matches and other items. They pulled fur for coats, curled feathers for hats and decorative aigrettes (headdresses), and mixed glue to bind books. Women managed all this work in crowded spaces, often one-room apartments with poor ventilation, dim light, and small children demanding attention and care.

More than any other type of outworker, the Victorian seamstress elicited the sympathy and attention of the middle-class public. The production of inexpensive textiles prompted an expansion of the dressmaking industry, causing needlewomen (including dressmakers, milliners, stay-makers, and embroiderers) to become one of the largest categories of female workers following domestic servants and factory workers. The profession was perceived as more respectable than factory work and was thus also a source of income for middle-class women in need, and yet on the whole, dressmakers earned less and worked longer hours than female factory workers. The work was highly seasonal depending on the demands of the fashionable classes. By the 1840s and 1850s, the distressed needlewoman—half-starved, freezing in a garret, suffering from failing eyesight, and perhaps even resorting to prostitution—emerged as a recognized figure in reform literature. She represented extreme poverty amidst England's industrial luxury and the limited employment opportunities for women. Dressmakers employed in workshops at the end of the century were limited to working 59 and a half hours per week, yet in no other industry was there such a routine use of illegal overtime. Girls of 12 and 13 years old were apprenticed to private dressmaker shops, sometimes paid nothing for the first year or longer, where they could work until 11 o'clock at night. Many women and girls took home extra sewing after their documented hours in workshops or produced entirely from their homes where there was no government oversight. The first major attempt to regulate outwork came in the early 20th century, when Winston Churchill introduced the Trades Boards Act of 1909, which regulated conditions and set minimum wages for the most common forms of sweated labor, including needlework, lace-making, cardboard-box making, and chain making.

## DOMESTIC SERVANTS

Domestic servants were by far the largest category of female workers. In 1851, there were over one million women and girls working as servants in England and Wales, one out of every four working women, nearly one-tenth of the entire female population. The growth of the commercial, industrial middle classes sparked a parallel growth in domestic service positions. At the same time, service developed into an increasingly feminized profession. In the early modern period, men made up the majority of servants, and male and female servants' work included a range of tasks associated with household production, such as animal husbandry and selling goods as well as cleaning. By the 19th century, however, most service positions concentrated on domestic tasks, most servants were women, and housework (now separated more distinctly from commercial or "productive" work) came to be primarily understood as "women's work." Victorian male servants—butlers, footmen, coachmen, grooms, and valets—were better paid and thus an important signifier of their employer's elite status.

Although often an overlooked category of workers, the presence of servants influenced nearly all aspects of Victorian life. Architectural designs of middle- and upper-class homes with their separate passages and stairs for servants, childrearing practices, and migration patterns all testify to the centrality of domestic service. In her childhood memoir of rural Oxfordshire, Flora Thompson (1876–1947) recalled that there were virtually no girls over 12 or 13 living in the village. Boys typically remained with their parents for several years after leaving school and contributed a small income to the family. Rural girls, however, often lacked similar local employment opportunities, so after leaving school at 10 or 11 and perhaps remaining home for another year to care for young children, they entered service. The girls' first positions, called "petty places," were typically in the homes of local tradesmen or schoolmasters. Here girls stayed for a year earning a small income along with room, board, and various payments in kind such as a Christmas dress or coat and cut material with which to sew undergarments before moving up to "gentlemen's service."[4]

The actual eventual placements of servants varied tremendously, from an aristocratic home that could hire between 30 and 50 servants to a working-class household employing a single maid-of-all-work from a local poor law school or charitable institution. *The Book of Household Management* (1861), Isabella Beeton's immensely popular guide for employers from the rising middle classes, outlined the various positions for female domestics. In elite households, the lady's maid served as part milliner, dressmaker, hairdresser, and decorator in charge of cleaning the dressing room and bedroom, as well as laundress who carefully brushed the mud from tweeds, rubbed silks with a square of merino, and gently shook muslins. Wealthy families also employed an assortment of other female servants: individual waiting maids for daughters 16 years and older, a general housekeeper (the highest paid female servant who oversaw the entire household), a head cook, kitchen maids, scullery maids, various upper and under house and laundry maids, maids-of-all-work, and nursemaids. The owners of grand country estates hired their own dairymaids and bakers, stable hands and coachmen, gardeners, and gamekeepers. Beeton estimated that an upper-middle-class family with a yearly income of £1,000 would hire a cook, an upper housemaid, a nursemaid, an under housemaid, and a manservant. A less prosperous upper-middle-class household earning £750 would hire a cook, a housemaid, a nursemaid, and a footboy. Most average middle-class households of £300 a year or less would employ one or two live-in servants: a maid-of-all-work and a nursemaid, or simply a general servant. The vast majority of female servants worked as maids-of-all-work or general servants in more modest middle- and upper-working-class households rather than in large estates.

The sheer multiplicity of distinct brushes and brooms illustrated in Beeton's guide—carpet brooms, stove brushes, banister brooms, staircase brooms, scrubbing brushes, long-hair brooms, furniture brushes, plate brushes, crumb brushes, cornice brushes, dusting brushes, etc.—suggests new standards of domestic cleanliness as well as the never-ending nature of the house servant's work. The general servant's workday extended from 6:00 or 6:30 in the morning until 11:00 at night or later, 6 days a week with a half-day on Sundays, for annual wages estimated by Beeton at £7 10s. to £11 plus room and board with an allowance for tea, sugar, and beer. The housekeeper and lady's maid of a wealthy home, by comparison, could earn respectively up to £45 and £25 per year.

The general servant Hannah Cullwick (1833–1909) provided a rare glimpse into the daily routines of domestics through her diaries, which she began keeping on the request of the upper-class barrister and writer Arthur Munby, whom she secretly married in 1873. With moments of sharp wit and social insight, Cullwick recounted days spent polishing boots, cleaning floors, lighting fires, emptying slops, and preparing meals. Many middle-class Victorians understood the physical labor and physicality of working women—their strength, muscles, and exposure to dirt and dust—as signs of inferiority and justification for exploitation. By calling Munby "Massa" and even at one point wearing a lock around her neck to which he held the only key, Cullwick also demonstrated how concepts of race intertwined with Victorian gender and class hierarchies in ways that help to explain the often-repeated references to domestic service as a form of English slavery.

**_The Diaries of Hannah Cullwick, Victorian Maidservant_, ed. by Liz Stanley (New Brunswick: Rutgers University Press, 1984), 110-111. Used by permission of Little, Brown Book Group.**

*Tuesday [31 July 1860]* Light the fire & clean'd the hearth & swept & dusted & clean'd 8 pairs of boots. Got breakfast up. Made the beds & emptied the slops. Clean'd & wash'd up the breakfast things. Swept the stairs & wash'd the lamp glasses & the things on the wash stands. Clean'd the knives & got dinner ready. Laid the cloth & took up the dinner & clean'd away. Clean'd the kitchen & passage & stairs & privy on my knees. Washed up in the scullery & clean'd the floor. Did some washing. Got tea; clean'd & wash'd up. Tied up the jam & got supper. Clean'd away & wash'd up & to bed.

This is the last day of July. I have cleaned 83 pairs of boots . . . Been to Massa ( ) times, to church not at all; been out no were [sic] but on errands. I met Thomas (in) the gardens by the public house & we had a bet about the weather & I won the sixpence of him, so he made me go in & spend it. So I went in & we had some beer. And the man that put up the boiler met me & ask'd me to go in with him to drink, but I didn't go. I have been to the dentist in this month I think, & he let his pupil see him stop my teeth. I suppose he wouldn't do so with a lady. I've been busy cleaning windows & glasses this month, for the flies & the dust makes so much dirt. My hands are very coarse & hardish, but not more so than usual. Mrs. J. has very white hands & she often comes & lays her hand lightly on mine for me to feel how cold they are—*we* say it's to show the difference more than anything else.

And yet, in spite of the physically demanding nature of the work, middle-class reformers continued to present domestic service as the ideal occupation for working women. Many girls had little choice but to enter domestic service, and poor law and charity schools trained girls with the sole expectation that they would become servants. As Cullwick's writings attest, the work of a servant could be equally physically demanding as the work of a factory worker (Cullwick took pride in her physical strength). Yet advocates of domestic service overlooked these "unfeminine" aspects, arguing instead that service provided female workers with an appropriate domestic setting. In his famous 1862 essay "Why Are Women Redundant?," William Rathbone Greg omitted domestic service from his list of occupations ill-suited for most women, declaring that service positions "fulfil [sic] both essentials of woman's being; *they are supported by, and they minister to, men.*"[5] Moreover, some bourgeois reformers drew on the language of liberal individualism to argue that in order to become full individuals separate from the impoverished masses, indeed to become fully human, poor girls needed to develop the characteristics of the ideal servant: most notably hard work, deference, and affection (not mere respect) for one's employers.

That many workers felt the strains of service and preferred other forms of work when given the option is evident from the "servant crisis" that developed in the second half of the 19th century as the demand for servants from the expanding middle classes exceeded the supply. Even as many servants welcomed the relative stability of the profession, they expressed much distress over the isolation, constant supervision, and separation from family members. Although reformers cited domestic upheaval and high infant mortality rates as arguments against female factory work and mining, the ways in which domestic service disrupted working-class family life went largely unrecognized until the end of the century. Most live-in servants were required to remain unmarried, which is why many women left service when they married. Single or widowed mothers seeking employment as servants needed to find alternative homes for their children, and the records of charities such as Thomas Coram's Foundling Hospital in London and Thomas Barnardo's boarding-out program list female servants as being among the main applicants. When, in 1894, George Moore published *Esther Waters*, his account of an unmarried servant seduced and left struggling to find a home for her infant son, England's largest bookseller refused to carry the book that explored how exploitation and domestic suffering could be fundamental aspects of servitude.

Domestic service remained the most popular employment for women and girls through the 19th century, but increasingly working women turned to other positions that gave them greater independence without separation from family members. The records of the Metropolitan Association for the Befriending of Young Servants trace girls after leaving poor law institutions and express a growing frustration in the 1880s and 1890s on the part of the elite female leaders faced with youths choosing other positions over live-in service. Many girls preferred work as day servants, yet others firmly rejected service altogether, working instead in factories, laundries, dress shops, public houses, and restaurants. Although white-collar jobs as shop assistants, clerical workers, and civil servants were generally not options for girls coming from workhouses or very impoverished backgrounds, these were the fastest growing professions for women in the last decades of the century.

## SHOP ASSISTANTS, CLERICAL WORKERS, AND CIVIL SERVANTS

Positions as shop assistants, civil servants, and clerks offered new opportunities for working- and middle-class women in the late-Victorian period, demonstrating England's overall growth in the service sector of the economy. These positions carried greater respectability than factory work or manual labor. Spurred by the rise of large department stores and expansion of retailing, the growth of government bureaucracies, and the availability of an educated workforce after the establishment of national education in 1870, shop owners and offices increasingly turned to less-expensive female workers. In the process, professions that had been dominated by male middle-class workers earlier in the century gradually declined in status, providing far fewer opportunities for career advancement for women. The expectation and, in some cases, legal requirement that women shop assistants, office workers, and civil servants remain unmarried was just one way in which institutional practices prohibited advancement, since the marriage ban (kept in place by the post office until 1963) deterred most women from developing a long-term career. Even when women workers remained single, they were often fired from these positions after reaching a certain age, so that companies could hire younger workers at lower wages.

Between 1870 and 1914, the Victorian shop assistant, a position that in the early-to-mid Victorian period still required an apprenticeship and extensive training, became one of the most popular employments for women. Fine work clothes, familiarity with consumer goods, and relatively little hard manual labor encouraged women to view the work as being higher in status than other forms of employment. For many shop workers, however, the promise of improved conditions was an illusion. Typical hours ranged from 75 to 90 hours a week, during which assistants remained standing with only short breaks for meals, and wages ranged from 18s.–£1 a week in an upscale London West End store to 7 or 8s. a week in smaller shops. Most assistants worked in mid-sized shops with 10 or more workers. In many parts of England, they were required to pay their employers for room and board in crowded, spare lodgings. Workers also complained of extensive, sometimes arbitrary fining practices that entitled employers to deduct 6d. or more from the women's wages if they returned to their living quarters after curfew, used the kitchen after hours, made a mistake in billing, left the counter because of illness, or arrived a minute late to work. Summing up her 1893 government study of working conditions for shop assistants, the Board of Trade labor correspondent Clara Collet (1860–1948) noted that while many factory women could not be convinced to leave their jobs after marriage, "the majority of shop assistants look upon marriage as their one hope of release, and would, as one girl expressed it, 'marry' anybody to get out of the business."[6]

The entry of female workers into clerical work and civil service similarly marked a transformation of these fields, not simply an opening of the doors to women. When first made available to significant numbers of women in the 1870s, such positions were initially conceived as providing an income for "redundant" or unmarried, educated women nominated from the professional middle classes and landed gentry. In 1881, however, the post office sparked a public stir when the Postmaster-General Henry Fawcett, husband of the suffrage leader Millicent Garrett Fawcett (1847–1929), abandoned the nomination process for women and instead based female clerking jobs on competitive exams, as was the practice for male postal employees. This, along with Fawcett's support for new grades of female postal workers, was an important innovation for the government's largest service employer. The purview of the post office extended into banking with the creation of the savings bank in 1861 as well as the country's telegraph operations, beginning in 1870, and telephone services by 1911. Women's high demand for clerical work was clear. In some cases, hundreds of women applied for a handful of openings. The popularization of shorthand transcription for business purposes in the 1850s and the development of commercial typewriters and telephones in the 1870s and 1880s also allowed for the standardization and subdivision of work and thus prompted an even greater reliance on female employees, although clerking and civil service positions continued to expand for male workers as well, just not at the same elevated rates.

Women not only filled government positions in the post office as clerks and telegraph workers, where the *Times* reported in 1882, they earned incomes of anywhere from £36 to £300 a year (though most women were concentrated at the lower end of the scale). They also worked as clerks, typists, telegraph, and telephone operators for private commercial houses and, to a lesser extent, for insurance companies, lawyers, and railway offices. By 1882, the *Times* asserted that women's aptitude for higher level administrative tasks was still undecided. The nation's leading newspaper emphasized, however, that women were well suited to simple routine clerking positions, particularly those normally staffed by boy clerks who would be better served by remaining in school longer to develop their professional futures. Unlike boy apprentices, however, female workers had little to no expectation of advancement, and changes in labor practices along with the greater supply of educated workers eventually made clerking and civil service less profitable for most male workers as well. By the turn of the century, secretarial work, the fastest growing occupation for women, had declined from its solidly professional status as a previously male-dominated occupation into a field characterized by routine, standardized tasks, low wages, and few opportunities for career advancement.

## PROSTITUTION

Victorians typically discussed prostitution in moral terms, but for those who worked in this profession it primarily illustrated the severe limitations on women's employment opportunities. The prostitute, commonly referred to as the "unfortunate," "social evil," "streetwalker," "public woman," or "fallen woman," provided a symbolic point of reference for Victorians wishing to raise fears about the dangers of women's economic activity and public presence. Critics of wage earning women at times drew on the rhetoric of prostitution, claiming that for any woman to accept money for her labor was a corruption of the feminine domestic ideal and hence a form of prostitution. Similarly, the frequent sexual accusations made against women in occupations that came to be viewed as unfeminine—agriculture, mining, and factory work—demonstrates how codes of sexual morality served to regulate women's access to paid labor.

At the same time, the realities of prostitution testified to the widespread insufficiency of wages for working women. Most actual prostitutes did not fit the fictional type of a young woman from the country seduced by an aristocratic man, then abandoned and forced by her "fallen" nature and economic necessity to follow a downward spiral of prostitution and death. They were often in fact paid workers—typically seamstresses, servants, shop assistants, and outworkers—pressed to turn to prostitution as a form of causal, intermittent income to supplement poor wages or survive during periods of unemployment. The rates of prostitution were seasonally linked to other forms of female employment, increasing in the winter when there was less work for dressmakers, for example, and decreasing in the summer during the busy social season. Yet the state's attempt to regulate prostitution through a series of laws known as the Contagious Diseases Acts of 1864, 1866, and 1869 (see Chapter 1) resulted in isolating prostitutes as a distinct class of workers from the rest of the casual working poor, since any woman examined under the acts was registered as a common prostitute, making it increasingly difficult for women to transition into another occupation.

Most prostitutes earned meager wages, as little as a shilling a night. For some women, the wages for prostitution were relatively high, if unreliable, and earnings might be supplemented by other amenities such as better clothing and entertainment in public houses and music halls—economic reasons that explain why women would choose prostitution given their otherwise bleak options. Courtesans such as Catherine "Skittles" Walters (1839–1920), daughter of a Liverpool customs worker, charmed London society as a regular rider in Hyde Park's Rotten Row in the late 1850s and 1860s. She served as the companion of such influential men as Lord Fitzwilliam (the hunting master of the Fitzwilliam hounds) and Lord Hartington (a future leader of the Liberal party), along with the poet Wilfrid Scawen Blunt, and Edward, Prince of Wales. Through such alliances, Walters usually commanded a house of her own as well as a large annual allowance in the thousands. By comparison, an elite prostitute working in London's West End during the mid-Victorian period earned on average £20–£30 a week, roughly twice what many servants earned in a year. However, all prostitutes remained vulnerable to the violent whims and demands of their clients. For the vast majority, life was characterized by poverty, ill health, and unstable living conditions as they negotiated their way between the common lodging house and the workhouse.

## MIDDLE-CLASS WOMEN AND PHILANTHROPY

Middle-class women also sought opportunities to work outside the home, and philanthropy provided them. Middle-class and elite English women worked as district visitors and charity bazaar organizers, Bible sellers, temperance advocates, and missionaries. In the second half of the century, middle-class women also increasingly sought out wage-earning employment, including positions not only as shop assistants and clerical workers, but also as professionals working in the usually (though not always) better-paid developing fields of social work, teaching, and nursing. Most of these positions were available only for single women. In the years just before World War I, unmarried and widowed women comprised over 85 percent of all paid female workers.

The Victorian debates about middle-class women and work focused primarily on whether single women should work and, if so, which occupations were deemed suitably respectable. These issues garnered widespread public interest after the published findings of the 1851 census. Writers such as Harriet Martineau (1802–1876) used the census to demonstrate the full breadth of female paid labor, arguing for a reexamination of woman's proper sphere along with continued expansion in female educational and employment opportunities. The 1851 census also reported a 500,000 "surplus" of single women over single men in England and Wales, likely related to normal population growth patterns, a later marrying age for men striving to secure a middle-class income prior to marriage, and higher male emigration rates. Feminists responded by calling for more paid work opportunities of substance for middle-class women in need of supporting themselves. In 1862, however, the journalist William Rathbone Greg argued in his popular essay "Why Are Women Redundant?" that society should instead encourage single women to marry. Greg reaffirmed a narrow view of women's role as helpmates to men by proposing that thousands of single women emigrate to Canada, the United States, and Australia as a route to marriage, and that those remaining in the country put aside the "morbid LUXURY of the age" and settle for a less-established mate.[7] While numerous Victorians challenged Greg's solutions, most supported the general view that a woman's primary role was to marry and raise children and, if she remained single, to care for her living family members.

However, alongside those who viewed women's paid work as an unnatural subversion of gender roles, others reinterpreted the rhetoric of separate spheres to expand the work opportunities available for middle-class women. Single women such as Harriet Martineau and Florence Nightingale (1820–1910), whose war service in Crimea from 1854 to 1856 did more than anything else to publicize the contributions of working women of the middle classes, joined married women such as Elizabeth Fry (1780–1845), the early-19th-century prison reformer, to argue that elite women were particularly qualified for work helping children and the poor, the sick and the elderly—in sum, any group traditionally associated with woman's care within the home. During the 1850s and following decades, elite, educated women increasingly expressed dissatisfaction with the narrow confines of woman's ideal role as wife and mother, challenging Greg's view of single women as "superfluous" or "redundant" members of society.

While these female reformers shared a fundamental belief in the need for women to apply domestic skills outside of their immediate homes, they often disagreed in their vision for women's public roles. Some thought women should limit their activities to philanthropic charity work, rejecting all paid employment—a position that clearly did not recognize the economic realities of many single, middle-class women. Others supported women's paid employment as long as they did not enter into "public" positions, which typically meant government positions or some other form of overtly political work, but could take on various nuanced meanings. Anna Jameson (1794–1860), literary and art critic, represented those who envisioned women's employment opportunities in the broadest terms. She developed the argument of "public housekeeping" in the 1850s, the idea that women should use their domestic skills for social reform. During this period, she worked closely with the Langham Place leaders and women's suffrage supporters Barbara Bodichon (1827–1891) and Bessie Parkes (1829–1925), who campaigned through the *English Woman's Journal* and the Society for Promoting the Employment of Women for improved working opportunities for women. Jameson called for government and private employers to hire more women as prison guards, workhouse assistants, hospital and war service nurses, reformatory school supervisors, and teachers. At the same time that Jameson proclaimed women's natural domestic skills, she ultimately blurred conventional boundaries between public and private, male and female, by suggesting that any knowledge useful to the family would be useful to society and vice versa. Drawing on liberal principles of individual development, she asserted that women required greater access to education, paid employment, and political influence on the basis that "the woman's sphere of knowledge and activity should be limited only by her capacities."[8]

**Anna Brownell Jameson, *Sisters of Charity and The Communion of Labour: Two Lectures on the Social Employments of Women*, new edition (London: Longman, Brown, Green, Longmans, and Roberts, 1859; Selection Originally Published as *Sisters of Charity Abroad and at Home*, 1855), xxx, xxxiv–xxxv**

Englishwomen require that in all public institutions, charitable, educational, sanitary, in which numbers of women and children are congregated and have to be managed and otherwise cared for, some part of the government should be in the hands of able and intelligent women; that the *maternal* as well as the *paternal* element should be made available, on the principle which I believe is now generally acknowledged, that the more you can carry out the family law, the "communion of labour," into all social institutions, the more harmonious and the more perfect will they be. This supposes, of course, that women so employed should be properly trained for their vocation. The recognition of this vocation, as coming within the "Woman's Sphere" of natural and necessary duties, would be a great public advantage; it would open a field of employment for the educated classes and it would incalculably benefit the humbler classes of women; but such employment must not be merely tolerated, it must be authorised. . . .

While pleading against the separation of the sexes in all social intercourse, and for their equal moral responsibility before God and the tribunals of their country, we Englishwomen agree with all intelligent men that there are vital differences which ought not to be lost sight of. We think it hard that such differences should be insisted on where they can be turned against us, and ignored where they ought to be recognised to our advantage; and we ask that these essential differences and requirements should be more considered, not only in the management of prisons, but in workhouses, asylums, factories, and all institutions in which men and women are relatively concerned.

The mid-Victorian reformers who followed Jameson's call to public service drew inspiration from the 18th- and early-19th-century philanthropists who established networks of female charity. Most notably, Elizabeth Fry set one of the century's most influential models for how women might apply their domestic, "feminine" qualities to social institutions and how men as well as women might put their religious faith into practice. The 4th of 12 children in a prominent Quaker family, Fry worked as a philanthropist in London and the surrounding area, distributing clothing, food, and information about smallpox vaccination. In 1813, Fry visited the female wards of

Newgate prison in London, notorious for corruption and abuse of prisoners housed without distinction of age or crime. At the time, it was practically unthinkable for a middle-class woman to enter such a place, where inmates and guards alike were renowned for violent outbursts, drinking, gambling, and sexual promiscuity. Through her campaigns, writings, and travels, Fry promoted the then uncommon idea that prisoners could be rehabilitated through kindness, individual attention, and a recognition of common humanity. In 1817, she founded the Ladies' Association for the Reformation of the Female Prisoners in Newgate, which expanded in 1821 into the British Ladies' Society for Promoting the Reformation of Female Prisoners. She also campaigned for abolition, religious toleration, and improved treatment of the mentally ill, and was among the first to address the appalling working conditions for British nurses by founding the Society of Nursing Sisters in 1840.

Although at the height of her international fame by the 1830s, government officials dismissed much of Fry's prison work as unprofessional and too focused on benevolence rather than punishment. Undeterred, she established a role for middle-class women visitors in public and private institutions largely by stressing their domestic skills. Her methods anticipated how middle-class domestic ideals and gender roles would become essential tools and measures within Victorian reform movements. At Newgate, for example, she promoted the idea that success at sewing and religious devotion served as positive signs of female inmates' rehabilitation. Female prisoners no doubt benefited from her humanitarian reforms: the schools she established for children imprisoned with their mothers, the improved sanitation, the income inmates earned from selling their sewing in the prison shop, and her personal Bible readings. All the while, the forms her benevolence took reflected her own gendered and classed identity as well as a practical realization of what instruction was required for a working-class woman to earn a living in 19th-century England.

Other 19th-century ladies' societies devoted to visiting local prisons, hospitals, asylums, charity schools, orphanages, and workhouses stressed the belief that institutions should be modeled on the domestic arrangements of middle-class family life. Women's proper calling, they argued, was to minister to the sick and nurture the young, to provide above all a moral guide and sympathetic support—services that female reformers lamented remained painfully absent from most state and charitable institutions governed by male officials. Like Fry, Mary Carpenter (1807–1877) argued that affection rather than punishment and smaller facilities based on middle-class family models, rather than mass institutions, were the best means to rehabilitate juvenile delinquents. Similarly, Louisa Twining (1820–1912), the Anglican descendant of the great tea merchant family, took up this mission as secretary of the Workhouse Visiting Society, founded in 1858 after several years of reform efforts inspired by a visit to her former nurse in the Strand union workhouse. Joined by her friend Anna Jameson, Twining and her cohort of well-connected women were horrified by the sight of poor law children referred to by number rather than by name. They set about bringing domestic influences to workhouses, focusing on the care of children and the sick.

As more women entered new types of charity work, the 1850s marked a shift toward greater professionalization of women's philanthropy. Some institutions already allotted female visiting societies a greater presence and control over fund-raising, an area where women were particularly successful, but poor law institutions, like prisons, proved stubbornly opposed to granting lady visitors significant authority over policy decisions. In many cases, local guardians refused all "interference" by lady visitors. Twining encouraged elite women to use their social connections along with arguments about women's domestic influence in order to persuade male poor law officials (typically from the more humble class of tradesmen, artisans, and, in rural areas, farmers) to accept women's participation. Gradually and unevenly, upper- and middle-class women gained influence over workhouse policies and slowly moved from volunteer into official positions. In 1873, James Stansfeld, supporter of many women's issues and president of the Local Government Board in charge of local administrative policy, commissioned Jane Elizabeth Nassau Senior (1828–1877) to conduct a study of girls in London poor law schools. Senior condemned the existing practices and, similar to Twining, argued for the restructuring of poor law institutions according to domestic models. Upper-level male poor law officials dismissed Senior's report as the work of an amateur lacking the authority of male professionals, someone so confined by her own strict definitions of middle-class femininity that she would censure a workhouse girl for wearing her hair down or otherwise not meeting the standards of middle-class respectability. Yet Stanfeld's controversial permanent appointment in 1874 of Senior as the first female inspector of workhouses and pauper schools was a major victory for women, although Senior resigned later that year because of ill health. The ideal that united many of these women—particularly in the earlier decades of their local government work—was the notion that the ideal bourgeois home should serve as the model for all social structures.

## WOMEN'S WORK AS EDUCATORS

During the first half of the century, finding a position as a governess was the most likely option for a single, middle-class woman in need of employment, a path initially taken by many prominent women, including the Brontë sisters, whose sympathy for the drudgery of the work imbues their fiction. After her first weeks as a family governess, Charlotte Brontë (1816–1855) declared, "I see now more clearly than I have ever done before that a private governess has no existence, is not considered as a living and rational being except as connected with the wearisome duties she has to fulfil [sic]."[9] A governess might have a position teaching in a school, travel daily to her employer's home, or like Brontë live with a family as a private tutor. An unmarried gentlewoman left without financial support would first apply to her friends and extended family for assistance in finding a position and only then, if necessary, to placement agencies such as the Governesses' Benevolent Institution (founded in 1843) before turning to newspaper advertisements as a last, disreputable resort. The average salary for a mid-century private governess varied between £20 and £45 a year plus room and board, well below the typical middle-class income, particularly considering that many governesses supported other family members as well. General duties ranged from the direction of children's formal lessons to full-time supervision and chaperoning of their activities, plus in some cases sewing or other work during the evenings.

The primary strains, however, arose not from the physical labor, but from the unclear nature of the governess' role and status as an employee within the bourgeois household. The desired governess was a gentlewoman, someone who could provide the appropriate training for elite children and highlight their mother's role as a person of leisure, but the very act of taking on paid employment placed the governess' genteel status in question. Set off from middle-class employers and household servants, governesses confused the strict Victorian classifications of rank. In some families, the governess would join the adults for dinner and be included in social events, while in others, they would eat with the children, who at their worst were unruly, arrogant, and even violent toward their educators. These social strains, combined with unstable employment arrangements and virtually no provisions for retirement besides the insufficient contributions from the Governesses' Benevolent Institution and other charities, help explain why former governesses were reported by Harriet Martineau to be the largest occupational group of women entering lunatic asylums (the second largest category being maids-of-all-work). By the 1840s and 1850s, middle-class women's dissatisfaction with governessing as their only reputable option helped fuel the campaign for better educational and work opportunities for middle-class women.

The 19th-century expansion of the school system created new professional positions for women. Middle-class women fulfilled the ideal feminine role of service to others as teachers in girls' boarding schools, dame schools, and the growing number of religious and charity schools founded by philanthropists such as Mary Carpenter. However, it was only after the 1870 Education Act created a system of national elementary schools that teaching developed into one of the largest and relatively well-paid professions for women. Initially, mainly working- and lower-middle-class women took on the new teaching positions in the state elementary schools charged with instructing children of the working classes. These teachers were less likely to justify their work with arguments referring to women's natural domestic talents and more likely to stress their economic necessity to work. Only gradually did the proportion of lower-middle-class and middle-class women increase as teaching gained status as a profession when conditions in the schools, educational standards, and provisions for teacher-training colleges improved in the last decades of the century. However, all female teachers still lagged behind men in their salaries, remained concentrated at the elementary levels, lacked opportunities for advancement, and in many localities experienced a marriage ban that allowed authorities to fire female teachers who announced plans to marry.

## WOMEN MEDICAL PROVIDERS: MIDWIVES, NURSES, AND DOCTORS

Like teachers, women working as medical providers negotiated expectations of women's natural attributes as caregivers against professional and social restrictions banning them from the most prominent positions. Women, mostly from the working classes, traditionally worked as midwives and healers offering a variety of informal services. Census records, local newspaper directories, and memoirs hint at the richness of women's largely unstudied medical work, listing women, often widows, employed as herbalists (sometimes selling abortifacients) and druggists, charm workers and spiritual healers, along with much rarer instances of female dentists and bonesetters. Many rural and urban communities relied on recognized medical women who were not certified in any formal way but nonetheless helped with childbirth, the laying of the dead, and the numerous medical needs in between that did not require emergency assistance from a male doctor. Unlike the middle-class district nurses who became regular visitors to poor neighborhoods in the late 19th century, medical women typically served people within their own communities. They understood the financial constraints of their patients and often came bearing needed supplies, such as a small bathing tub for infants, rather than the condescension at times associated with district nurses.

Midwives cared for women during pregnancy, assisted with births, and often returned to help mothers and infants in the days following (see Chapter 5). Members of a low-paying, low-status vocation, midwives were often remembered kindly by patients, yet viciously portrayed by the medical establishment as poorly trained, dirty, gin-drinking hacks. "Accouchers," or male midwives, became more common in the 18th and early 19th centuries, generally claiming better training and charging higher fees than women. Male doctors, still uneasy about their own claims to professional status, attempted to regulate the practice of midwives through licensing. Eventually, after significant resistance, parliament passed the 1902 Midwives' Act requiring all new midwives to acquire a degree from the Obstetrical Society and become licensed by the Midwives' Board. But meanwhile, women of the middle classes and even some working-class women were much more likely to secure a male doctor, rather than a female midwife, for childbirth.

Most early-Victorian nurses came from the working classes, but by the end of the century, nursing emerged as a professional field for middle-class as well as for working-class women. Nurses worked in a variety of settings, including hospitals, poor law institutions, and private homes, and their labor typically involved menial cleaning tasks along with medical care. During the Crimean War, nursing achieved greater status when Florence Nightingale—from an elite, well-connected family—organized a group of 38 women including Anglican and Roman Catholic sisters trained as nurses to assist wounded soldiers and tackle horrific hygienic practices at the wartime hospitals in Scutari, Turkey. Despite resistance from male doctors and military officials, Nightingale gained respect as a skilled administrator. On meeting her, Queen Victoria remarked, "Such

Originally from Jamaica, the nurse Mary Seacole (1805–1881) received medals for her service during the Crimean War and eventually settled in London. (Universal History Archive/Getty Images)

a *head*! I wish we had her at the War Office."[10] The English public revered Nightingale as "the Lady of the Lamp" for her nightly ministering to patients, but her discipline and sense of authority equally contributed to her success in reforming the Army Medical Service and England's hospitals. Like her more famous counterpart, the nurse Mary Seacole (1805–1881), daughter of a white Scottish officer and a black Jamaican herbalist, became a British heroine—"Mother Seacole"—for her work during the Crimean War. When her application to join Nightingale's nurses was rejected, Seacole set out on her own. She established her "British Hotel" near the front catering to soldiers and regularly rode into the battlefields to care for wounded men. By the end of the century, there were training schools for English nurses and several professional organizations, including the Royal British Nurses' Association, founded in 1891. No longer tainted by associations with moral laxity or sexual promiscuity as had been the case before the accomplishments of

A portrait from 1839 of the military surgeon James Barry (ca. 1799–1865). Barry attended the University of Edinburgh and rose to the position of Inspector General of Hospitals as a man, but was identified as anatomically female on his death. (Hulton Archive/ Stringer)

Nightingale and Seacole, nursing became celebrated as a respectable profession for women from all classes.

Few Victorian women gained recognition as doctors, and those who did faced growing resistance from the medical profession until the 1870s. Examples of female "surgeonesses" (general practitioners) and apothecaries existed in the 18th century, as well as unlicensed female "doctresses" into the 1830s and 1840s. However, the male medical profession, as it developed during this period, sought to exclude women from such positions. The handful of Victorian women who achieved careers as licensed doctors did so through unconventional means. The talented young James Barry (ca. 1799–1865), who was born female and presented himself as a man from the age of 10, graduated from the University of Edinburgh with a medical degree in 1812 before working at St. Thomas's Hospital in London. He joined the army, eventually becoming a staff surgeon and ultimately inspector general of hospitals, serving posts in Cape Town, Mauritius, Jamaica, St. Helena, Malta, Corfu, and Canada, before retiring in England. Only after his death did the papers report that Barry had been a woman.

Women seeking to become doctors identified loopholes in the professional regulations that excluded them. While British medical schools still refused female students, Elizabeth Blackwell (1821–1910) attended Geneva Medical College in New York and became the first woman to graduate from medical school in the United States, where her family had emigrated when she was a child. Blackwell returned to England and became the only woman included on the medical registrar of qualified practitioners when it was established by the Medical Act of 1858. Elizabeth Garrett Anderson (1836–1917), the second woman recognized by the medical registrar, followed a similarly circuitous route. Rejected by British medical schools, she registered by becoming the first woman to pass the Society of Apothecaries' exam in 1865 (after which point the society effectively banned women from taking the exam). Garrett Anderson later completed her medical degree at the University of Paris, but Sophia Jex-Blake (1840–1912) along with several other women seeking their degrees campaigned for women's admission to British schools by first successfully matriculating as medical students at the University of Edinburgh in 1869 and then facing down the male students preventing them from entering the Surgeons' Hall to take an examination the following year. In 1873, Scottish courts supported the exclusion of female medical students. Despite many differences in their tactical and medical approaches, Blackwell, Garrett Anderson, and Jex-Blake recognized the dire need for women's medical training and together supported the founding of the London School of Medicine for Women in 1874. Jex-Blake completed her training and entered the medical registrar in 1877. By 1901, the census listed 214 women as physicians, surgeons, or general practitioners in England and Wales.

## NOTES

1. Friedrich Engels, *The Condition of the Working Class in England* (Harmondsworth, U.K.: Penguin Books, 1987; 1845), 167–168.

2. Children's Employment Commission, *First Report of the Commissioners—Mines*, evidence from Sarah Gooder, No. 116 (London: William Clowes and Sons, 1842), House of Commons Sessional Papers, 252–253.

3. "Colliery Pit Women and Girls," *The Leisure Hour* (September 1887): 642.

4. Flora Thompson, *Lark Rise to Candleford* (London: Penguin, 1973; 1939), 155–157.

5. William Rathbone Greg, "Why Are Women Redundant?" *National Review* (April 1862): 451, emphasis in original.

6. *The Employment of Women: Reports by Miss Eliza Orme, Miss Clara E. Collet, Miss May E. Abraham, and Miss Margaret H. Irwin on the Conditions of Work in Various Industries in England, Wales, Scotland, and Ireland* (London: H.M. Stationary Office, 1893), 89.

7. Greg, "Why Are Women Redundant?" 446.

8. Anna Brownell Jameson, *Sisters of Charity and the Communion of Labour: Two Lectures on the Social Employments of Women*, new edition (London: Longman, Brown, Green, Longmans, and Roberts, 1859), lii.

9. *Letters of Charlotte Brontë*, 191, as quoted in Christine Alexander, "Brontë, Charlotte (1816–1855)," in *Oxford Dictionary of National Biography* (Oxford: Oxford University Press, September 2004).

10. Queen Victoria, as quoted in Lytton Strachey, *Eminent Victorians* (New York: Modern Library, 1918), 162, emphasis in original.

# 7

# URBAN LIFE

According to one late-Victorian etiquette manual advising women how to comport themselves in the street, "one can almost invariably distinguish the well-bred girl at the first glance, whether she is walking, shopping, in an omnibus, descending from a carriage or a cab, or sauntering up and down in the Park." Even amidst urban crowds, such "well-bred" women were supposedly immediately recognizable not simply because of their fine health and dress, but also because of their restrained manner of walking, their quiet tones, their refusal to make lively gestures or glance about, and above all their "self-effacement."[1] With the growth of Victorian cities, guidebooks and manuals such as this provided explicit instructions for how women and men should negotiate urban spaces in a manner fitting to the expectations of their gender and class. And yet, at the same time, many Victorians recognized that the relative anonymity of cities compared with rural settings offered greater opportunities for reinvention and experimentation with one's identity. By necessity and by choice, women living in cities exposed the contradictions inherent in the Victorian gender ideal of separate spheres that identified women's primary realm as the private domain of the home and family, and men's realm as the public world of commerce, politics, and business. Through their work, leisure, and political activities in cities, women entered public spaces

Victorian era music hall star, Anna Held, receives instruction in how to ride a bicycle, July 30, 1898. (Bettmann/Corbis)

and came together in close proximity with people from different backgrounds in ways that revealed the shifting, ambiguous nature of gender, race, and class in the Victorian era.

## URBAN GROWTH AND THE IMPERIAL CITY

The growth of Victorian cities increased rapidly with industrialization, and over the course of the 19th century, the British population shifted from being primarily rural to being primarily urban. The census of 1851 reported for the first time that more English people lived in cities than in rural areas. In 1800, London, which had a population of approximately one million, was the only British city with a concentration over 100,000. Urbanization continued steadily, resulting in 5 British cities with populations over 100,000 by 1837 and 30 such cities by 1901. The greater London metropolis included a population of 6.6 million by 1901. The most marked urban expansion took place in the North of England. Cities such as Birmingham, Liverpool, Leeds, Sheffield, Bradford, and, most of all, Manchester dramatically increased as a result of the demand for industrial workers, particularly within the cotton textile industry. City populations grew mainly from rural migration rather than internal population increase, and women, especially those between 15 and 20, were more likely than men to travel short distances to move to cities in search of employment, marriage opportunities, and increased independence.

By the 1840s, social critics focused on England's northern industrial cities, condemning the harsh realities of urban life and factory work. Such critiques represented a broad range of political perspectives, including Benjamin Disraeli's *Coningsby* (1844), Friedrich Engels's *The Condition of the Working Class in England* (1845), Elizabeth Gaskell's *Mary Barton* (1848) and *North and South* (1855), and Charles Dickens's *Hard Times* (1854).

By the 1880s and 1890s, London served not only as Britain's major port and capital city, but also as the heart of the British Empire. Irish immigration to England increased dramatically in the first half of the 19th century, reaching a height during and immediately following the devastating years of the Irish Potato Famine (1845–1854), creating significant Irish communities in Manchester, Liverpool, Glasgow, and, most of all, London. Younger single Irish women were more likely than men to immigrate to London, where they could find work in wealthier neighborhoods as domestic servants. Entire families also immigrated, the mother and children often joining the father after he secured housing and funds to transport the rest of the family. The Irish represented by far the largest immigrant community in London, but by the late 19th century, the city was also home to a substantial Jewish community as over 100,000 immigrants fleeing Russia and Eastern Europe joined the smaller, well-established Anglo-Jewish communities. People also came to London from all parts of the empire—especially South Asia, the West Indies, and Africa—to settle permanently or reside temporarily in search of work, professional training, or respite on the way to some other destination.

As an imperial city, London was the place where many of the structures and the challenges to imperialism took shape. City inhabitants supported imperial museum displays and exhibitions, black minstrel performances, and Christian missionary magic lantern slide shows with titles such as "Celestials and Barbarians," "Glimpses of India," and "Heroes and Fanatics of the Sudan." By the 1880s, urban reformers shifted their primary attention away from the northern industrial cities to London, and their public appeals demonstrated the pervasiveness of empire as reformers applied imperial rhetoric to describe domestic class relations. Tracts such as the Salvation Army founder William Booth's *In Darkest England and the Way Out* (1890) directly drew on the popularity of the African explorer H.M. Stanley's best-seller *Through the Dark Continent* (1878) to portray life in London's poorer districts, concentrated in the East End, as a world apart from the rest of England. At the same time, however, the city also served as an organizational center for anti-imperial groups. In 1900, for example, black Londoners organized the first Pan-African conference, which included influential women such as the American Anna Julia Cooper (1858–1964) along with W.E.B. Dubois among the delegates.

## TRANSPORTATION AND NAVIGATING THE CITY

Transportation methods changed dramatically during Victoria's reign. Private investors began funding passenger railway construction in the 1830s and, after the "railway mania" of 1844–1847, England had a national railway network that largely replaced passengers' earlier reliance on horse-drawn carriages for long-distance trips. Trains were divided into first-, second-, and third-class cars until the 1870s, when companies did away with second-class accommodations. First-class carriages contained private compartments, while those of the third-class initially consisted merely of open boxcars with benches. In the 1840s and 1850s, the middle and upper classes were the primary users of trains, but by the end of the century, most passengers were from the working classes—a shift prompted by the Cheap Trains Act of 1883, which made less expensive fares for workers compulsory.

As they traveled throughout the city, women negotiated the social demands of feminine dress, behavior, and decorum with the realities of crowded streets and urban filth. Some rail companies maintained separate entrances, waiting rooms, refreshment areas, and lavatories for different classes of passengers in an effort to enforce social distinctions, and some trains reserved separate compartments for women traveling without male companions. The invention of rail travel sparked public concern about opportunities for sexual impropriety, particularly in the private compartments, and women were warned to refrain from close proximity or signs of familiarity with gentlemen travelers. "The Unprotected Female," or single woman traveling alone, became a special subject of anxiety and some mockery by the 1850s as *Punch* and other periodicals detailed the dangers women travelers faced ranging from intruders' sexual advances to stolen luggage, missed stations, and train accidents. At least one male author demanded help for "The Unprotected Male" train traveler as well, who was "not a prey to male vultures only," but also to "female harpies."[2]

**"Ought Women to Travel by Train at All? (A Pendent to a Current Controversy)," *Punch* (May 5, 1894): 208**

DEAR MR. PUNCH,—I notice in the columns of a popular newspaper a discussion under the heading "The Ladies' Invasion," in which it is asked whether women have any right to invade the men's smoking compartments. This suggests a much wider question. Why should women want to travel by train at all? I've been brought up to think that a woman's place is *her home*, and if that's true, what does she want to go trapesing about in a railway carriage, smoking or not smoking? Women nowadays are bold and brazen enough to do anything. Why my own daughter—a quiet little thing to look at, too—actually travelled *alone* the other day from Sloane Square to South Kensington! When I asked her how she *dared* to do such a thing, she actually said that she couldn't see where the harm came in, and that she didn't see what else she was to do. No! Let woman stick to her own sphere—the common round, the daily task—and there will be no more of this bother about men not having room to smoke, or not caring to because ladies are present. I enclose my card, and am,

Yours, only an old-fashioned Woman,
A MAYFAIR MOTHER.

For transportation within cities, most people relied on some form of horse-drawn carriage. As with train travel, these forms of urban transportation put pressure on social expectations about women's sexuality and their presence in the public sphere. Only the wealthy could afford to maintain a private carriage. Nonelite women might travel with companions in privately rented four-wheel hackney carriages, which were good for larger groups carrying luggage, but expensive and notoriously dirty, since they were also sometimes used as ambulances and transport for corpses and convicts. The faster, lighter, two-wheeled "safety cabs," or hansoms, patented in 1834, presented more popular options for those who could afford them. In 1829, the first horse-drawn omnibuses carrying up to 22 passengers began operating in London, and by the 1840s, most omnibuses also included rooftop seats offering views of the

MAY 28, 1864.] PUNCH, OR THE LONDON CHARIVARI. 227

UNDERGROUND RAILWAY.

*Old Lady.* "WELL, I'M SURE NO WOMAN WITH THE LEAST SENSE OF DECENCY WOULD THINK OF GOING DOWN *THAT* WAY TO IT."

*Punch* (1864) explores new urban spaces including the underground: Old Lady. "Well, I'm sure no woman with the least sense of decency would think of going down that way to it." (Vassar College Library)

city. By the end of the century, London contained over 200 regular omnibus routes in service from eight in the morning until midnight. Construction on the London underground began in 1854. The Metropolitan line opened in 1863, providing a more affordable means of transportation that gradually extended throughout the city and suburban areas.

Women as well as men relied on these various forms of transport to move throughout the city. Guidebooks and etiquette manuals advised women on how to maintain their respectability and personal space even when pressed against strangers. The very construction of these new methods of transport acknowledged women consumers by, for example, placing modesty guards along the stairs of omnibuses to protect women from indiscrete glances as they boarded. Popular literature poked fun at the difficulties women faced as they struggled to climb aboard omnibuses while wearing broad crinolines or at women's fears that descending into the depths of the underground might compromise feminine decency.

Such concerns demonstrated that new urban systems of transportation challenged existing feminine ideals and, at the same time, provided new spaces in which women developed a public, urban presence. By the 1860s, more and more middle-class women traveled throughout the city unchaperoned without compromising their sense of respectability. In a lithograph from 1865, a clergyman approaches a well-dressed woman waiting in Piccadilly Circus under a clearly marked sign for omnibuses. He mistakes her for a prostitute and offers her the Bible, advising, "Take it home and read it attentively. I am sure it will benefit you." The lady replies, "Bless me, Sir, you're mistaken. I am not a social evil, I am only waiting for a bus."[3] Middle-class women alone in mid- and late-Victorian cities were at times mistaken for prostitutes, and this was a major cause for their objection to the Contagious Diseases Acts of the 1860s. However, the clergyman's misunderstanding of the situation—his failure to read the actual signs or see the omnibus rounding the corner—also satirizes those Victorians who remained oblivious to the social transformations that allowed women of all classes to have greater independence and visibility in public urban spaces.

Walking was the primary means of moving through the city for most working-class women and a popular activity for women of the middle and upper classes as well. Wealthier neighborhoods, such as London's West End, contained large parks for promenades. Hyde Park provided a favorite locale for walks, horse riding, and carriage rides. Here, stylish women joined the Church Parade on Sundays between morning service and luncheon to display London's finest fashions. Despite improvements in sanitation, however, most city streets remained dusty and filthy. Horse-drawn transportation along with the influx of hundreds of thousands of livestock each year to feed urban populations left the streets covered in animal manure. Blood from butchers' shops, industrial filth from factories, and even human sewage from homes littered the streets. Long skirts and trains, when in fashion, collected the dirt of the streets, so that women (or their maids) had to brush off the dried mud when returning from walks. In 1851, a humorous article in *Punch* praised the self-sacrifice of ladies who swept the London streets as they walked through public thoroughfares wearing long dresses, suggesting fashionable women should organize brigades of "female street orderlies" for this municipal service.[4] In reality, crossing busy streets proved challenging, and unaccompanied middle-class women often relied on nearby gentlemen for assistance or crossing sweeps, who not only cleared the path but also negotiated through the chaotic traffic for a small tip.

The hundreds of etiquette manuals published in the second half of the 19th century aimed at middle-class women provided explicit instructions on how to maintain distinctions of class, gender, and sexuality in the streets. It was considered proper, for example, for a married woman to address a single woman first and for the woman of the higher station to initiate the first sign of recognition with a slight bow. Guidebooks also provided women with intricate systems of greetings imbued with moral meanings as they met gentlemen in the streets. If a woman passed a gentleman whom she was pleased to accept as an acquaintance, she was to make the first bow. If, however, she disapproved of his moral character, she was to bow very coldly on the first meeting and then afterward refuse to recognize him in what was known as a "cut."

**"Manners in the Street and Public Places," in *The Etiquette of Modern Society: A Guide to Good Manners in Every Possible Situation* (London: Ward, Lock, and Co., 1881), 17–18**

If you meet a lady with whom you have become but slightly acquainted, and had merely a little conversation (for instance, at a party or a morning visit), and who moves in a circle somewhat higher or more fashionable than your own, it is proper to wait till she recognises you. It is not expected that all intimacies formed at watering-places should continue after the parties have returned to town. A mutual bow when meeting is sufficient; but there is no interchanging of visits unless ladies have, before parting, testified a desire to continue the acquaintance. In this case the lady who is the senior, or palpably highest in station, makes the first call. It is not customary for a young lady to make the first visit to a married lady. When meeting them in the street, always speak first to your dressmaker, milliner, seamstress, or to any one you have been in the habit of employing. To pass without notice servants whom you know is rude and unfeeling. When meeting a gentleman whom a lady has no objection to numbering among her acquaintances, she denotes it by bowing first. If she has any reason to disapprove of his character or habits, let her bow very coldly the first time, and after that not at all. When a lady is walking between two gentlemen she should divide her conversation as equally as practicable, or address most of it to the greater stranger to her. A lady should never take the arms of two gentlemen at the same time. To speak loudly in the street is unladylike, and to call across the way to an acquaintance is in execrable taste. A lady may shake hands with gentlemen who are intimate acquaintances, but the action must be very quickly and gently performed. It is sufficient that a young lady places her hand in that of the gentleman with but little of other action. On being escorted home by a gentleman a lady expects he will not leave her till he has waited until she is actually in the house.

As prescriptive literature, such guidebooks offered a basis for social exchanges, but the realities of street interactions were no doubt significantly more complex and ambiguous. Along with the etiquette manuals that envisioned a clearly decipherable social hierarchy in which all city dwellers fit specific class and moral categories, urban guides stressed the greater anonymity of cities. Guidebooks from the first half of the 19th century described city life as a form of daily theater in which no one's identity remained secure. The promenades in Hyde Park became playful masquerades in which tradespeople might appear more fashionable than aristocrats. Similarly, the begging women who looked pregnant by day might merely have filled their fronts with straw to arouse sympathy. Victorians understood cities as places where close, daily proximity with strangers from different backgrounds created opportunities for experimenting with one's identity—opportunities that might alternatively be guarded against or welcomed. For women in particular, the 19th-century city provided new kinds of public spaces in which they might explore evolving models of feminine behavior.

## MIDDLE-CLASS WOMEN AND THE CITY

For middle-class women, cities presented opportunities to question the social expectation that women's proper role was in the home and at the same time to fulfill the feminine domestic ideal in new ways as they pursued their philanthropic work, household duties, and cultural activities in public, urban settings. In some cases, cities offered women a sense of liberation, independence, and pleasure as the very nature of urban space blurred clear distinctions between male and female spheres. The city was the obvious home to the late-Victorian New Woman, who directly confronted gender norms with her intellectual pursuits, professional status, and greater economic independence. At the same time, however, many middle-class women also conducted their public explorations of the city according to evolving definitions of what was considered to be appropriate feminine behavior. Elite women typically supported their public urban activities by appealing to a sense of their greater domestic, religious, and moral duties. They stressed various ways women could improve and domesticate the city—a form of rhetoric that sought to continue distinctions between male and female ideals while also allowing women of the middle and upper classes to play a more active role in public life.

### Female Philanthropists and the Urban Poor

By the last decades of the 19th century, the working-class home had become a regular site of middle-class female assistance as a host of volunteers and government officials joined the district visitors and the Biblewomen (see Chapters 2 and 6). Many of these new officials gained their positions from the mid-Victorian expansion of government regulations, such as the 1848 Public Health Act, the 1866 Sanitary Act, and national education in the 1870s. They included a mix of paid and volunteer professionals: district nurses, poor law officers, sanitary inspectors, and school board workers. Middle-class women valued such philanthropic work as a practical outlet for their religious beliefs and, perhaps equally important, an escape from the tedium many experienced as they fulfilled their primary domestic duties within the home.

Some women eventually built entire careers based on their experiences with district visiting and contributed to the general movement toward professionalization. The housing reformer Octavia Hill (1838–1912) is one such example. Like most district visitors, she expressed a belief in self-help and individual reform rather than any desire to question what others saw as fundamental inequalities inherent within industrial capitalism. In the mid-1860s, with financial support from the art critic and writer John Ruskin, Hill bought her first block of London houses, which she transformed into affordable homes for the poor. By the 1880s, when many reformers argued for greater government intervention and subsidies, Hill proclaimed that private philanthropy and moral reform remained the best solutions to improve England's worst slums. She reinvested all profits into her properties and directed her female volunteer rent collectors to instruct tenants on everything from the value of industry and religion to the art of flower arrangement.

A supporter of public urban parks and the "garden city," Hill called on women's domestic influences as she hoped to transform urban slums by introducing color, light, and beauty into the daily lives of workers. Hill's career also demonstrated the complex and different ways in which women approached their work in urban spaces. Even as she became one of England's best-known philanthropists, she considered her work improving domestic conditions for the poor to be essentially private rather than public, an extension of what she understood to be woman's proper realm. Hill remained staunchly opposed to women's suffrage and other demands for women's political input on national and imperial issues.

While Hill's form of capitalist philanthropy did little in the end to address the vast problems of urban overcrowding, she raised awareness and helped train a cohort of female workers dedicated to housing and urban reform. "Slumming" became a popular activity for middle-class women and men by the 1880s. In an attempt to experience working-class life more directly, women visited impoverished districts, where they sometimes disguised themselves and took on new identities in the name of research. The Fabian socialist Beatrice (Potter) Webb (1858–1943), for example, first served as a female rent collector before assisting her cousin Charles Booth in his study of London poverty, *Life and Labour of the People in London* (1889–1903). She moved to East London and worked in disguise as a seamstress, gathering material for her "Pages from a Work-Girl's Diary," published in *The Nineteenth Century* in 1888. Although Potter later became dismissive of this form of reporting, she also recognized the freedoms and excitement that urban exploration offered women and men of the middle classes.

The settlement house movement created another opportunity for elite men and women to promote cross-class alliances and reform by living in poorer neighborhoods. Reverend Canon Samuel Barnett and his wife Henrietta Barnett (1851–1936), Octavia Hill's close friend, founded the first settlement house, Toynbee Hall, in Whitechapel, London, in 1884. It served as a place where male students from Oxford and Cambridge could live as they ideally created friendships with local residents, taught classes, and provided professional training. A number of settlement houses specifically for single women opened soon thereafter, including the 1887 Women's University Settlement in Southwark. Settlements drew on a model of colonization in which England's elite moved into working-class neighborhoods. Elite volunteers provided training and resources, but also prescribed what they considered to be proper behavior and culture for the working poor. While male settlement workers typically taught classes in the arts and literature, along with offering professional or legal expertise, women settlement workers headed clubs for girls and focused on instruction in domestic areas involving childcare, housekeeping, food preparation, and hygiene. The routines of women settlement workers' lives remained influenced by middle-class expectations. They sometimes brought servants with them and maintained such customs as dressing for dinner. At the same time, however, these women traveled to parts of the city they would otherwise likely never have seen, and worked with people outside of their social circles. They also discarded some of the more immediate signs (if not all the luxuries) of female respectability, such as wearing gloves and a hat when walking in the streets.

### Shopping

Like philanthropy, shopping served as an activity that increasingly enabled middle-class women to explore the city on their own without male companions. In the early Victorian period, most elite woman shopped with male chaperones or servants, and often even requested the shopkeeper to bring goods to their carriages for private view. However, shopping gradually took on new forms as women developed new practices as consumers. By the 1860s, London's West End was England's foremost shopping locality for fashionable bourgeois women, a center of pleasure and consumerism in which women claimed a variety of public spaces. Regent Street, completed in 1820, was designed as a promenade and shopping area featuring small stores selling luxury items such as silks, fans, and parasols at a time when most of London's commercial activities remained located in the financial district contained within the City of London. The expansion of public transportation in the 1850s along with the production of ready-made clothing promoted the creation of the first department stores. In 1863, the draper William Whiteley opened a store selling ribbons and luxury materials in Bayswater. By the late 1870s, Whiteley's had transformed into a "universal provider," England's first department store, selling everything from beef and other foodstuffs to jewelry, furniture, and complete wedding trousseaus at varying price levels. Harrod's, founded by a tea merchant in 1849, developed from a grocery into one of the world's largest retailers. Liberty's first opened on Regent

Street in 1875 under the name East India House, specializing in the sale of Indian silks and Japanese finery, before expanding into a full-scale department store. It drew in shoppers with exoticized portrayals of colonial subjects in its Eastern Bazaar and even in 1885 created an "Indian Village" in Battersea Park for advertising. By the 1880s, the department store came to represent British modern life, industrial progress, and imperial power as well as women's changing public roles.

The experience of shopping allowed women to walk through the city and look with pleasure at shop windows, displays, and goods for sale, and at the same time sparked larger debates about women's proper economic, legal, and social position. Shopping became a recognized form of entertainment and leisure associated with bourgeois women, rather than simply a household duty. Store owners tapped into the growing consumer power of women shoppers by increasingly hiring women shop girls, rather than male assistants who required higher wages. The growth of department stores spurred the creation of all sorts of new public spaces for women—restaurants, tea rooms, and public female lavatories—that recognized women's needs and served as alternatives to the pubs, taverns, and clubs primarily oriented toward a male clientele. At the same time, there was a clear backlash against the increasing visibility of middle-class women exploring the city as consumers. More often than not, such criticism took the form of sexualized threats, casting middle-class female shoppers in the role of public women or prostitutes as a way to suggest that any association with economic transactions or public life would necessarily undermine bourgeois feminine respectability.

### Civic Spaces

Long before elite women's growing urban presence as philanthropists and shoppers in the last decades of the century, they engaged in a variety of activities within civic cultural spaces. Middle-class women regularly attended art galleries, museums, concert halls, and theaters as part of their social life. In these characteristically urban venues, women crowded together with men and, in some cases, people from a spectrum of social backgrounds. Over the course of the Victorian period, such activities gained even greater importance as signs of middle-class culture and respectability, underscoring how the public sphere helped shape women's class and gender identities.

Middle-class women's increasing access to reading rooms illustrates how women ventured from their homes into a variety of civic spaces, often despite male resistance. The British Museum, founded in 1759 as a national institution free and open to the public, also contained the British Museum Library, which transformed over the 19th century from a haphazardly developed specialist collection into one of the world's premier research libraries. In 1839, *The London Saturday Journal* noted that on average, 220 readers used the British Museum reading room each day, a marked increase from previous decades, and that these visitors were "mostly all of the 'sterner sex,' for the daily average number of ladies attending the rooms is not more than eight." By the 1880s, however, women readers became a noticeable, if not always welcome presence. An 1880 article in *Leisure Hour* warned potential visitors, "There are no reserved seats except for ladies, who, we may remark in passing, frequently do not use them, and encroach on the space intended for others."[5] Women such as Eleanor Marx (1855–1898) and the New Woman novelist Olive Schreiner (1855–1920)—and before them Anna Jameson (1794–1860), who died from pneumonia developed while walking home in the snow after many hours working in the British Library—regularly claimed seats in the reading room. They redefined the British Library as a public, notably national urban space so that what had once effectively been the sole preserve of men became a space in which women also pursued their intellectual interests. The transformation of the British Museum Library was part of a much larger Victorian movement to improve library access through the promotion of a variety of different sorts of free, subscription, and municipal libraries, some of which advertised separate reading rooms for women. By the 1870s, even some department stores had created reading rooms specifically for female employees.

Some elite and middle-class women preferred a more comfortable setting for their public reading, one also suitable to dining, socializing, and networking. In the last decades of the century, these women remodeled the male bastion of political and social power—the gentlemen's club—into a site that offered necessary comforts for women as they engaged in urban activities while also promoting their professional and political pursuits. London clubs for men flourished in the Victorian period. They became associated with specific interests, such as the Anthenaeum (officially founded in 1824) for intellectuals, the Garrick (1831) for artists, the Carlton

(1832) for Tories, and the Reform (1836) for Whigs. The elite male clubs were primarily located in grand buildings along Pall Mall, Piccadilly, and St. James's. Most clubs excluded women, although mixed male and female discussion clubs, such as the socialist Fabian Society and the radical Men and Women's Club, became more popular in the 1880s. The radical Unitarian Whittington Club, opened in 1846, provided a much earlier example of a vibrant mixed club dedicated to providing the luxuries of the elite gentleman's club along with lectures, entertainment, and reading rooms for men and women from the rising middle classes. By 1850, almost one fifth of its members were women.

Notably, one of the first clubs for women, the Berners Club, was founded in 1860 by women connected with the Langham Place Circle, the group including Bessie Parkes (1829–1925), Barbara Bodichon (1827–1891), and Emily Davies (1830–1921) that campaigned in the 1850s and 1860s to reform women's property laws, education, and voting rights. Other major female clubs opened in the last decades of the 19th century and early 20th century: the Alexandra (1884), the Primrose League's separate branch for Tory women (1885), the Pioneer (1892) associated with feminism and temperance work, the Women Writers' Club (1892) on Fleet Street, the Victoria (1894), and the Lyceum Club (1904) for writers and artists. There were also places, such as the Enterprise Club (1889), specifically for lower-middle-class working women. Clubs offered women a place of rest in the city, a public yet also peaceful setting where they might read in the library, enjoy a meal, attend a lecture, join in a debate, and possibly even arrange for overnight lodgings. Celebrating the expansion of female clubs, the poet Amy Levy (1861–1889) wrote, "Here, at last is a haven or refuge, where we can write our letters and read the news, undisturbed by the importunities of a family circle."[6] Many critics disapprovingly associated clubs with feminism, female consumerism, or, as Levy's sentiment suggests, a disavowal of women's domestic ideal. Still, by the 1890s, these clubs were increasingly acceptable outlets for women seeking social, political, and professional support.

## WORKING-CLASS WOMEN AND THE CITY

Unlike elite women, working-class women throughout the 19th century by necessity spent much of their lives unaccompanied by men in urban public spaces. Day servants and seamstresses, factory workers and laundresses, along with the thousands of homeless women and children regularly inhabited the open spaces of Victorian cities. Women beggars appealed for contributions along street corners, and female entertainers—acrobats, musicians, and artists—joined women street sellers and prostitutes as important Victorian examples of women who were public participants in the urban economy as workers and sellers, not just as consumers.

In conjunction with the expansion of cities and the growth of public transportation, new spaces developed for women workers. After the spread of railways, for example, pubs and restaurants employing female barmaids opened along the platforms. These women worked on their feet for up to 11 hours a day before making what could often be the long trek home along the streets after midnight. As the century progressed and middle-class women ventured out into the city in greater numbers, the omnipresence of working women in urban, public spaces became a growing concern for Victorian reformers, who presented working-class women's public presence, economic activities, and domestic arrangements as a threat to middle-class gender ideals.

The overcrowded conditions of many working-class homes caused families to engage public spaces in a manner that often shocked middle-class district visitors and reformers. Living in a one-room London East End apartment measuring 12 by 10 feet with his parents and two siblings, Arthur Harding recalled how his mother would send him out into the streets with his food to eat so that she could continue her piecework making matchboxes. The streets, rather than the middle-class nursery, were the primary place of play for children of the working classes. In the second half of the 19th century, philanthropic tracts such as *The Little London Arabs* (1870) and *A Plea for Our Street-Arabs: Grace Triumphant, or the Dying Match-Seller* (1895) applied imperial rhetoric to describe poor urban children as "street Arabs"—a term implying that children's alternative domestic arrangements were somehow foreign and "un-English."

Working women also relied on public urban spaces in their daily domestic lives. Courtyards, despite the filth and lack of ventilation, served as places to hang laundry and socialize. In their rightful condemnations of the sanitary conditions within working-class neighborhoods, many middle-class reformers were equally concerned with the ways in which these living arrangements defied middle-class domestic ideals. The lack of privacy or clear

Two girls play on a lamppost swing in this illustration from Dorothy Stanley's book, *London Street Arabs*, published in 1890. (Stanley, Dorothy. *London Street Arabs*, 1890)

segregation between domestic and urban public spaces within the homes of the poor served as signs of urban disorder.

Female costermongers, or street sellers, were among the most visible working-class women in the Victorian city. Even after the creation of large department stores, many people continued to purchase goods from small specialty shops as well as from street peddlers who set up carts at local markets or traveled with their merchandise throughout the city. Women and girls worked alongside men and boys selling a wide array of household goods. According to Henry Mayhew's mid-Victorian study of London street life, women sellers had many specialties: the sale of "fish (including shrimps and oysters), fruit and vegetables (widows selling on their own account), fire-screens and ornaments, laces, millinery, artificial flowers (but not in any great majority over the male traders), cut flowers, boot and stay-laces and small wares, wash-leathers, towels, burnt linen, combs, bonnets, pin-cushions, tea and coffee, rice-milk, curds and whey, sheeps'-trotters, and dressed and undressed dolls."[7] The least profits came from the sale of goods such as watercresses and matches, relatively common and inexpensive items of which women and girls also tended to be the primary peddlers. Irishwomen as well as Englishwomen comprised a large portion of London's street sellers. According to Mayhew, roughly half of the women street traders were married to or in established relationships with male street sellers. Children often set up stalls in close proximity to their parents, from whom they learned the trade. In addition to street selling, women and girls worked in a variety of other street trades as ballad singers and entertainers, crossing sweepers, beggars, rag collectors, and mudlarks, who searched the river banks for resalable items. The female street workers interviewed by Mayhew were often quick to stress their respectability even as Mayhew, like other Victorian reformers, intimated that the public sale of any sort of goods placed women on the path to prostitution. Sexual impropriety remained the typical or unspoken charge against all women in public.

The 1888 Jack-the-Ripper murders, known at the time as the Whitechapel murders for the East End London neighborhood where most of the attacks took place, brutally demonstrated the dangers women faced in public. All of the known female victims—Martha Tabram, Polly Nicholls, Annie Chapman, Catherine Eddowes, Elizabeth Stride, and Mary Kelly—were members of the working poor who had occasionally earned money as prostitutes. While some local East End newspapers expressed sympathy for the victims and stressed their connections to local communities, most reports implied that by working as prostitutes and earning the "wages of sin" these women caused their own deaths. Press reports about the physical mutilation and dissection of women's bodies in notably public spaces such as courtyards and streets highlighted the violence women faced if they stepped out of their prescribed domestic roles. Reporters tended to detail the instability of family life among the poor and emphasize the ways in which the victims failed to meet the standards of middle-class domesticity. Little was said about victims' roles as mothers, for example, although several of the women had children ranging in age from 6 or 7 to their early 20s. The overwhelming solutions discussed in the press included calls for more police officers, neighborhood patrols by predominantly male vigilance committees, the repression of prostitution, and warnings against women not to venture out alone. Such reforms did little in the end to make cities safer for women. The Victorian responses to the Whitechapel murders reinforced the idea that public urban spaces were for men and private domestic spaces for women, even as this ideal clearly did not match the realities of Victorians' lives, particularly for working-class women.

## WOMEN'S POLITICAL LIVES AND THE CLAIMING OF PUBLIC URBAN SPACES

At the same time that women renegotiated the boundaries and meanings of urban public spaces as sites of pleasure and work, some women also claimed public spaces as a way to demonstrate their political rights. The city street, square, and park had long been associated with predominantly male political activities: demonstrations, marches, speeches, and canvassing. However, by the end of Queen Victoria's life, a wide array of women representing many different political standpoints in addition to suffragettes orchestrated political activities in urban public spaces. They did so as a way both to appeal to greater numbers of voters in the era of expanding mass politics and, in the case of women's suffrage workers, to redefine women's relationship to the state.

Aristocratic women presented some of the earliest examples of women taking on prominent public political roles. There are pre-Victorian examples of aristocratic women who became renowned political campaigners and public speakers, most notably Georgiana Cavendish, the fashionable Duchess of Devonshire (1757–1806). Attacked by her social peers, the press, and cartoonists for spending all her days in the streets campaigning and supposedly winning votes with kisses, she nonetheless was much appreciated by the Whig politicians she helped elect to parliament. Elite women's access to politicians and society also created opportunities for ceremonial political statements made through public displays. Caroline Norton (1808–1877), for example, recalled how a group of politically minded Tory ladies created a public scandal when they hissed at Queen Victoria's carriages passing over the racecourse at Ascot in an effort to express contempt for Her Majesty's Prime Minister Lord Melbourne. In less scandalous but likely more effective settings, elite women also publicly exerted their political influence over tenants and local voters through letter writing and canvassing. This role for women expanded greatly when, in 1883, the Corrupt

Practices Act outlawed the payment of political canvassers. Political parties founded auxiliary female organizations in the 1880s, such as the highly successful Tory Primrose League, through which female volunteers practiced door-to-door canvassing and organized other social events.

Queen Victoria's jubilee celebrations of her 50th and 60th years of rule in 1887 and 1897 illustrate how, by the end of the century, women participated in political spectacles that increasingly aimed to reach not only the political elite, but also a mass audience including the expanded electorate enfranchised by the Second and Third Reform Acts of 1867 and 1884. Royal public ceremonies in the early and mid-Victorian period tended to be poorly orchestrated, but Victoria's Golden Jubilee in the summer of 1887 was a precisely coordinated affair, recognized as the grandest state ceremony of its time, and celebrated with parades and speeches around the world. Victoria, despite her reservations, greeted crowds of thousands from her carriage as she rode through West End London along with her extended family and other state dignitaries. The Diamond Jubilee of 1897 similarly became a celebration of the British Empire as troops from all different colonial territories joined the processions in London. At the same time, the Queen's image became a popular icon for advertisers selling all sorts of mass consumer goods, everything from perfume to pills. The jubilee celebrations solidified Victoria's return to the public realm after her retreat following Albert's death in 1861. Not only the Queen took on a new public political role, but also, by the end of the century, women such as Nancy Lord—the heroine of George Gissing's *In the Year of Jubilee* (1894)—who relished the royal celebrations as occasions for women to experience the tremendous freedom as well as the anonymity of mixing amidst urban crowds.

In comparison to elite women, working-class women had a long history of turning to urban streets and public spaces as sites for making political statements. In the 18th and early 19th centuries, women joined radical parades as well as the carefully organized food riots in many urban centers. Early and mid-Victorian political movements such as Chartism ultimately limited women to more clearly domestic roles in an attempt to gain respectability, although certainly many female Chartists joined in public demonstrations, as did women in other popular political movements, such as the anti–Poor Law movement and the anti-vaccination movement (see Chapter 1).

By the last decades of the 19th century, working-class women orchestrated their own marches and protests highlighting the specific concerns of women workers. Female demonstrators gained widespread public attention in the 1888 Match Girls' Strike of workers from Bryant and May's match factory in Bow, East London. The strike heralded a new era for women workers and marked the rise of new unionism, the movement through which unions reached out to unskilled workers along with the skilled workers who had previously dominated trade unions. In July, just weeks before the first notice of the Whitechapel murders, 1,400 match girls (who were typically in their early 20s or younger) went on strike to oppose exploitative working conditions. They protested poor wages of approximately 4–8s. a week (of which half could go to rent), punitive fines for offenses ranging from talking to arriving at work with dirty feet, and dangerous working conditions. Exposure to phosphorus caused necrosis or "phossy jaw," a relatively common condition among matchmakers resulting in the painful, disfiguring decay of their jaws and teeth. The middle-class socialist and spiritualist writer Annie Besant (1847–1933) helped the match workers' cause by publishing articles on their working conditions and the strike. She also promoted a boycott of Bryant and May matches, collected a strike fund, and supported workers in their negotiations with union leaders and factory owners. The match workers, however, including many from Irish backgrounds, were the ones to initiate and sustain the strike on their own. Girls and women typically represented as prime examples of London's street waifs—alone and helpless—gained national attention by joining together to march through the city streets carrying banners, holding a rally in Regent's Park, and leading a procession to the House of Commons, where they were interviewed by members of parliament. The end of the three-week strike marked a victory for the workers, who achieved the creation of the Matchmakers' Union as well as higher wages and improved conditions, although phosphorus exposure continued to debilitate matchmakers until it was banned by parliament 20 years later. Still, these accomplishments by some of the poorest paid, unskilled, young, and female workers signaled the rise of a mass workers' protest movement culminating in the successful strike of some 10,000 London dockworkers the following year.

Women from all classes also turned to the streets in what was by far the most controversial use of urban public space: the women's

Members of the Matchmakers' Union on strike in 1888. From *Annie Besant: An Autobiography* (1893). (Vassar College Library)

suffrage movement (see Chapter 1). Supporters of women's suffrage strategically used public spaces to convey their messages to large numbers of people and to challenge the very notion that women should have only a limited role in the public sphere. Even at an early age, the future women's suffrage leader Emmeline Pankhurst (1858–1928) perceived opportunities for public political work. In her ghost-written memoir, *My Own Story* (1914), she recalled how during the first election after the 1867 Second Reform Act she and her younger sister marched up and down the street before a Manchester polling booth, lifting up their new green winter dresses to expose their red petticoats beneath—hoping the red and green colors of the Liberal party would persuade voters. The moment of joyful political campaigning soon ended, when their unhappy nursemaid snatched them up and took them home.

From the mid-1860s until World War I (1914–1918), women from various organizations, including the more moderate National Union of Women's Suffrage Societies led by Millicent Garrett

Fawcett (1847–1929) and, after Queen Victoria's death, the more militant Women's Social and Political Union (WSPU) led by Pankhurst, trained women in the art of giving public speeches, planned protest rallies, and organized door-to-door canvassing in support of women's suffrage. Through such seemingly mundane acts as writing "Votes for Women" in chalk on the pavement, supporters of women's suffrage laid claim to public spaces as they conveyed their message. Yet even such basic public expressions could inspire personal attacks. When, for example, women stood in the streets to sell copies of WSPU newspapers, they received an endless stream of physical abuse and sexual insults from male passersby. In some cases, if women sellers ventured from the gutters onto the main pavement, police threatened to charge them with public obstruction. On a grander scale, women's suffrage activists nonetheless made use of spectacular public pageants, elaborate parades that featured floats, pantomime displays, and hundreds of women marching in line and wearing white to signify sexual purity and respectability in contrast to the dominant image of women in public—the prostitute.

In their more militant forms of public protest from 1912 until the outbreak of World War I, suffragettes directly attacked the public infrastructure. Feminist supporters of the WSPU disrupted postal services by putting bombs, acid, and black ink in the mailboxes of major cities. They cut telegraph and telephone wires, slashed paintings in art galleries, poured acid on golf courses, shattered the windows of London's West End department stores and clubs, and chained themselves to the gates of Hyde Park and Buckingham Palace. Through such actions women expressed the mixed message that property was less important than women's right to vote and that as consumers women could put pressure on business owners and politicians to support women's suffrage. Above all, such tactics of the women's suffrage movement challenged assumptions of women's submissiveness and ensured that the public recognized women as a forceful presence in the modern urban public sphere.

Women's participation in public urban life—riding omnibuses and walking the streets, visiting a museum and going shopping, canvassing and joining a political rally—demonstrates how any simple notion of separate spheres fails to describe the complexity of Victorian life. Women's gender identities were formed in public spaces as well as in their private homes. Some women adapted new meanings of femininity to the public realm, so that they could pursue their work and leisure in the city while still remaining suitably feminine. They could maintain a sense of "self-effacement" even while surrounded by thousands of strangers. They extended their domestic roles to assist the urban poor, children, the sick, and others in need of womanly care. For other women, however, the city offered an alternative to the middle-class domestic ideal as they sought out public spaces for intellectual engagement and pleasure as well as a necessary source of income. By the end of the Victorian period, when the safety bicycle popularized in the 1880s became a symbol of the New Woman's mobility, women of all classes representing a range of political perspectives not only participated in urban life, but also transformed many (though certainly not all) public urban spaces into locales that were home to women as well as to men. For the women matchmakers and suffragettes, the district visitors, and West End shoppers, claiming this public identity was part of a woman's daily experience.

**Amy Levy, "Ballade of an Omnibus," in *A London Plane-Tree and Other Verse* (London: T. Fisher Unwin, 1889), 21–22**

To see my love suffices me.
—*Ballades in Blue China*

Some men to carriages aspire;
On some the costly hansoms wait;
Some seek a fly, on job or hire;
Some mount the trotting steed, elate.
I envy not the rich and great,
A wandering minstrel, poor and free,
I am contented with my fate—
An omnibus suffices me.

In winter days of rain and mire
I find within a corner strait;
The 'busmen know me and my lyre
From Brompton to the Bull-and-Gate.
When summer comes, I mount in state
The topmost summit, whence I see
Croesus look up, compassionate—
An omnibus suffices me.

I mark, untroubled by desire,
Lucullus' phaeton and its freight.
The scene whereof I cannot tire,
The human tale of love and hate,
The city pageant, early and late
Unfolds itself, rolls by, to be
A pleasure deep and delicate.
An omnibus suffices me.

Princess, your splendour you require,
I, my simplicity; agree
Neither to rate lower nor higher.
An omnibus suffices me.

## NOTES

1. C. E. Humphry, *Manners for Women*, 2nd ed. (London: James Bowden, 1897), 18.
2. "The Unprotected Male," *The London Review* (August 20, 1864): 199.
3. See Lynda Nead, *Victorian Babylon: People, Streets and Images in Nineteenth-Century London* (New Haven, CT: Yale University Press), 63–64.
4. "The Female Street Orderlies," *Punch* (July 12, 1851): 26.
5. "The Library and Reading-Room of the British Museum," *The London Saturday Journal* (April 6, 1839): 220 and "The Reading-Room of the British Museum," *Leisure Hour* (October 23, 1880): 686.
6. Amy Levy, as quoted in Erika Diane Rappaport, *Shopping for Pleasure: Women in the Making of London's West End* (Princeton, NJ: Princeton University Press, 2000), 89.
7. Henry Mayhew, *London Labour and the London Poor*, Vol. 1 (New York: Dover Publications, 1968; 1861–1862), 457.

# 8

# WOMEN AND EMPIRE

Like many imperial writings, *Africana, or the Heart of Heathen Africa* (1882)—a text by the Presbyterian missionary Duff MacDonald—rallied support for the British presence in Africa by appealing to Victorian understandings of gender and the role of women. The tract, framed as an early anthropological survey of African customs and beliefs, asserted vast generalizations about Africans and their differences from Europeans, ignoring the obvious similarities as well as the internal divisions within each of these imagined communities. Again and again, MacDonald cited examples of how the natives of Central Africa defied Victorian gender binaries as proof of their supposed need for reform and instruction. The "dress of a man," he claimed, "does not differ from that of a woman, except that the latter may occasionally cover her breasts." In other areas, MacDonald presumed to identify a complete reversal of Victorian middle-class gender roles. He wrote that in the afternoons, it was the men who "do light work, as sewing, but a great many remain quite idle," while the women "will be found pounding maize. They are nearly as strong and tall as the men, perhaps owing to the heavy work they do." Most of all, however, like so many other colonizers, MacDonald justified imperialism with an appeal to British chivalry and an account of women's suffering. In a section titled "The Inferior Position of Women," he claimed that African women were treated as "beasts of burden," forced to kneel when addressing men—a practice, according to MacDonald, that along with slavery had "very rapidly disappeared in the region of the missionaries."[1]

*Africana, or the Heart of Heathen Africa* was by no means an exceptional text. During the 19th century, British missionaries and explorers created very similar accounts of colonized peoples throughout Africa, Asia, and all parts of the empire, using gender ideals to justify British imperialism. British officials portrayed colonized men alternatively as effeminate or brutish and colonized women as overly masculine, overtly sexualized, or as helpless victims of their own societies in need of British protection. Many Englishwomen defined their identities by drawing contrasts with women in the colonies. Still others gained national prominence by taking up reform issues in solidarity with colonized women—sometimes drowning out the very voices of the women whom they claimed to represent. Of course, Englishwomen held multiple, changing, sometimes contradictory views on the empire ranging from full support to open opposition to ignorance. In all cases, the empire emerged during this period as a major influence on Englishwomen's daily lives—affecting their political activities, their economic choices, and their leisure and entertainment. Imperialism fundamentally contributed to the context that shaped what it meant to be a woman in Victorian England.

By the 19th century, after the loss of the American colonies, India—the "jewel in the crown"—was Britain's most important colony in terms of economic riches, military resources, and cultural influences. English imperialism in India began under the East India Company, chartered by Queen Elizabeth in 1600. The company traded first mainly in Indian spices and cotton, then by the 18th century also in coffee and tea, and eventually by the 19th century in opium. By the mid-18th century, however, the East India Company responded to growing competition from French traders and the instability of Mughal rule by claiming greater administrative and territorial control. Company directors collected taxes and organized small armies for local Indian rulers, gradually extending their influence from the three main forts at Calcutta, Madras, and Bombay. In the 1770s and 1780s, the British government established more direct oversight of the actions of the East India Company (stipulating, for example, that the company could no longer declare war on its own initiative), but local traders maintained great independence at a time when it still took some six months to send a communication from Britain to India. During the early

19th century and first years of Victoria's reign, the East India Company took on even greater powers of political rule in much of South Asia. Company rulers intervened more directly in the lives of Indians by, for example, banning the practice of sati (in which a widow would burn herself on her husband's funeral pyre) in 1829, allowing Christian missionaries free movement to proselytize after 1833, and, according to Lord Thomas Babington Macaulay's famous 1835 Minute on Education, promoting the instruction of elite Indian men in English rather than in Sanskrit and Arabic.

While clearly the East India Company was involved in much more than trade by the Victorian period, two mid-Victorian crises in empire marked a shift in British imperial interests from trading empires to more direct control. The first was the Indian Rebellion, what Victorians often referred to as the "Sepoy Mutiny," beginning in May 1857. The conflict erupted as native members of the East India Company army refused to use Enfield rifle bullets greased with fat from cows and pigs (a practice abhorrent to Hindus and Muslims), but stemmed from much broader political causes related to the company's expansive territorial control. The British press reported extensively on the conflict, highlighting and exaggerating accounts of white British women killed and sexually assaulted. There was no firsthand evidence of Englishwomen raped by Indian men, despite the widespread focus on this topic by English writers. The British military responded with indiscriminate violence: burning entire villages, hanging prisoners, and shooting captured rebels from cannons. Hundreds of thousands of Indian men and civilians died during the conflict, along with approximately 11,000 British soldiers. In August 1858, the Government of India Act stripped the East India Company of all ruling powers and established formal control of much of India as a direct colony, while maintaining indirect rule of territories remaining under approximately 500 Indian princes.

The second major crisis of empire was the 1865 rebellion in Morant Bay, Jamaica. In October 1865, several hundred black Jamaicans led by the Baptist deacon Paul Bogle marched into Morant Bay to protest their continued oppression over three decades after the 1833 act of parliament abolished slavery in British colonies. The British colonial governor Edward Eyre responded by drawing on the example of the Indian Rebellion even though the Jamaican protesters exhibited far less violence and were far fewer in number. Governor Eyre declared martial law under which colonial officials tried and executed 354 Jamaicans. An additional 85 people were killed without trial. Colonial officials flogged hundreds of Jamaican men and women, and burned many of their houses. The Jamaican Rebellion sparked intense debate in England, resulting in the eventual creation of two factions: the Eyre Defense Aid supporting Governor Eyre's actions and the Jamaica Committee that initiated an ultimately unsuccessful campaign to have Eyre tried for murder. These debates revealed different models of British imperial rule and became intertwined with ongoing domestic debates about working-class male suffrage and women's rights. John Stuart Mill, a leading critic of Eyre, demanded that the rule of law be extended to the empire as in England. On the other side of the debate, John Ruskin and other major literary men such as Thomas Carlyle, Charles Dickens, and Alfred Lord Tennyson celebrated Eyre as an example of a heroic and strong masculine imperial ruler.

Together, the imperial crises of the Indian and Jamaican rebellions shifted the direction of British imperialism. The distinctions between the "responsible, self-governing" settler colonies that formed Canada, Australia, New Zealand, and South Africa and the predominantly nonwhite "dependent" colonies grew even starker. After these crises, British imperialists became less supportive of proposals to assimilate colonial subjects and increasingly adopted racist beliefs proclaiming that nonwhite subjects were incapable of self-government. Such views gained support from the works of scientific racists and anthropologists professionalizing in the second half of the century and, as we shall see, in some instances from English feminists as well.

These racial hierarchies served as the foundation for the imperial expansion that took place in Africa during the last decades of the 19th century. Until the early 1880s, European outposts in Africa mostly remained isolated in select West African trading coastal areas with few exceptions, including the British Cape Colony in the south and French Algeria in the north. Following the Berlin Conference on Africa (1884–1885) that set the imperial policy of recognizing territorial claims based upon "effective occupation" and "treaties of protection" signed by local leaders, Europeans raced to establish administrative and military dominion of the continent in the "Scramble for Africa." As in India, chartered trading companies first led the way for British imperial expansion. But rapidly, from the time of the Berlin Conference to the outbreak of World War I in 1914, European nations claimed control over the entire continent of Africa with the sole exceptions of Ethiopia and Liberia.

## WOMEN AND THE BRITISH ANTISLAVERY MOVEMENT

Many Englishwomen first became conscious of the scope of Britain's global power and expanding territorial possessions through their awareness of slavery. From the mid-15th century to the late 19th century, approximately 12 million men, women, and children were enslaved and shipped from Africa to the Americas. By 1670, English traders began a domination of the transatlantic slave trade that would continue to grow until the late 18th century and the eventual outlawing of the British slave trade by parliament in 1807. Profits from slavery fueled Britain's industrial economy. The goods produced on colonial slave plantations in the West Indies and North America—especially cotton, tobacco, and sugar, Britain's leading import from the 1750s to the 1820s—brought wealth to British merchants and manufacturers and new consumer goods to the general British public. The growth of the slave trade also altered the British population, particularly in port cities such as London and Liverpool, so that by the mid-to-late 18th century there were over 10,000 black Britons living in the country.

The law and court decisions proved contradictory and ambiguous as to the legality of slavery in England. In 1772, however, Lord Justice Mansfield set a crucial precedent by ruling that James Somerset, a former slave who had escaped from his master while living in England, could not be forced back into slavery in Jamaica. The Somerset case effectively established that slavery was illegal in England, but it was not until 1833 that parliament outlawed slavery in British colonies. The 1833 emancipation did not fully do away with all forms of forced labor. In fact, the law required freed slaves to continue to work for their former masters as unpaid "apprentices"—a system that lasted until 1838—and did not address forms of slavery in India or the conditions of forced indentured laborers. Slavery remained legal in some British territories, especially in Africa, until the 20th century. Furthermore, even after 1833, British manufacturers and traders profited from slave-produced cotton, sugar, and other commodities from the United States, South America, and elsewhere. Yet, despite these fundamental limitations, the 1833 emancipation presented a major victory and precedent for enslaved peoples and British abolitionists.

British women galvanized the abolition movement from its very beginnings in the late 1780s. As early as the 1790s, feminist writers such as Mary Wollstonecraft (1759–1797) linked the movements for women's rights and abolition in their demands for full equality. More often, female abolitionists such as Hannah More (1745–1833) and Sarah Stickney Ellis (1799–1872) gained support by highlighting women's distinct domestic roles as caretakers of their families and as moral, religious guides. Starting with the first major campaign of 1791, women led boycotts of slave-produced sugar, which over the course of the 18th century had transformed from a luxury good into a daily commodity in the diets of most English families. In 1800, *An Appeal to Englishwomen* called on the women of England to "reflect seriously upon their power, privilege, and responsibility" and to take action by boycotting all slave-produced products, including cotton calico for dresses as well as sugar.[2] At a time when William Wilberforce and most other male abolitionists still called for a gradualist approach, the Quaker Elizabeth Heyrick (1769–1831) demanded an immediate end to slavery. By the 1820s, Heyrick and other women abolitionists organized methods of direct political action that could involve the entire population, not only those with a voice in parliament. In addition to boycotting West Indian sugar, women wrote pamphlets, canvassed neighborhoods, and raised money through sewing groups, fundraising bazaars, and tea parties complete with custom-made china by Wedgewood and other manufacturers depicting the sufferings of enslaved women and children. Women abolitionists used such tactics to challenge male domination of the movement and to demonstrate women's power to take hold of political debate in the public sphere through economic and moral decisions made in the domestic realm.

In 1831, the former slave Mary Prince (b. 1788) brought widespread attention to the particular sufferings of women under slavery by publishing her life account, *The History of Mary Prince, a West Indian Slave*, the first and only known slave narrative by a woman from Britain's Caribbean colonies. Prince appealed directly to the English public to recognize and put an end to slavery. Her history, recorded by the writer Susanna Strickland (1803–1885) and privately published by the secretary of the Anti-Slavery Society, Thomas Pringle, told of her direct experience of slavery in Bermuda, Turks Island, and Antigua, before she eventually escaped from her owners while visiting London and claimed her freedom in 1828. Prince stressed the brutality of slavery—the inhumanity, beatings, sexual exploitation, degradation, and endless work. She also underscored how slavery debased Christian and domestic values. She herself had married the freeman Daniel James in

The radical 18th-century British writer Mary Wollstonecraft condemned slavery and women's lack of rights in her famous book on female equality, *A Vindication of the Rights of Women*, published in 1792. Drawing after a portrait by John Opie, ca. 1797. (Library of Congress)

Antigua, but was prevented from rejoining him since returning to the British colony would mean giving up her legal freedom in England. It was eventually revealed that Prince's narrative omitted details of her past that may have disrupted middle-class ideals of respectability, including her seven-year relationship with another man before her marriage—a point used by supporters of slavery in an attempt to discredit Prince. Overall, however, Prince's history proved an immensely popular and successful document detailing her resistance, survival, and moral decency in the face of shameless and cruel masters. Sold by female members of antislavery societies and widely read, *The History of Mary Prince* went into three editions the very first year of publication, stirring support for the 1833 Emancipation Act.

**Mary Prince, *The History of Mary Prince, a West Indian Slave*, ed. by Sara Salih (London: Penguin Books, 2004; 1831), 37–38**

I am often much vexed, and I feel great sorrow when I hear some people in this country say, that the slaves do not need better usage, and do not want to be free. They believe the foreign people [West Indians], who deceive them, and say slaves are happy. I say, Not so. How can slaves be happy when they have the halter round their neck and the whip upon their back? and are disgraced and thought no more of than beasts?—and are separated from their mothers, and husbands, and children, and sisters, just as cattle are sold and separated? Is it happiness for a driver in the field to take down his wife or sister or child, and strip them, and whip them in such a disgraceful manner?—women that have had children exposed in the open field to shame! There is no modesty or decency shown by the owner to his slaves; men, women, and children are exposed alike. Since I have been here I have often wondered how English people can go out into the West Indies and act in such a beastly manner. But when they go to the West Indies, they forget God and all feeling of shame, I think, since they can see and do such things. They tie up slaves like hogs—moor them up like cattle, and they lick them, so as hogs, or cattle, or horses never were flogged;—and yet they come home and say, and make some good people believe, that slaves don't want to get out of slavery. But they put a cloak about the truth. It is not so. All slaves want to be free—to be free is very sweet. I will say the truth to English people who may read this history that my good friend, Miss S - -, is now writing down for me. I have been a slave myself—I know what slaves feel—I can tell by myself what other slaves feel, and by what they have told me. The man that says slaves be quite happy in slavery—that they don't want to be free—that man is either ignorant or a lying person. I never heard a slave say so. I never heard a Buckra [white] man say so, till I heard tell of it in England. Such people ought to be ashamed of themselves. They can't do without slaves, they say. What's the reason they can't do without slaves as well as in England? No slaves here—no whips—no stocks—no punishment, except for wicked people. They hire servants in England; and if they don't like them, they send them away: they can't lick them. Let them work ever so hard in England, they are far better off than slaves. If they get a bad master, they give warning and go hire to another. They have their liberty. That's just what *we* want. We don't mind hard work, if we had proper treatment, and proper wages like English servants, and proper time given in the week to keep us from breaking the Sabbath. But they won't give it: they will have work—work—work, night and day, sick or well, till we are quite done up; and we must not speak up nor look amiss, however much we be abused. And then when we are quite done up, who cares for us, more than for a lame horse? This is slavery. I tell it, to let English people know the truth; and I hope they will never leave off to pray God, and call loud to the great King of England, till all the poor blacks be given free, and slavery done up for evermore.

After 1833, women abolitionists focused on the global campaign to end slavery and, through this political process, became increasingly aware of the limited rights of women. In 1838, over 700,000 women signed petitions to Queen Victoria opposing the apprenticeship system that replaced slavery—marking a major shift that occurred in the 1830s toward increasing acceptability of women as signers of political petitions. The first women's antislavery society was founded in Birmingham in 1825, and by the 1850s, there were more female than male societies. Participation as officers in these organizations trained women in key political skills and made them all the more aware of the restrictions placed on their rights. When, in 1840, the British Foreign Anti-Slavery Society held the first World Anti-Slavery Convention in London, male leaders banned female U.S. representatives from speaking or taking their seats as delegates. The moment became legendary, spurring the rebuffed U.S. representative Lucretia Mott (1793–1880) and her companion Elizabeth Cady Stanton (1815–1902) to organize the Seneca Falls Convention for women's rights eight years later.

British abolitionists remained divided over the role of women, but more and more women claimed a public voice in meetings and publications. Prominent writers, such as Harriet Martineau (1802–1876), Fanny Kemble (1809–1893), Barbara Bodichon (1827–1891), and Frances Power Cobbe (1822–1904), highlighted the wrongs of slavery against women. After the publication of her best-selling novel, *Uncle Tom's Cabin* (1852), Harriet Beecher Stowe toured England in 1853, 1856, and 1859, where she spoke against slavery at domestic gatherings and met with major figures including Queen Victoria. Stowe's sentimental portrayal proved a sensational hit in England, inspiring local theatrical performances, public readings, and household reenactments. Such events were often more entertaining than political, but they nonetheless brought unprecedented awareness to the abolition movement, rousing over half a million Englishwomen to sign a petition in 1852 appealing to their American sisters to end slavery.

### "Slavery in the United States," *Times* (November 29, 1852): 8

*This petition, written by Lord Shaftsbury, called for a gradual end to slavery. The official position of most British abolitionists at the time favored immediate abolition. Many objected to the original petition's wording and circulated revised versions demanding immediate emancipation. Over half a million women signed this version, and some 200,000 women signed the revised petitions.*

#### The Affectionate and Christian Address of Many Thousands of the Women of England to their Sisters, the Women of the United States of America

A common origin, a common faith, and, we sincerely believe, a common cause, urge us, at the present moment, to address you on the subject of that system of negro slavery which still prevails so extensively, and, even under kindly-disposed masters, with such frightful results, in many of the vast regions of the western world.

We will not dwell on the ordinary topics,—on the progress of civilization, on the advance of freedom everywhere, on the rights and requirements of the nineteenth century,—but we appeal to you very seriously to reflect, and to ask counsel of God how far such a state of things is in accordance with His holy word, the inalienable rights of immortal souls, and the pure and merciful spirit of the Christian religion.

We do not shut our eyes to the difficulties, nay, the dangers, that might beset the immediate abolition of that long established system; we see and admit the necessity of preparation for so great an event; but, in speaking of indispensable preliminaries, we cannot be silent on those laws of your country which, in direct contravention of God's own law, "instituted in the time of man's innocency [sic]," deny in effect to the slave the sanctity of marriage, with all its joys, rights, and obligations; which separate, at the will of the master, the wife from the husband, and the children from the parents. Nor can we be silent on that awful system which, either by statute or by custom, interdicts to any race of man, or any portion of the human family, education in the truths of the Gospel and the ordinances of Christianity.

A remedy applied to these two evils alone would commence the amelioration of their sad condition. We appeal to you, then, as sisters, as wives, and as mothers, to raise your voices to your fellow-citizens, and your prayers to God, for the removal of this affliction from the Christian world. We do not say these things in a spirit of

> self-complacency, as though our nation were free from the guilt it perceives in others. We acknowledge, with grief and shame, our heavy share in this great sin. We acknowledge that our forefathers introduced, nay, compelled, the adoption of slavery in those mighty colonies. We humbly confess it before Almighty God; and it is because we so deeply feel, and so unfeignedly avow, our own complicity, that we now venture to implore your aid to wipe away our common crime and our common dishonour.

Thousands also came to hear the radical abolitionist Sarah Parker Remond (1826–1894), a free black woman from Salem, Massachusetts, who was the first woman to speak publicly in Britain against slavery. After training with her brother Charles Lenox Remond, one of the few male delegates along with William Garrison who opposed the decision to exclude women from the 1840 World Anti-Slavery Convention, Sarah Remond emphasized the condition of enslaved women in her British antislavery speeches. She remained in England from 1859 to 1866, based in London where she attended Bedford College for Women, living with the college's founder Elisabeth Reid (1789–1866). Remond continued her work as a popular speaker during the American Civil War (1861–1865), countering the arguments of Southern Confederate supporters who sought British assistance. She was also one of the signers of the 1866 Ladies' Petition calling for women's suffrage.

Englishwomen proved essential to the abolitionist cause, but this did not necessarily translate into an opposition to imperialism. Indeed, many British abolitionists supported imperialism with the belief that British rule could hasten the end to global slavery. As the British Empire significantly expanded in Asia and Africa during the second half of the 19th century, racist paternalism and the rhetoric of benevolent imperialism more often replaced the early 19th-century radical abolitionist arguments of equality and human rights. Especially following the 1857 Indian Rebellion and the 1865 Jamaican Rebellion, popular racism gained greater influence in England.

In the aftermath of the Jamaican Rebellion as the public and parliament debated Governor Eyre's actions, Sarah Remond wrote in November 1865 to the London *Daily News* protesting the widespread defense of Eyre in the English press. Remond reminded English readers that Eyre's punishment of Jamaicans—including the hangings without trial, floggings, and destruction of property—directly contradicted the fundamental ideal upheld in the 1772 Somerset case: that all people, regardless of color, should be treated equally before the law. Although Remond initially celebrated the sisterhood and relative freedom from prejudice she experienced in England, she left the country in 1866 disillusioned by a sense of the growing popular racism and violence inherent within Britain's expanding empire.

## FEMALE EMIGRANTS, MISSIONARIES, AND REFORMERS

As with the abolition movement, British responses to imperialism revealed key disagreements concerning the Victorian "Woman Question." The 19th-century expansion of empire prompted debate over Englishwomen's public roles, their domestic duties, and their moral influence. The empire provided new geographical and intellectual spaces for Victorian women who traveled abroad or established new lives as emigrants. Although most Englishwomen never actually physically left the country, the existence of colonial territories nonetheless framed understandings of what it meant to be a woman in Victorian England.

Most emigrants leaving the country were single men. (This was not true for Ireland, where during the famine more women than men emigrated, many of them going to the United States in search of work as domestic servants.) Beginning in the 1830s, however, large numbers of Englishwomen emigrated, demonstrating the fluid boundaries between England and its existing and former colonies. Female emigrants primarily came from the working classes. Married and single women left England, seeking new opportunities chiefly in the United States and in British settler colonies with significant European populations: Australia, Canada, New Zealand, and South Africa. Despite advertisements promising new homes and riches, many women faced extreme hardship, starting with the emigrant ships widely condemned as scenes of sexual vice and violence. Still, given their limited options in England, most women made the decision to emigrate freely, sometimes with assistance from various philanthropic groups, such as the Family Colonisation Society, founded in 1849 by Caroline Chisholm (1808–1877).

**"Female Emigrant Ships,"** ***Times*** **(December 28, 1849): 6**

**To the Editor of the Times**

Sir,

Perceiving from your paper that a large sum has been lately raised in aid of female emigration, applicable in the first instance to the removal to Australia of the distressed needlewomen of London, I take it for granted that any information tending to throw light on their future destiny will be valued by those on whom the moral and general superintendence of this emigration will devolve. I hope, therefore, that you will give publicity to the enclosed extract from a letter recently received from Mr. Brookes King, a graduate of Cambridge, who was appointed in February last, on the recommendation of the Colonization Society, to the office of religious teacher on board the James Gibb emigrant ship, bound for New South Wales:

(Extract,)

"Off Sydney, June 11, 1849.

There were shocking scenes on board; continued attempts at mutiny, only put down by the strong arm, and threats of the pistol; while the coarse indecency of the women was most revolting. My idea of an emigrant ship, from what I have seen and heard since our arrival (our own is a favourable instance, from the strict discipline maintained), is that it is the hotbed of vice and brutality. The lowest prostitutes from the streets of London, with others of doubtful character, are found mixed with a few poor innocent girls, who find themselves pent up with such characters as these; the men, poor broken-down mechanics, or Chartists who have been once in York Castle; while young men and women just married are going out on a pure speculation, unable to do anything in particular, though they have passed themselves off for agriculturists. We are the latest of the arrivals. In some ships the scenes that have taken place are not to be told for depravity. The crew of the — have been imprisoned on arrival here, it being found that they had paired off with the single women, each taking his mate for the voyage, and the captain and officers the same. I know from my own eyesight that such was very nearly the case in the —. Gambling goes on to a great extent even with us, but we have at least kept up the appearance of good conduct on board."

However, other English adults and children emigrated not by choice but by force. Between 1787 and 1868, the government ordered the transportation of thousands of female convicts to Australia.

Women found guilty of stealing items as seemingly insignificant as a roll of flannel cloth could be transported for seven years or more. Women were more likely than men to be transported for their first charge of petty theft. In addition, during the last decades of the 19th century and well into the 20th, charity societies and state poor law unions sent tens of thousands of poor English girls and boys to settler colonies (in many cases without their parents' knowledge), where they worked as farm laborers and servants, often in isolated, abusive settings.

**"Trial of Amelia Payne,"** ***Old Bailey Proceedings Online*** **(January 1840), www.oldbaileyonline.org**

507. AMELIA PAYNE was indicted for stealing, on the 23rd of December, 1 handkerchief, value 3*s*., 3 sovereigns, 2 half-sovereigns, 1 half-crown, and 1 5*l*. promissory-note, the property of Henry Cook, from his person.

HENRY COOK. I am a labourer, I live in Yorkshire. I came up to London to buy some onions, and met the prisoner on the 23rd of December, at one o'clock in the morning—she spoke to me first, and asked me to give her a drop of gin—we went to the Three Tuns, public-house, and I gave her a little—I afterwards went with her to a house in West-street, and we went up stairs—I gave her a shilling, and the woman of the house a shilling—I was only to stay a short time—I was on the bed with threa [sic] prisoner—I had a pocket-book in my waistcoat-pocket, containing three sovereigns, two half-sovereigns, a half-crown, and a 5*l*. promissory-note—I fell asleep till about seven o'clock—the prisoner was then gone, and another woman came up, awoke me, and said some other persons wanted the bed—I did not seem willing to go, and she pushed me down—when I got to the passage I put my hand to my pocket, and found my money was gone—I saw the prisoner in the lower room with two men—I was pushed out—I went and told the policeman—I lost a handkerchief, which was taken from my hat—the prisoner was taken that morning, and my handkerchief was found on her neck, under her shawl—I never gave it to her—my money and note was gone—I did not take my waistcoat off.

*Prisoner*. You say you met me in Smithfield, which is false—you did not, and you had been with another female before me, in the early part of the night—you made a remark to me, in Farringdon-street, that Smithfield was a fine place to lose your pocket-book in—you gave me the shilling, and then you gave me the handkerchief, and said you would make it up to me next time you saw me—you said it was a 5*l*. note, and then a 10*l*. note, and now you differ again in your story. *Witness.* No, I did not—I met her in Smithfield—I had not been with another female—I did not say that Smithfield was a fine place to lose my pocket-book—I did not give her the handkerchief.

JOHN CALE (*City police-constable, No,* 236.) The prosecutor stated to me that he had been robbed—I went in search of the prisoner—I found her at No. 2, West-street, Smithfield—she had on a shawl, and the handkerchief taken from the prosecutor was taken off her neck at the watchhouse—the end of the handkerchief was visible under the shawl she had over it—I took her in the same house where the prosecutor had been—she was with another woman and two men.

*Prisoner's Defence.* He was very drunk at the time—I am innocent.

GUILTY. Aged 24.—Transported for Ten Years.

By the 1850s and 1860s (the period of the emerging women's movement), English writers drew attention to another social group along with convicts and the poor whose plight they imagined would best be solved by emigration, rather than domestic reform: unmarried middle-class women. The censuses of 1851 and 1861 showed that unmarried women outnumbered unmarried men and that the numbers of single women were increasing. Responding to the census data, the essayist William Rathbone Greg published a piece in *The National Review* asking "Why Are Women Redundant?" (1862). According to Greg, "there were in *England and Wales*, in 1851, 1,248,000 women in the prime of life, *i.e.* between the ages of twenty and forty years, who were unmarried, out of a total number of rather less than 3,000,000." Many of these single women would marry before the age of thirty, Greg acknowledged, but he proclaimed roughly 750,000 would remain "spinsters" because of "social disorders." "There is an enormous and increasing number of single women in the nation," Greg asserted, "a number quite disproportionate and quite abnormal; a number which, positively and relatively, is indicative of an unwholesome social state, and is both productive and prognostic of much wretchedness and wrong." Greg's greatest concern was that single women were "proportionally most numerous in the middle and upper classes," and that these were women "who have to earn their own living, instead of spending and husbanding the earnings of men; who, not having the natural duties and labours of wives and mothers, have to carve out artificial and painfully-sought occupations for themselves; who, in place of completing, sweetening, and embellishing the existence of others, are compelled to lead an independent and incomplete existence of their own." Colonial emigration was Greg's solution; he urged England's "redundant," "superfluous" single women to put aside their love of luxury—the "dainty living, splendid dressing, large houses, carriages *ad libitum*, gay society"—and embark on simpler though still respectable lives as potential wives in settler colonies where the proportion of single British men far outnumbered women.[3]

Even before Greg published his influential essay, various reformers pursued emigration as a response to deal with the increasing numbers of single, middle-class women in England. In 1851, the feminist Harriet Martineau wrote a series of articles arguing that educated, middle-class single women might find employment as governesses in Australia and eventually become the mothers of a new British imperial population. Ten years later, Maria Rye (1829–1903), a member of the Langham Place group and founder of the Society for Promoting the Employment of Women (1859), stressed the colonies' important role as potential sites of employment, rather than marriage, for genteel women. She personally assisted dozens of women emigrate and in 1862 created the Female Middle Class Emigration Society (which became administered by the Colonial Emigration Society in 1886 and then the British Women's Emigration Association) to help emigrant women find housing and employment and provide them with interest-free loans. Rye heralded the greater independence and opportunities for female emigrants, although she, much more so than Martineau, still believed that women should limit their paid employment to "feminine" positions such as teachers and governesses. Rye also drew on English domestic ideologies by professing that middle-class women—in contrast to working-class and Irish emigrants and indigenous women—would bring a much-needed "civilizing," moral influence to the colonies.

The quantifiable results of Rye's efforts remained limited. By 1879, the Female Middle Class Emigration Society had assisted only 215 women—a number that reached only a few hundred by the mid-1880s. Colonial farm laborers and servants were in much greater demand than governesses and teachers. However, the greater significance of such programs existed in the ways they shaped domestic English debates on women's work and independence. Moreover, even as writers such as Greg and reformers such as Martineau and Rye disagreed on the issue of women's employment, they shared an overall belief that elite women should be promoters of Britain's imperial mission—as purveyors of English values, moral influence, and ethnic heritage. The issues of colonial emigration and empire more generally served to coalesce and give prominence to mid-Victorian English feminists. In turn, this prominence reinforced the view of white, middle-class Englishwomen as the key symbol of Britain's so-called imperial "civilizing mission."

Englishwomen who traveled to imperial destinations as the wives and daughters of military officers, civil servants, and traders typically embraced this role even more openly. Unlike most female emigrants to settler colonies, these groups of women retained much closer ties to England. Englishwomen in India, for example, returned intermittently with their families to their home country for schooling, leaves, and retirement. The numbers of Englishwomen who traveled to colonial outposts in Asia, Africa, and the Middle East increased significantly over the course of the 19th century. At the beginning of the century, the population of Englishwomen living in India was negligible. Long-term interracial relationships between European men and native women were common, if not always publicly acknowledged. However, as the East India Company expanded its colonial governing powers in the early 19th century, it placed greater restrictions on family and sexual relations between rulers and ruled. By the end of Victoria's reign, there were tens of thousands of Englishwomen living in India.

In part, Englishwomen took advantage of improved travel. Steamships, the development of an overland route across Egypt, and eventually the opening of the Suez Canal in 1869 shortened what had been a trip of as long as six months around the Cape of Good Hope to a journey of several weeks. The 1858 Government of India Act establishing India as a colony, followed by the 1876 declaration of Queen Victoria as Empress of India, also marked the formal shift from trading empire to colonial rule. White women, or memsahibs, emerged as central actors in this process. Englishwomen in India raised children to become the next generation of imperial rulers and within their growing but in many ways increasingly insular communities they celebrated the artifacts of English culture. For example, the frequently republished *Complete Indian Housekeeper and Cook* (1888), jointly written by Flora Annie Steel (1847–1929) and Grace Gardiner (d. 1919), provided a sort of *Mrs. Beeton's Book of Household Management* for young memsahibs—complete with instructions on how to communicate with and discipline servants, treat scorpion and snake bites, prepare a proper English meal, and even cultivate English roses and strawberries in the hot Indian climate.

A Victorian lady poses with a hookah before a backdrop of the Egyptian pyramids, ca. 1880. (Hulton Archive/Getty Images)

During the 19th century, greater numbers of Englishwomen engaged in Christian missionary work, both based in England and traveling throughout the empire. At the very beginning of the evangelical missionary movement in the late 1780s, women such as the abolitionist Hannah More and her sisters directly linked missionary work in Africa and other foreign lands with their local efforts to reform England's poor "heathens." They promoted Sunday schools, sewing classes for girls, and women's benefit societies that taught domestic skills and Christian doctrine. The first foreign missionary societies formally barred women from serving as ordained missionaries, since nearly all Protestant denominations—except for the Quakers and others such as the Primitive Methodists—forbid female preachers. Women were also prevented from holding positions on the national committees, but they created their own auxiliary organizations, starting with such early groups as the Female Missionary Society in Northampton, established in 1805 as a wing of the Baptist Missionary Society. Missionary organizations actively recruited married men by the 1820s with the belief that their wives modeled values central to the vision of British civilization that missionary groups sought to impose—particularly the ideals of domesticity and separate spheres for men and women. Yet the actual work of these married women along with their single female counterparts extended far beyond the home as they significantly contributed to early missionary work as domestic visitors, pamphleteers, fund-raisers, writers for missionary journals, and teachers.

From the late 1850s to the 1870s, Englishwomen began to take an even greater role in foreign missionary service as Protestant evangelical sects became more accepting of female preaching (see Chapter 2). The Wesleyan Methodist Missionary Society was the first to engage single women officially as missionaries in 1858. Other missionary groups followed suit: the Baptist Missionary Society in 1866, the London Missionary Society in 1875, and the Church Missionary Society in 1887. The English Zenana Missionary Society and the Baptist Zenana Mission specifically recruited Englishwomen to provide medical care to Indian women. (Zenanas were parts of the household exclusively reserved for women in some, usually more elite Hindu and Muslim families.) By 1900, two thirds of foreign missionaries were women.

Early and mid-Victorian female missionaries and reformers typically approached their imperial service from a perspective that accepted the dominant ideal of separate spheres. Englishwomen paradoxically expanded upon this belief to justify their public social work in England and abroad by claiming their maternal role in relation to colonial subjects, above all to colonial girls and women. Throughout the 19th century, many Englishwomen based their imperial reforms on the assumption that colonial women remained voiceless, helpless, and thus in dire need of foreign assistance. The dominant evangelical approach thus reinforced notions of Englishwomen's proper association with domesticity as well as their alleged superiority over "heathen," or "savage" colonial women, rather than prompting any sustained questioning of women's status in England or Britain's imperial power abroad.

In India, for example, Englishwomen advocated reforms to improve the lives of Indian women and girls—and their efforts demonstrate how issues related to women and the family provided key contexts for the establishment of British imperial power. In 1829, the East India Company outlawed the practice of sati—an act that became synonymous with Indian culture, but was actually largely isolated to a minority of Hindus in the area around Calcutta. The women of England signed and sent petitions to parliament in support of the 1829 ban and collected funds to publicize the cause. Sati became a major issue for the British missionaries first granted access to India in 1813 and then allowed greater freedom of movement throughout the subcontinent in 1833 as they began a widespread attack on "Indian" cultural practices and traditions deemed contrary and inferior to British values.

From the ban on sati, British missionaries and reformers turned their attention to Indian female education. By the 1830s, Englishwomen took a leading role in creating schools and orphanages for girls in imperial contexts, working through such organizations as the Society for Promoting Female Education in China, India, and the East—an interdenominational missionary organization founded in 1834 that by the end of the century extended its scope to include Palestine, Syria, Japan, and parts of Africa. In addition to education, female reformers organized around issues of infanticide, child marriage, Hindu widow remarriage, polygamy, and age of consent legislation. Some, such as Mary Carpenter (1807–1877), who traveled to India several times during the 1860s and 1870s to establish schools for girls, created alliances with local Indian reformers. Even Carpenter, however, insisted that Indian schools needed Englishwomen to train local teachers. All of these various imperial campaigns generally shared a view of colonized cultural traditions as the source of female oppression, British intervention as the source of justice and female protection. A writer for *The Sentinel*, a Christian reform periodical, expressed this dominant assumption, claiming that the Indian population "looks mainly to England, and especially to the women of England, to guide and to sustain the efforts that are being made in India" to improve the lives of women and girls.[4]

**Mrs. Bayle Bernard, "The Position of Women in India," *The Englishwoman's Review* (July 1, 1868): 472–473, 482**

*This article provides a review of Mary Carpenter's influential book,* Six Months in India, *2 vols. (1868), which described her plan to establish schools for Indian girls and recruit Englishwomen to serve as teachers.*

"From the first to the last day of a residence in India," exclaims Miss Carpenter, "the point which most painfully strikes the mind is the position of Hindoo women;" and from all the evidence that is forthcoming we can well imagine that every benevolent heart must be similarly impressed. For girls of the lower class, literally no means of

> education whatever are provided (except a few mission schools for the children of converts), while the amount of maternal care they can receive may be judged by the fact that upon their mothers devolve the hardest of labours and lowest of tasks. Women of this class are employed as masons' labourers, mounting ladders, and carrying hods, while they are held in such degraded estimation that their very touch is deemed pollution, and accidental contact with any male workman exposes them to the vilest abuse. . . .
>
> If one Englishwoman [Mary Carpenter], who was only able to snatch a few months from the pressure of many other labours, to pay a short visit to that distant land, could yet excite so much interest and exercise so much influence, what might not be looked for if all who are passing years of leisure on the spot were to emulate her noble example? Let them throw their hearts and souls into the work, and determine never to rest until they have raised their Eastern sisters to their own level; and then may the women of India at last attain a position honourable to themselves and to England, instead of, as is now so generally the case, filling one which can only be contemplated with feelings of shame and sorrow.

There were, however, some who challenged such clear-cut divisions between "East" and "West" represented by portrayals of oppressed colonial women and enlightened Englishwomen. Fanny Parks (1794–1875), for example, lived in India with her husband, a civil servant for the East India Company, from 1822 to 1845. Her two-volume account of her life and travels in India, *Wanderings of a Pilgrim in Search of the Picturesque* (1850), highlighted the universal oppression of all women, rather than the exceptional exploitation of Indian women. Parks presented sati as a patriarchal practice—rather than an inherently Indian or religious rite—that stemmed from the desire to deprive widows of their property. She also favorably contrasted the Indian treatment of women to the English in several areas, noting that while Indian dress allowed women freedom of movement, stays bound Englishwomen by restricting their bodies "as a lobster in its shell." Comparing the fates of Hindu and English married women and widows with her friend the Baiza Bai, the former queen of Gwalior, Parks stressed "the severity of the laws of England with respect to married women, how completely *by law* they are the slaves of their husbands, and how little hope there is of redress." The two women concluded: "The fate of women and of melons is alike. 'Whether the melon falls on the knife or the knife on the melon, the melon is the sufferer.' "[5]

Yet this sort of universalism remained rare. For the most part, Englishwomen who traveled throughout the empire as well as those who remained in England drew on images of oppressed colonial women to justify British imperial expansion. Even many British feminists who challenged the very idea of separate spheres and campaigned for greater rights for women in the second half of the century did so by stressing their unique knowledge and authority to speak for women in India, Africa, the Middle East, and other imperial territories. These "imperial feminists" supported the empire, but claimed that British women needed suffrage to ensure the protection of colonial women more often than not represented as silent victims.

Josephine Butler (1828–1906), for instance, had led the crusade for the 1886 repeal of the Contagious Diseases Acts in Britain, which regulated prostitution and sought to curb the spread of venereal disease by detaining women identified as prostitutes for medical examinations (see Chapter 1). Imperial governments passed similar legislation throughout the British Empire—in Hong Kong (1857 and 1867), Corfu (1861), India (1864 and 1868), Canada (1865), Ceylon (1867), Jamaica (1867), Queensland (1868), Barbados (1868), Cape Colony (1868 and 1885), New Zealand (1869), Trinidad (1869), Singapore (1870), Victoria (1878), Tasmania (1879), and Fiji (1882), among other locales. After 1886, Butler turned her attention to the repeal the Indian Cantonments Act of 1864 and the Indian Contagious Diseases Act of 1868. She stood as a harsh critic of the corrupt imperial government that supported regulation, while prophesying that benevolent rule recognizing women's rights would ultimately strengthen Britain's empire. Butler proclaimed in 1893 that repeal in India—dependent in her view on the tireless efforts of Englishwomen—would be "a just and purifying victory for Imperial England."[6] Such nationalist, imperialist arguments became mainstays in women's journals, especially *The Englishwoman's Review* (1866–1910), which developed as the principal feminist periodical following the *English Woman's Journal* (1858–1864).

The imperial context provided one of the most influential foundations for late-Victorian feminist activists and readers, shaping arguments on suffrage, employment, education, legal reform, and access to the public sphere for the vast majority of Englishwomen who never traveled beyond the country's borders. At the same time, antisuffragists such as Eliza Lynn Linton (1822–1898) often framed their critique of English feminists by asserting that they presented an unnaturally independent, disruptive example of feminine behavior for women in the colonies—an example that could ultimately weaken rather than strengthen British imperial authority.

**Eliza Lynn Linton, "The Wild Women as Social Insurgents,"**
***The Nineteenth Century* (October 1891): 604**

Unlike the female doctors, who, we believe, undertake no proselytising, and are content to merely heal the bodies while leaving alone the souls and lives of the "purdah-women," the zenana missionaries go out with the express purpose of teaching Christian theology and personal independence. We hold each to be an impertinence. Like the Jews, the Hindu men have ample means of judging of our Christianity, and what it has done for the world which professes it. They also have ample means of judging the effects of our womanly independence, and what class of persons we turn out to roam about the world alone. If they prefer this to that, they have only to say so, and the reform will come from within, as it ought—as all reforms must, to be of value. If they do not, it is not for our Wild Women to carry the burden of their unrest into the quiet homes of the East; which homes, too, are further protected by the oath taken by the sovereign to respect the religion of these Eastern subjects. When we have taught the Hindu women to hunt and drive, play golf and cricket, dance the cancan on a public stage, make speeches in Parliament, cherish "dear boys" at five-o'clock tea, and do all that our Wild Women do, shall we have advanced matters very far? Shall we have made the home happier, the family purer, the women themselves more modest, more chaste? Had we not better cease to pull at ropes which move machinery of which we know neither the force nor the possible action? Why all this interference with others? Why not let the various peoples of the earth manage their domestic matters as they think fit? Are our Wild Women the ideal of female perfection? Heaven forbid! But to this distorted likeness they and their backers are doing their best to reduce all others.

## THE EMPIRE IN ENGLAND: PEOPLE, CONSUMPTION, ENTERTAINMENT, AND IDENTITY

The empire affected the lives of women living in England everyday in numerous, often more subtle, unrecognized ways that extended beyond the political and religious movements for abolition, imperial reform, and women's rights. Whether or not Englishwomen explicitly supported or questioned Britain's imperial power, their daily routines, leisure activities, and very notions of identity developed within the context of imperialism.

In urban areas, the demographic and economic connections of empire grew visible in more diverse metropolitan populations. While the "English" people had continuously been reshaped by immigration, by the 19th century, diasporic communities of colonial migrants from Asia, Africa, and the Caribbean reflected the growth of the British Empire. Many colonial peoples came to England temporarily—as skilled workers, servants, entertainers, activists, and students. Others established homes and raised families in England. Such communities at times suffered violent attacks and exclusion, particularly during periods of imperial crisis, but at other moments experienced greater integration. Fanny Eaton (ca. 1835–ca. 1924), for example, a "mixed race" woman born in Jamaica, settled in London in the 1850s where she married

An 1861 portrait of the Pre-Raphaelite model Fanny Eaton, by Joanna Boyce Wells. (Yale Center for British Art, Paul Mellon Fund)

a portrait photographer and worked as a charwoman. During the late 1850s and 1860s, Eaton supplemented her income by sitting as a model for several artists associated with the Pre-Raphaelite movement, including the siblings Simeon (1840–1905) and Rebecca Solomon (1832–1886), Albert Moore (1841–1893), Joanna Wells (1831–1861), John Everett Millais (1829–1896), and Dante Gabriel Rossetti (1828–1882), who celebrated Eaton as a striking beauty comparable to the famous model Jane Morris (1839–1914). Little is known about Eaton's life beyond the paintings that remain, but she went on to raise at least seven children, living in London and, for a period, on the Isle of Wight, working as a seamstress and a cook.

In rural as well as urban areas, the empire involved Englishwomen in new commercial networks and commodity cultures—a point that female abolitionists made explicit in their boycotts of slave-produced sugar and textiles. Drawing on the abolitionists and the more general philanthropic tradition of charity bazaars, late-Victorian women developed global commercial networks to promote their humanitarian causes. In Constantinople, for instance, Quaker women led the humanitarian effort to aid victims of the 1896 Armenian massacres by setting up missions where orphans and widows manufactured toys, rugs, and needlework—products then distributed to the English public through "Drawingroom Sales made by the many kind ladies in England."[7]

Without necessarily sharing such awareness of the global context behind their daily routines, women in England also gained access to a greater variety of foods and other products dependent on colonial networks: sugar, tea, coffee, cocoa, wheat, dairy products, and meat (see Chapter 3) as well as baby bottle nipples made from Indian rubber, soap from West African palm oil, and textiles from Indian and Egyptian cotton or Australian and South African wool. During the second half of the 19th century as the overall English standard of living rose, new patterns of consumption included an ever-wider array of imperial products for sale in English homes.

The advertisements—many of them aimed at women—that developed alongside these new consumer goods reinforced the social and cultural values of imperialism. Such advertisements popularized the racist ideologies that gained prominence in anthropological and scientific circles after the 1850s, sending messages that reinforced racial hierarchies to all classes of the English population, not only to the intellectual elite. Particularly during the last decades of the century, the growth of mass advertising brought endless images of empire into women's homes. Tins of Huntley and Palmers' biscuits, for example, displayed a group of British men taking a break from their hunting expedition in India; they sit on crates, served tea and biscuits by effeminate looking Indian servants, while regal, tamed elephants carry the limp bodies of shot tigers in the background. Epps's Cocoa displayed a jolly John Bull—Britain's Uncle Sam figure representing the people—drinking a hot cup of cocoa while sitting astride the globe.

Most of all, soap advertisements appealed to customers by selling cleanliness, racial "purity," and imperial supremacy. In the mid-1880s, just at the beginning of the European "Scramble for Africa" following the Berlin Conference (1884–1885), Pears soap launched a series of advertisements in which black or white working-class children and adults were made "clean." In one characteristic example, a young though notably voluptuous white child washes the face of a black woman. These and other racist advertisements sold products by selling empire and by encouraging Englishwomen to define themselves as "pure," "white," moral, and powerful in comparison

An 1887 Pears' Soap advertisement from *Puck* (English edition) aligning whiteness with cleanliness. (Beinecke Library)

to the colonial "other" represented as irrational, infantile, and in need of guidance.

English popular culture mirrored these distinctions in a manner that often stressed women's roles as representatives alternatively of colonial "savagery" and of English "civilization." Early in the 19th century, the Khoisan woman known by her Afrikaans and Anglicized names as Saartjie or Sara Baartman (ca. 1770s–1815) was brought by two men—one a former British naval surgeon and doctor at the Cape Town Slave Lodge—from South Africa to London. For several years starting in 1810, Baartman toured as a performer in variety shows, where she became known to the public as the Hottentot Venus. "Hottentot" was a derogatory colonial term for the Khosian people. Humiliated and literally treated as a caged spectacle, Baartman's very title evoked contrasts between "savage" and "civilized" physical ideals. The English public and later scientific accounts fixated on Baartman's sexual organs, postulating that she more closely resembled the orangutan than her fellow human. She left London for Paris in 1814, where she continued to be exhibited. Reduced to a type representing "Hottentot women," and, for some, the supposedly deviant sexuality of all women, she became a common reference point in the writings of scientific racists, such as Robert Knox's influential *Races of Men* (1850). After her death, the preeminent French naturalist and anatomist Georges Cuvier dissected her corpse, embalming select organs and reconstructing her skeleton for display at Paris museums. He also made a full plaster cast of her body as well as wax details of her genitals and buttocks. From May through October 1889, just months after the brutal Jack-the-Ripper murders in London involving the public dismemberment of victims' bodies, millions of visitors viewed a massive illustration of Sara Baartman's figure at the Universal Exhibition of Paris. Only in 2002 did the Musée de l'Homme finally return Baartman's remains to South Africa for burial.

Baartman provides one of the clearest examples of how scientific and popular racism combined ideas of racial and sexual deviancy, but her case was by no means an isolated incident. Victorian museum displays and colonial exhibitions presented objects from around the world alongside narratives of British military force, technological expertise, commercial strength, and moral superiority—typically conveyed by sexualized accounts of polygamy, harems, and zenanas. The rapid expansion of the British Empire during the 1880s and 1890s made such themes ubiquitous in imperial exhibits featuring live representatives on tour from the colonies. Other pervasive entertainments—music hall shows, blackface minstrels, popular songs, melodramas, pantomimes, magic lantern slide presentations, children's games, and literature—similarly promoted ideas of British imperial superiority based on the supposed racial and sexual inferiority of colonized peoples.

By the end of the century, women played a greater role as authorities influencing the work of major British imperial and scientific societies, marking an extension of their engagement from the social sphere to the professional—yet this greater professional voice for women met equal amounts of celebration and censure. Middle-class women trained in geography and cartography had long specialized in writing children's primers outlining the territories and peoples of Britain's empire. These women focused their talents in a suitably feminine field when denied the liberty and resources to travel abroad themselves. During the last decades of the century, several women gained fame as imperial explorers in their own right. Born in Yorkshire, Isabella Bishop (née Bird, 1831–1904) traveled before and after her brief, yet happy marriage to John Bishop that lasted from 1881 until his death in 1886. Bishop explored many parts of Britain's former and expanding empire and other parts of the globe, including the United States, Canada, Tibet, Persia, Korea, and China. In 1892, she was the first woman to be admitted as a fellow to the Royal Geographical Society. Like Bishop, Mary Kingsley (1862–1900) emerged as one of England's most influential travel writers. Kingsley spent the first decades of her life isolated in her middle-class home, caring for her ailing parents in the years before they died in 1892. After their death, Kingsley set out alone to explore the West African coast. Her *Travels in West Africa* (1897) soon established her as an expert with popular and scientific audiences. However, Kingsley rejected all suggestions that she represented the New Woman. In 1899, she refused to sign a petition demanding women's full and equal admission to learned societies, writing to the Royal Geographical Society's secretary, "these androgynes I have no use for."[8]

**Mary Kingsley, *Travels in West Africa*, abridged and introduced by Elspeth Huxley (London: Everyman, 1987; 1897), 14–15**

It was the beginning of August '93 when I first left England for "the Coast". . . . So with a feeling of foreboding gloom I left London for Liverpool—none the more cheerful for the matter-of-fact manner in which

> the steamboat agents had informed me that they did not issue return tickets by the West African lines of steamers.
>
> I will not go into the details of that voyage here, much as I am given to discursiveness. They are more amusing than instructive, for on my first voyage out I did not know the Coast, and the Coast did not know me, and we mutually terrified each other. I fully expected to get killed by the local nobility and gentry; they thought I was connected with the World's Women's Temperance Association, and collecting shocking details for subsequent magic-lantern lectures on the liquor traffic; so fearful misunderstandings arose, but we gradually educated each other, and I had the best of the affair; for all I had got to teach them was that I was only a beetle and fetish hunter, and so forth, while they had to teach me a new world, and a very fascinating course of study I found it. And whatever the Coast may have to say against me—for my continual desire for hairpins, and other pins, my intolerable habit of getting into water, the abominations full of ants, that I brought into their houses, or things emitting at unexpectedly short notice vivid and awful stenches—they cannot but say that I was a diligent pupil, who honestly tried to learn the lessons they taught me so kindly, though some of those lessons were hard to a person who had never previously been even in a tame bit of tropics, and whose life for many years had been an entirely domestic one in a University town.
>
> One by one I took my old ideas derived from books and thoughts based on imperfect knowledge and weighed them against the real life around me, and found them either worthless or wanting.

Women's experiences with imperialism were thus notably diverse, but they nonetheless highlight the global context influencing English domestic life and the multiple points at which racial and gender identity intersected. For many Englishwomen, the causes of racial and gender equality existed hand in hand. For others, the empire provided a platform from which to argue for Englishwomen's greater access to public debate and political power in ways that often silenced the voices of colonized women. Still others such as Mary Kingsley made extensive use of their imperial role to break out of the home without ever explicitly challenging many of the social and political confines placed on women—although Kingsley herself also sought and gained political influence over government policies in West Africa. For women of color, England offered the extremes of imperial violence and liberation along with all of the daily routines that made them part of English society. Until recently in some cases, there exists relatively little or no historical scholarship on the lives of women such as Sara Baartman, Mary Prince,

Fanny Eaton, and Sarah Remond, in contrast to the revived interest in the Crimean nurse Mary Seacole (1805-1881), voted in 2004 to be the greatest Black Briton. Despite her status as a best-selling author, Mary Prince disappears from the historical record after 1833. Rather than interpreting these silences as absence, it is best to understand such gaps in the historical record—as they exist unevenly for all women in comparison to men—as signs of the power relations of the period that demand greater reflection and consideration.

*****

In all aspects of their daily lives, Victorian women of very different backgrounds negotiated the fluid boundaries between public and private worlds in ways that made any solid demarcation of these divisions impossible. George Eliot (1819–1880) stressed this fundamental point in her novel *Felix Holt, the Radical* (1866), declaring "There is no private life which has not been determined by a wider public life."[9] This was particularly true in matters of gender. Food preparation, for example, connected women with commercial exchanges taking place in city markets and imperial territories. It was through the newspaper used to wrap butter brought into the home where the Pre-Raphaelite model Elizabeth Siddal (1829–1862) worked as a servant that she first discovered Tennyson's poems and realized she wanted to write poetry. Women engaged the wider world by sending letters through the penny post and riding aloft omnibuses. Miners and match girls marched through London's streets, as did middle-class philanthropists and temperance workers. Some women traveled to and from imperial vistas, and all women in England lived lives influenced by the larger context of empire.

That some women described such actions beyond the home as remaining within the private domestic sphere suggests more about the Victorian ideal of womanhood than women's daily lives. For many Victorian women, the ideal of female domesticity served to provide them access to new venues in England and abroad. At the same time, this ideal restricted women's economic and intellectual freedoms. Women of varied political, class, and racial backgrounds confronted the legal and cultural treatment of women as non-persons. What this meant for individual women ranged from actual slavery for Mary Prince (b. 1788) to inequality under the law for Caroline Norton (1808–1877) to the lack of suffrage for Emmeline Pankhurst (1858–1928). Appreciating the diverse ways in which women both felt the limits of and employed concepts of femininity challenges overly simplified models of separate spheres for men and women, which present women as isolated and largely absent from history, as silent bystanders who remained uninvolved and unaffected by major events. This book demonstrates that rather than enduring isolation, women sustained vibrant female-oriented networks extending beyond the home: women's friendships, their religious communities, their work, and their social ties. They also redefined the terms and tactics of political action to reveal the essential contributions coming from women such as those who petitioned against the New Poor Law, boycotted sugar, or went on "strike" against bearing more children without the resources to raise them. In the end, George Eliot was right: Victorian women from all walks of life merged their public and private worlds to fundamentally shape the age in which they lived.

## NOTES

1. Duff MacDonald, *Africana, or the Heart of Heathen Africa,* Vol. 1 (London: Dawsons of Pall Mall, 1969; 1882), 15, 29, 35. The term "imagined communities" referring to the cultural construction of national identities comes from Benedict Anderson's *Imagined Communities: Reflections on the Origins and Spread of Nationalism* (London: Verso, 1983).
2. *An Appeal to Englishwomen* (London: Jarrold and Sons, 1800), 3.
3. William Rathbone Greg, "Why Are Women Redundant?" *The National Review* 28 (April 1862): 441, 436, 447, emphasis in original.
4. "Infant Marriage and Enforced Widowhood in India," *The Sentinel* 12 (September 1890): 102.
5. Fanny Parkes [Parks], *Begums, Thugs and White Mughals: The Journals of Fanny Parkes,* selected and introduced by William Dalrymple (London: Sickle Moon Books, 2002), 202, 256, emphasis in original.
6. Josephine Butler, as quoted in Antoinette Burton, *Burdens of History: British Feminists, Indian Women, and Imperial Culture, 1865–1915* (Chapel Hill: University of North Carolina Press, 1994), 150.
7. Ann Mary Burgess (1904), as quoted in Michelle Tusan, "The Business of Relief Work: A Victorian Quaker in Constantinople and Her Circle," *Victorian Studies* 51.4 (Summer 2009): 645.
8. Mary Kingsley, letter to Scott Keltie (November 29, 1899), as quoted in Cheryl McEwan, *Gender, Geography and Empire: Victorian Women Travellers in West Africa* (Burlington, VT: Ashgate, 2000), 57 and D. J. Birkett, "Kingsley, Mary Henrietta (1862–1900)," in *Oxford Dictionary of National Biography* (Oxford: Oxford University Press, September 2004; online edition, January 2008).
9. George Eliot, *Felix Holt, the Radical* (1866), as quoted in Rosemary Ashton, "Evans, Marian [George Eliot] (1819–1880)," *Oxford Dictionary of National Biography* (Oxford University Press, 2004; online edition 2008).

# FURTHER READING

*Sources are listed only once under the most appropriate section, although many are relevant to multiple chapters.*

## INTRODUCTION: VICTORIAN CONTEXTS AND IDEALS OF WOMANHOOD


Cannadine, David. *The Decline and Fall of the British Aristocracy*. New Haven, CT: Yale University Press, 1990.

Davidoff, Leonore. "Gender and the Great Divide: Public and Private in British Gender History." *Journal of Women's History* 15, no. 1 (2003): 11–27.

Gleadle, Kathryn. *British Women in the Nineteenth Century*. New York: Palgrave, 2001.

Lewis, Jane. *Women in England, 1870–1950: Sexual Divisions and Social Change*. Bloomington: Indiana University Press, 1984.

Matthew, Colin, ed. *The Nineteenth Century: The British Isles, 1815–1901*. Oxford: Oxford University Press, 2000.

McCord, Norman. *British History, 1815–1906*. Oxford: Oxford University Press, 1991.

Mitchell, Brian R., and Phyllis Deane. *Abstract of British Historical Statistics*. Cambridge, U.K.: Cambridge University Press, 1971.

Mitchell, Sally. *Daily Life in Victorian England*. Westport, CT: Greenwood Press, 1996.

Perkin, Joan. *Victorian Women*. New York: New York University Press, 1995.

Rendall, Jane. "Women and the Public Sphere." *Gender and History* 11, no. 3 (1999): 475–488.

Ross, Ellen. "Adventures among the Poor." In *Slum Travelers: Ladies and London Poverty, 1860–1920*. Berkeley: University of California Press, 2007.

Ruskin, John. *Sesame and Lilies*, edited and with an introduction by Deborah Epstein Nord and with essays by Elizabeth Helsinger, Seth Koven, and Jan Marsh. New Haven, CT: Yale University Press, 2002.

Steinbach, Susie. *Women in England, 1760–1914: A Social History*. London: Weidenfeld and Nicholson, 2004.

Steinbach, Susie. *Understanding the Victorians: Politics, Culture and Society in Nineteenth-Century Britain*. London: Routledge, 2012.

Vickery, Amanda. "Historiographical Review: Golden Age to Separate Spheres? A Review of the Categories and Chronology of English Women's History." *Historical Journal* 36, no. 2 (1993): 383–414.

## CHAPTER 1: WOMEN AND THE STATE

Clark, Anna. *The Struggle for the Breeches: Gender and the Making of the British Working Class*. Berkeley: University of California Press, 1995.

Durbach, Nadja. *Bodily Matters: The Anti-Vaccination Movement in England, 1853–1907*. Durham, NC: Duke University Press, 2005.

Epstein, James, and Dorothy Thompson, eds. *The Chartist Experience: Studies in Working-Class Radicalism and Culture, 1830–1860*. London: Macmillan Press Ltd., 1982.

Fraser, Stuart. "Leicester and Smallpox: The Leicester Method." *Medical History* 24, no. 3 (1980): 315–332.

Gleadle, Kathryn. *Borderline Citizens: Women, Gender, and Political Culture in Britain, 1815–1867*. Oxford: Oxford University Press, 2009.

Gleadle, Kathryn, and Sarah Richardson, eds. *Women in British Politics, 1760–1860: The Power of the Petticoat*. New York: St. Martin's Press, 2000.

Hall, Catherine, Keith McClelland, and Jane Rendall. *Defining the Victorian Nation: Class, Race, Gender and the Reform Act of 1867*. Cambridge, U.K.: Cambridge University Press, 2000.

Hammerton, James A. *Cruelty and Companionship: Conflict in Nineteenth-Century Married Life*. London: Routledge, 1992.

Holcombe, Lee. *Wives and Property: Reform of the Married Women's Property Law in Nineteenth-Century England*. Toronto, ON: University of Toronto Press, 1983.

Hollis, Patricia. *Ladies Elect: Women in English Local Government, 1865–1914*. Oxford: Clarendon Press, 1987.

Holton, Sandra Stanley. *Suffrage Days: Stories from the Women's Suffrage Movement*. London: Routledge, 1996.

Jones, David. "Women and Chartism." *History* 68, no. 222 (1983): 1–21.

Kidd, Alan. *State, Society and the Poor in Nineteenth-Century England*. New York: St. Martin's Press, 1999.

Lees, Lynn Hollen. *The Solidarities of Strangers: The English Poor Laws and the People, 1700–1948*. Cambridge, U.K.: Cambridge University Press, 1998.

Norton, Caroline. *Caroline Norton's Defense: English Laws for Women in the Nineteenth Century*, introduced by Joan Huddleston. Chicago: Academy, 1982.

Purvis, June, and Sandra Stanley Holton, eds. *Votes for Women*. London: Routledge, 2000.

Schwarzkopf, Jutta. *Women in the Chartist Movement*. New York: St. Martin's Press, 1991.

Shanley, Mary Lyndon. *Feminism, Marriage, and the Law in Victorian England*. Princeton, NJ: Princeton University Press, 1989.

Surridge, Lisa. *Bleak Houses: Marital Violence in Victorian Fiction*. Athens: Ohio University Press, 2005.

Thompson, Dorothy. *The Chartists: Popular Politics in the Industrial Revolution*. New York: Pantheon Books, 1984.

Walkowitz, Judith. *Prostitution and Victorian Society: Women, Class, and the State*. Cambridge, U.K.: Cambridge University Press, 1980.

## CHAPTER 2: RELIGION, SPIRITUALISM, AND DEATH

Garnett, Jane. "Religious and Intellectual Life." In *The Nineteenth Century: The British Isles, 1815–1901*, edited by Colin Matthew, 192–227. Oxford: Oxford University Press, 2000.

Herringer, Carol Engelhardt. "The Revival of the Religious Life: The Sisterhoods." In *The Oxford Handbook of the Oxford Movement*, edited by Stewart J. Brown, Peter Nockles, and James Pereiro. Oxford: Oxford University Press, forthcoming 2014.

Herringer, Carol Engelhardt. *Victorians and the Virgin Mary: Religion and Gender in England, 1830–85*. Manchester, U.K.: Manchester University Press, 2008.

Inglis, Kenneth Stanley. *Churches and the Working Classes in Victorian England*. London: Routledge and Kegan Paul, 1963.

Jalland, Pat. *Death in the Victorian Family*. Oxford: Oxford University Press, 1996.

Larsen, Timothy. *A People of One Book: The Bible and the Victorians*. Oxford: Oxford University Press, 2011.

Lloyd, Jennifer. *Women and the Shaping of British Methodism: Persistent Preachers, 1807–1907*. Manchester, U.K.: Manchester University Press, 2009.

Malmgreen, Gail, ed. *Religion in the Lives of English Women, 1760–1930*. Bloomington: Indiana University Press, 1986.

Mangion, Carmen. *Contested Identities: Catholic Women Religious in Nineteenth-Century England and Wales*. Manchester, U.K.: Manchester University Press, 2008.

McLeod, Hugh. *Class and Religion in the Late Victorian City*. London: Croom Helm, 1974.

McLeod, Hugh. *Religion and Society in England, 1850–1914*. New York: St. Martin's Press, 1996.

Melnyk, Julie. *Victorian Religion: Faith and Life in Britain*. Westport, CT: Praeger, 2008.

Morgan, Sue, and Jacqueline deVries, eds. *Women, Gender and Religious Cultures in Britain, 1800–1940*. London: Routledge, 2010.

Murdoch, Lydia. "'Suppressed Grief': Mourning the Death of British Children and the Memory of the 1857 Indian Rebellion." *The Journal of British Studies* 51, no.2 (2012): 364–392.

Prochaska, Frank K. *Women and Philanthropy in Nineteenth-Century England*. Oxford: Clarendon Press, 1980.

Strange, Julie-Marie. *Death, Grief and Poverty in Britain, 1870–1914*. Cambridge, U.K.: Cambridge University Press, 2005.

Tromp, Marlene. "Spirited Sexuality: Sex, Marriage, and Victorian Spiritualism." *Victorian Literature and Culture* 31, no. 1 (2003): 67–81.

Valman, Nadia. "Women Writers and the Campaign for Jewish Civil Rights in Early Victorian England." In *Women in British Politics, 1760–1860*, edited by Kathryn Gleadle and Sarah Richardson, 93–114. New York: St. Martin's Press, 2000.

Walker, Pamela. *Pulling the Devil's Kingdom Down: The Salvation Army in Victorian Britain*. Berkeley: University of California Press, 2001.

## CHAPTER 3: FAMILY, HOME, AND LEISURE

Adams, Annmarie. *Architecture in the Family Way: Doctors, Houses, and Women, 1870–1900*. Buffalo, NY: McGill-Queen's University Press, 1996.

Auerbach, Jeffrey. *The Great Exhibition of 1851: A Nation on Display*. New Haven, CT: Yale University Press, 1999.

Bailey, Peter. *Leisure and Class in Victorian England: Rational Recreation and the Contest for Control, 1830–1885*. London: Routledge and Kegan Paul, 1978.

Bailey, Peter. *Popular Culture and Performance in the Victorian City*. Cambridge, U.K.: Cambridge University Press, 1998.

Banks, Joseph Ambrose. *Prosperity and Parenthood: A Study of Family Planning among the Victorian Middle Classes*. London: Routledge and Kegan Paul, 1954.

Cohen, Deborah. *Household Gods: The British and Their Possessions*. New Haven, CT: Yale University Press, 2006.

Davidoff, Leonore. *Thicker Than Water: Siblings and Their Relations, 1780–1920*. Oxford: Oxford University Press, 2012.

Davidoff, Leonore, and Catherine Hall. *Family Fortunes: Men and Women of the English Middle Class, 1780–1850*. Chicago: University of Chicago Press, 1987.

Flanders, Judith. *Inside the Victorian Home: A Portrait of Domestic Life in Victorian England*. New York: W. W. Norton, 2003.

Flanders, Judith. *Consuming Passions: Leisure and Pleasure in Victorian Britain*. London: Harper Press, 2006.

Frost, Ginger. *Promises Broken: Courtship, Class, and Gender in Victorian England*. Charlottesville: University Press of Virginia, 1995.

Frost, Ginger. *Living in Sin: Cohabitation as Husband and Wife in Nineteenth-Century England*. Manchester, U.K.: Manchester University Press, 2008.

Gerard, Jessica. *Country House Life: Family and Servants, 1815–1914*. Oxford: Blackwell, 1994.

Gillett, Paula. *Musical Women in England, 1870–1914: "Encroaching on All Man's Privileges."* New York: St. Martin's Press, 2000.

Gillis, John. *For Better, for Worse: British Marriages, 1600 to the Present*. Oxford: Oxford University Press, 1985.

Girouard, Mark. *The Victorian Country House*. New Haven, CT: Yale University Press, 1979.

Golden, Catherine. *Posting It: The Victorian Revolution in Letter Writing*. Gainesville: University Press of Florida, 2009.

Hamlett, Jane. *Material Relations: Domestic Interiors and Middle-Class Families in England, 1850–1910*. Manchester, U.K.: Manchester University Press, 2010.

Kriegel, Lara. *Grand Designs: Labor, Empire, and the Museum in Victorian Culture*. Durham, NC: Duke University Press, 2007.

McLaren, Angus. *Birth Control in Nineteenth-Century England*. New York: Holmes and Meier, 1978.

McLaren, Angus. *A History of Contraception: From Antiquity to the Present Day*. Oxford: Basil Blackwell, 1990.

Peterson, M. Jeanne. *Family, Love, and Work in the Lives of Victorian Gentlewomen*. Bloomington: Indiana University Press, 1989.

Ross, Ellen. *Love and Toil: Motherhood in Outcast London, 1870–1918*. Oxford: Oxford University Press, 1993.

Thompson, F.M.L. *The Rise of Respectable Society: A Social History of Victorian Britain, 1830–1900*. Cambridge, MA: Harvard University Press, 1988.

Wohl, Anthony. *The Eternal Slum: Housing and Social Policy in Victorian London*. London: E. Arnold, 1977.

## CHAPTER 4: HEALTH AND SEXUALITY

Borsay, Anne. *Disability and Social Policy in Britain since 1750*. New York: Palgrave Macmillan, 2005.

Clark, Anna. *Desire: A History of European Sexuality*. London: Routledge, 2008.

Cunnington, C. Willett. *English Women's Clothing in the Nineteenth Century*. London: Faber and Faber, 1948.

Hall, Lesley, ed. *Outspoken Women: An Anthology of Women's Writing on Sex, 1870–1969*. London: Routledge, 2005.

Levene, Alysa, Thomas Nutt, and Samantha Williams, eds. *Illegitimacy in Britain, 1700–1920*. New York: Palgrave Macmillan, 2005.

Levine-Clark, Marjorie. *Beyond the Reproductive Body: The Politics of Women's Heath and Work in Early Victorian England*. Columbus: Ohio State University Press, 2004.

Marcus, Sharon. *Between Women: Friendship, Desire, and Marriage in Victorian England*. Princeton, NJ: Princeton University Press, 2007.

Oppenheim, Janet. *"Shattered Nerves": Doctors, Patients, and Depression in Victorian England*. New York: Oxford University Press, 1991.

Peterson, M. Jeanne. *The Medical Profession in Mid-Victorian London*. Berkeley: University of California Press, 1978.

Roberts, Elizabeth. *A Woman's Place: An Oral History of Working-Class Women, 1890–1940*. New York: B. Blackwell, 1984.

Scull, Andrew. *Hysteria: The Biography*. Oxford: Oxford University Press, 2009.

Showalter, Elaine. *The Female Malady: Women, Madness, and English Culture, 1830–1980*. New York: Pantheon Books, 1985.

Smith, Francis Barrymore. *The People's Health, 1830–1910*. New York: Holmes & Meier Publishers, Inc., 1979.

Steele, Valerie. *The Corset: A Cultural History*. New Haven, CT: Yale University Press, 2001.

Summers, Leigh. *Bound to Please: A History of the Victorian Corset*. Oxford: Berg, 2001.

Vicinus, Martha. *Intimate Friends: Women Who Loved Women, 1778–1928*. Chicago: University of Chicago Press, 2004.

Wohl, Anthony. *Endangered Lives: Public Health in Victorian Britain*. Cambridge, MA: Harvard University Press, 1983.

Wright, David. *Mental Disability in Victorian England: The Earlswood Asylum, 1847–1901*. New York: Oxford University Press, 2001.

## CHAPTER 5: CHILDREARING, YOUTH, AND EDUCATION

Behlmer, George. *Child Abuse and Moral Reform in England, 1870–1908*. Stanford, CA: Stanford University Press, 1982.

Burnett, John. *Destiny Obscure: Autobiographies of Childhood, Education and Family from the 1820s to the 1920s*. New York: Penguin, 1984.

Cunningham, Hugh. *The Children of the Poor: Representations of Childhood since the Seventeenth Century*. Oxford: Blackwell, 1992.

Cunningham, Hugh. *Children and Childhood in Western Society since 1500.* London: Longman, 1995.

Davin, Anna. *Growing Up Poor: Home, School and Street in London, 1870–1914.* London: Rivers Oram Press, 1996.

Dyhouse, Carol. *Girls Growing Up in Late Victorian and Edwardian England.* London: Routledge and Kegan Paul, 1981.

Flegel, Monica. *Conceptualizing Cruelty to Children in Nineteenth-Century England: Literature, Representation, and the NSPCC.* Burlington, VT: Ashgate, 2009.

Frost, Ginger. *Victorian Childhoods.* Westport, CT: Praeger, 2009.

Gorham, Deborah. *The Victorian Girl and the Feminine Ideal.* Bloomington: Indiana University Press, 1982.

Hendrick, Harry. *Child Welfare: England, 1872–1989.* London: Routledge, 1994.

Hopkins, Eric. *Childhood Transformed: Working-Class Children in Nineteenth-Century England.* Manchester, U.K.: Manchester University Press, 1994.

Horn, Pamela. *The Victorian Town Child.* Stroud, U.K.: Sutton Publishing, 1997.

Jackson, Louise. *Child Sexual Abuse in Victorian England.* London: Routledge, 2000.

Lewis, Judith Schneid. *In the Family Way: Childbearing in the British Aristocracy, 1760–1860.* New Brunswick, NJ: Rutgers University Press, 1986.

Murdoch, Lydia. *Imagined Orphans: Poor Families, Child Welfare, and Contested Citizenship in London.* New Brunswick, NJ: Rutgers University Press, 2006.

Pinchbeck, Ivy, and Margaret Hewitt. *Children in English Society*, 2 vols. London: Routledge and Kegan Paul, 1969.

Rubenstein, David. "Socialization and the London School Board, 1870–1904: Aims, Methods, and Public Opinion." In *Popular Education and Socialization in the Nineteenth Century*, edited by Philip McCann, 231–264. London: Methuen, 1977.

## CHAPTER 6: WAGE LABOR AND PROFESSIONAL WORK

Bennett, Judith. *History Matters: Patriarchy and the Challenge of Feminism.* Philadelphia: University of Pennsylvania Press, 2006.

Copelman, Dina. *London's Women Teachers: Gender, Class and Feminism, 1870–1930.* London: Routledge, 1996.

Elliott, Dorice Williams. *The Angel Out of the House: Philanthropy and Gender in Nineteenth-Century England.* Charlottesville: University Press of Virginia, 2002.

Goose, Nigel, ed. *Women's Work in Industrial England: Regional and Local Perspectives.* Hatfield, U.K.: Local Publication Studies, 2007.

Hiley, Michael. *Victorian Working Women: Portraits from Life*. London: Gordon Fraser, 1979.

Holcombe, Lee. *Victorian Ladies at Work: Middle-Class Working Women in England and Wales, 1850–1914*. Hamden, CT: Archon Books, 1973.

Honeyman, Katrina. *Women, Gender and Industrialisation in England, 1700–1870*. London: Macmillan Press, 2000.

Horn, Pamela. *Victorian Countrywomen*. Oxford: Basil Blackwell, 1991.

Paravisini-Gerbert, Lizabeth. "Mrs. Seacole's *Wonderful Adventures in Many Lands* and the Consciousness of Transit." In *Black Victorians, Black Victoriana*, edited by Gretchen Holbrook Gerzina, 71–87. New Brunswick, NJ: Rutgers University Press, 2003.

Parliamentary Papers. "England and Wales—Occupations of Females at Different Periods of Age." In *Accounts and Papers: Forty-Eight Volumes, Part I—Population (England and Wales)*, Table XX, 320–329. London: House of Commons, 1863.

Peterson, M. Jeanne. "The Victorian Governess: Status Incongruence in Family and Society." In *Suffer and Be Still: Women in the Victorian Age*, edited by Martha Vicinus, 3–19. Bloomington: Indiana University Press, 1972.

Pinchbeck, Ivy. *Women Workers and the Industrial Revolution, 1750–1850*. London: Frank Cass, 1969; 1930.

Rappaport, Helen. *No Place for Ladies: The Untold Story of Women in the Crimean War*. London: Aurum, 2007.

Rose, Sonya. *Limited Livelihoods: Gender and Class in Nineteenth-Century England*. Berkeley: University of California Press, 1992.

Valenze, Deborah. *The First Industrial Woman*. New York: Oxford University Press, 1995.

Vicinus, Martha. *Independent Women: Work and Community for Single Women, 1850–1920*. Chicago: University of Chicago Press, 1985.

## CHAPTER 7: URBAN LIFE

Briggs, Asa. *Victorian Cities*. London: Odhams Books, 1963.

Copelman, Dina. "The Gendered Metropolis: Fin-de-Siècle London." *Radical History Review* 60 (1994): 38–56.

Curtis, Perry. *Jack the Ripper and the London Press*. New Haven, CT: Yale University Press, 2001.

Dyos, Harold J., and Michael Woolf, eds. *The Victorian City: Images and Realities*, 2 vols. London: Routledge and Kegan Paul, 1973.

Freeman, Michael. *Railways and the Victorian Imagination*. New Haven, CT: Yale University Press, 1999.

Jones, Gareth Stedman. *Outcast London: A Study in the Relationship between Classes in Victorian Society*. Oxford: Clarendon Press, 1971.

Koven, Seth. *Slumming: Sexual and Social Politics in Victorian London*. Princeton, NJ: Princeton University Press, 2004.

Lees, Lynn Hollen. *Exiles of Erin: Irish Migrants in Victorian London*. Ithaca, NY: Cornell University Press, 1979.

Nead, Lynda. *Victorian Babylon: People, Streets and Images in Nineteenth-Century London*. New Haven, CT: Yale University Press, 2000.

Nord, Deborah Epstein. *Walking the Victorian Streets: Women, Representation, and the City*. Ithaca, NY: Cornell University Press, 1995.

Purvis, June. "'Deeds, Not Words': Daily Life in the Women's Social and Political Union in Edwardian Britain." In *Votes for Women*, edited by June Purvis and Sandra Stanley Holton, 135–158. London: Routledge, 2000.

Rappaport, Erika. *Shopping for Pleasure: Women in the Making of London's West End*. Princeton, NJ: Princeton University Press, 2000.

Raw, Louise. *Striking a Light: The Bryant and May Matchwomen and Their Place in Labour History*. London: Continuum, 2009.

Richards, Thomas. *The Commodity Culture of Victorian England: Advertising and Spectacle, 1850–1914*. Stanford, CA: Stanford University Press, 1990.

Ross, Ellen, ed. *Slum Travelers: Ladies and London Poverty, 1860–1920*. Berkeley: University of California Press, 2007.

Ryan, Mary P. *Women in Public: Between Banners and Ballots, 1825–1880*. Baltimore, MD: Johns Hopkins University Press, 1990.

Schneer, Jonathan. *London 1900: The Imperial Metropolis*. New Haven, CT: Yale University Press, 1999.

Walkowitz, Judith. *City of Dreadful Delight: Narratives of Sexual Danger in Late-Victorian London*. Chicago: University of Chicago Press, 1992.

Wilson, Elizabeth. *The Sphinx in the City: Urban Life, the Control of Disorder, and Women*. Berkeley: University of California Press, 1992.

## CHAPTER 8: WOMEN AND EMPIRE

Buettner, Elizabeth. *Empire Families: Britons and Late Imperial India*. Oxford: Oxford University Press, 2004.

Burton, Antoinette. *Burdens of History: British Feminists, Indian Women, and Imperial Culture, 1865–1915*. Chapel Hill: University of North Carolina Press, 1994.

Coombes, Annie. *Reinventing Africa: Museums, Material Culture, and Popular Imagination in Late Victorian and Edwardian England*. New Haven, CT: Yale University Press, 1994.

Crais, Clifton, and Pamela Scully. *Sara Baartman and the Hottentot Venus: A Ghost Story and a Biography*. Princeton, NJ: Princeton University Press, 2009.

Gerzina, Gretchen Holbrook, ed. *Black Victorians, Black Victoriana*. New Brunswick, NJ: Rutgers University Press, 2003.

Ghosh, Durba. *Sex and the Family in Colonial India: The Making of Empire*. Cambridge, U.K.: Cambridge University Press, 2006.

Hall, Catherine, and Sonya O. Rose, eds. *At Home with the Empire: Metropolitan Culture and the Imperial World*. Cambridge, U.K.: Cambridge University Press, 2006.

Kranidis, Rita. *The Victorian Spinster and Colonial Emigration*. New York: St. Martin's Press, 1999.

Levine, Philippa. *Prostitution, Race and Politics: Policing Venereal Disease in the British Empire*. London: Routledge, 2003.

Levine, Philippa. *The British Empire: Sunrise to Sunset*. Harlow, U.K.: Pearson, 2007.

Mackenzie, John. *Propaganda and Empire: The Manipulation of British Public Opinion, 1880–1960*. Manchester, U.K.: Manchester University Press, 1984.

MacMillan, Margaret. *Women of the Raj*. New York: Thames and Hudson, 1988.

Marsh, Jan, ed. *Black Victorians: Black People in British Art, 1800–1900*. Aldershot, U.K.: Lund Humphries, 2005.

McClintock, Anne. *Imperial Leather: Race, Gender and Sexuality in the Colonial Contest*. London: Routledge, 1995.

McEwan, Cheryl. *Gender, Geography and Empire: Victorian Women Travellers in West Africa*. Aldershot, U.K.: Ashgate, 2000.

Midgley, Clare. *Women against Slavery: The British Campaigns, 1780–1870*. London: Routledge, 1992.

Midgley, Clare. *Feminism and Empire: Women Activists in Imperial Britain, 1790–1865*. London: Routledge, 2007.

Norcia, Megan. *X Marks the Spot: Women Writers Map the Empire for British Children, 1790–1895*. Athens: Ohio University Press, 2010.

Nunn, Pamela Gerrish. "Artist and Model: Joanna Mary Boyce's *Mulatto Woman*." *Journal of Pre-Raphaelite Studies* 2 (1993): 12–15.

Parsons, Timothy. *The British Imperial Century, 1815–1914*. Boulder, CO: Rowman and Littlefield, 1999.

Prince, Mary. *The History of Mary Prince, a West Indian Slave*, edited with an introduction by Sara Salih. London: Penguin Books, 2004.

Sinha, Mrinalini. *Colonial Masculinity: The "Manly Englishman" and the "Effeminate Bengali" in the Late Nineteenth Century*. Manchester, U.K.: University of Manchester Press, 1995.

Thorne, Susan. *Congregational Missions and the Making of an Imperial Culture in Nineteenth-Century England*. Stanford: Stanford University Press, 1999.

Tusan, Michelle. "The Business of Relief Work: A Victorian Quaker in Constantinople and Her Circle." *Victorian Studies* 51, no. 4 (2009): 633–661.

Twells, Alison. *The Civilizing Mission and the English Middle Class, 1792–1850: The "Heathen" at Home and Overseas*. New York: Palgrave Macmillan, 2009.

Woollacott, Angela. *Gender and Empire*. New York: Palgrave Macmillan, 2006.

# INDEX

**About the Author**

LYDIA MURDOCH is an associate professor of History and the former director of Women's Studies at Vassar College. She is the author of *Imagined Orphans: Poor Families, Child Welfare, and Contested Citizenship in London* (2006) and is currently writing a book about Victorian responses to child mortality.